Making Projects Work

Effective Stakeholder and Communication Management

T0313107

Making Projects Work

Effective Stakeholder and Communication Management

Lynda Bourne

CRC Press
Taylor & Francis Group
Boca Raton London New York

CRC Press is an imprint of the
Taylor & Francis Group, an **informa** business

AN AUERBACH BOOK

CRC Press
Taylor & Francis Group
6000 Broken Sound Parkway NW, Suite 300
Boca Raton, FL 33487-2742

First issued in paperback 2022

© 2015 by Taylor & Francis Group, LLC
CRC Press is an imprint of Taylor & Francis Group, an Informa business

No claim to original U.S. Government works

ISBN-13: 978-1-482-20666-1 (hbk)
ISBN-13: 978-1-03-234018-0 (pbk)
DOI: 10.1201/b18100

Library of Congress Cataloging-in-Publication Data

Bourne, Lynda.
  Making projects work : effective stakeholder and communication management / Lynda Bourne.
     pages cm. -- (Best practices and advances in program management series)
  Includes bibliographical references and index.
  ISBN 978-1-4822-0666-1 (alk. paper)
  1. Project management. 2. Communication in management. I. Title.

HD69.P75B677 2015
658.4'04--dc23   2014041678

Visit the Taylor & Francis Web site at
http://www.taylorandfrancis.com

and the CRC Press Web site at
http://www.crcpress.com

Contents

Introduction

The high point of my career in project management came in the late 1990s when I managed a project that really was successful. *Everybody* wanted it, and everybody was prepared to contribute to its successful implementation. My team and I received as much cooperation from all our stakeholders as we could desire. This project succeeded because everybody wanted the outcomes of the project and were prepared to collaborate with us to achieve them. They were willing to work with us to ensure that their needs were met—*and* they knew what they wanted.

My project was the development of an interface between the project management software selected by the organization (and loved by the project managers) and a corporate-wide enterprise resource planning (ERP) application.

THE COMPONENTS OF SUCCESS

The main feature contributing to the success of this project was the perception of how it would add value to the three main groups within the organization as well as to the vendors:

- *The finance and accounting community*: These individuals would benefit from an increasingly timely understanding of the expenditure incurred by projects expressed in a way that fitted the finance and accounting processes defined through the ERP system.
- *Senior management*: Senior management would benefit from more timely and accurate data about revenue and expenditure. This was part of the reason for the original decision to implement ERP so that the organization could keep track in a more timely fashion of revenue and expenditure in a way that best suited its reporting needs (internal and external). Senior management also appreciated more timely data on the progress and effectiveness and efficiency of the project.
- *The project team*: These individuals would benefit by avoiding duplicate data entry. Simply by the routine maintenance of time and cost

needed for the day-to-day management of the project, the new interface provided the ERP with useful organizational data.

- *The suppliers of the project management software*: These suppliers
would benefit from contractual arrangements that allowed this company to market the interface as an additional solution for clients who
have purchased the ERP software.

Kahneman (2011) defined success as a combination of hard work, skill
and knowledge, and luck. This was also the case with this project—and any
project. We learn so much from failure: In the world of projects, there are
plenty of opportunities to learn. We also need a few successes; the memories of these successes are what enable us to continue to work on projects.

Those in the project management profession, both practitioners and
academics, continue to seek to understand the factors that are essential
to project success.* Many hypotheses have been developed; they all have
merit but still do not answer the question, Why are we not learning from
the past? At the time of writing, the spotlight was beginning to focus on
relationships, the people side of planning, execution, and implementation
of the outputs of the project or other organizational activity. This was my
experience with the ERP interface—even though all stakeholders were
supportive of the project's outcomes, we still had to communicate to share
information and to build relationships.

Experienced project managers still love to return for new project
"challenges," and a little self-deception goes a long way. The cultural
myths of organizations and project management allow executives and
governors of organizations to believe their own wishful thinking or the
unrealistic promises made by proposers of something new. Management
within the organization continues to delude itself that this time it will be
different†—and so does the project manager.

This facility of self-deception is how we are able to take on challenges
such as complex, difficult projects knowing (from the last time) that there
will be minimal support and many issues standing between the project
manager and team and acknowledged success of the project. The generation of such false beliefs is a function of how the brain makes sense of the

---

* My research boundaries were from Pinto and Prescott (1990) to Samphire (2014) at the time
of writing this book.
† The saying "insanity is repeating the same mistakes and expecting different results" has been
attributed to Albert Einstein (but there is no reference to support it). Whoever said it clearly
understood the nature of self-delusion.

environment. It is also a function of hope and optimism that excites us as we contemplate the unknown or the semi-unknown.

There are still many questions to be addressed: Who is responsible for managing the realization of the benefits to achieve the outcomes that will provide value to the organization? What are the boundaries of a project and therefore the boundaries of a project manager's responsibility? Defining the project boundaries provides clarity for the project team and the project's stakeholders. With this definition, everyone in the organization is clear on all the roles and responsibilities necessary for successful delivery of the project outcomes. If the boundaries are too restrictive, opportunity for the project manager to influence how the project is planned and implemented are also restricted.

The purpose of this book is to explore project relationships in the expectation that it will be read by project management students, practitioners, and possibly even those who have a project role as stakeholder, with a view to creating a pragmatic framework for routinely achieving project success.

Chapter 1, Making Projects Work, introduces the idea of the organization's communication ecosystem where information flows freely and readily within and among all the layers of the organization. Communication is the tool that builds and maintains relationships within the organization. There is a strong connection between these relationships and successful outcomes, particularly in the realm of programs and projects, because *projects are done by people for the benefit of other people.* To be successful, the relationships between the people involved in programs or projects (stakeholders) must be robust, sustainable, and effective. The involvement of stakeholders from all levels both within and outside the organization within the framework of the communication ecosystem is required to make projects successful.

In attempting to define how this might work, the rest of the chapter contains a discussion of the current state of thinking about how to make traditional project management more effective. Should we be defining the boundaries of a project in a different way? Should we be thinking about project success as more than delivering the project's output within time and budget constraints and to required scope and quality? By redefining how we think about projects and their function within the organization, we may also be able to improve the conditions in which projects are constructed and implemented. This redefinition includes recognizing the importance of the communication ecosystem and the role that everyone within that ecosystem must play to achieve value for the organization. It examines the culture of project management as it is understood today—testing the commonly accepted beliefs about how project management should be performed and how the project manager should conduct the work of the project to deliver value to the organization.

Chapter 2, Stakeholders and Organizational Value, explores the importance of the relationships with the project's stakeholder community as keys to project success. The focus of this chapter is to define the stakeholder community and develop an approach to building those essential, but often unstable, relationships. Until the stakeholder community is known, efforts for meeting stakeholder expectations and building relationships with them will be less than effective. The task of defining the project's stakeholders depends on understanding who can be stakeholders. By revisiting the work of Freeman et al. (2010), the connection between the success of the organization and shareholder value is broken, and a stronger link between organizational success and delivering *stakeholder value* is proposed.

Definitions of stakeholders are discussed as a starting point to identification of the members of the project's stakeholder community, followed by descriptions of communication approaches to engage them. Effective stakeholder engagement delivers value to the organization and to the stakeholders and supports the work of the project in delivering successful project outcomes that add value to the organization.

Chapter 3, Focus on Leadership: Theories for Leading and Managing describes the theoretical underpinnings of leadership: What are the characteristics of effective leadership? The successful project manager needs to *be* a leader (of the team) and *understand* what a leader of stakeholders from all parts of the organization and outside does and must do. This chapter is a broad brush of theoretical approaches. Leaders may consciously or unconsciously use different approaches depending on their personality or considered responses to current circumstances or the characteristics of the stakeholder groups. A leader or potential leader can learn from the many different approaches defined in leadership theory, selecting the approaches that best fit the leader's circumstances or the current situation to meet the needs of the followers or the project.

Chapter 4, Focus on Downwards: *The Practicalities of Leading the Project Team,* begins the detailed analysis of the project's stakeholder community. Team members (and an organization's employees) are stakeholders—in many ways the most important stakeholders. They contribute to the success of the project through their knowledge, skills, and contribution to the work. For optimal contribution, they need an effective work environment.

This is the leadership role and responsibility of the project manager. The effective leader selects the appropriate style and behaviors to meet the needs of the team within the framework of the organization's culture and the type of project. At best, the leader's actions and behaviors foster collaboration and cooperation and minimize the distractions of conflict.

A team is formed when each team member is operating within an interdependent set of relationships with the other team members. Success depends on each member taking responsibility for the team's success, both individually and together as a team. In addition, success of the team depends on the actions and behaviors of the leader in creating an environment that nurtures the team members' interdependence and effective working. Included in this chapter are discussions of the more practical aspects of leading and managing downwards, such as the emotional intelligence (EI) of individuals and teams. Theories of team formation and suggestions for practical interventions in the process of team formation may reduce conflict and increase the effectiveness of the team's work. The essential skills for engaging downwards stakeholders—motivation, giving feedback, and managing conflict—are discussed.

Chapter 5, Focus on Managing Upwards, provides a perspective, and some guidelines, for understanding the project's senior stakeholders that will assist in developing credible and effective relationships with these stakeholders. The leadership theories described in Chapter 3 will also prove useful in helping the project manager understand the roles, responsibilities, and motivations of the senior stakeholders. A description of the "manager's dilemma" will help to build empathy through understanding the pressures of the roles and responsibilities of senior stakeholders.

Some of the most common problems facing the project team when dealing with senior managers are identified and guidelines offered to assist with building a reputation of credibility, dealing with difficult people (bosses), and learning to say 'no' to senior stakeholders.

Chapter 6, Focus on Sidewards *and* Outwards *Stakeholders,* describes and analyses relationships between the project team and the final two types of stakeholders: *sidewards* and *outwards*. Sidewards stakeholders are the peers of the project manager, and outwards stakeholders are all of the other stakeholders outside the project—the list is long, but includes government, suppliers, end users, and the public. Sometimes, it is not possible to directly influence these relationships, and other options become necessary, such as building alliances with third parties, utilizing networks to influence stakeholders that the project manager or team are not directly connected with, or negotiation. Discussion of the theory and application of negotiation techniques will assist the project team to acquire scarce resources and support for the project from peers, "outsiders," and senior managers.

Chapter 7, Culture and Other Factors that Influence Communication, attempts to answer the question, "What makes us who we are and how we operate in our social world?" The answer lies somewhere in a complex web of our own "reality" formed by how our brain makes sense of our experiences, our culture, and our gender. It influences how we live, work, and relate to others. Within the work environment, the culture of organizations also affects the project and its stakeholders and often defines the methods and formats of formal communication with stakeholders.

What we "perceive" and how we make sense of that will also be affected by our personality and our preferences. The complexity of the multiple influences of culture must be understood to the extent that we are aware of cultural or personality differences—our own and other stakeholders—without making the mistake of assuming that we can then predict how any particular stakeholder will prefer to receive information or what the nature of that relationship will be. Understanding the complexity of these influences is necessary to make us aware of the variations within the stakeholder community that we must address when developing communication strategies and plans.

Finally, *Chapter 8, Communication,* does not describe processes or define forms—that information can be sourced from many different places. What this chapter does provide is guidance on developing the appropriate messages to meet the needs of the project and its stakeholders. Included in the chapter are the foundations of communication: the three types of stakeholder communication (reporting, project relations [PR]), and directed communication; a definition of communication; and descriptions of the mechanisms of communication. The communication strategies developed will take into account the type of stakeholder and the aspects that make each stakeholder unique, such as the different cultures, personalities, and expectations of important stakeholders. Finally, ways of measuring successful (and effective) communication are described.

About the Author

Dr. Lynda Bourne FAIM, FACS, PMP is a senior management consultant, professional speaker, trainer, and an award-winning project manager with more than 30 years of professional industry experience. She is the CEO and Managing Director of Stakeholder Management Pty Ltd focusing on the delivery of stakeholder engagement and other project- and organization-related consultancy, mentoring and training for clients worldwide. Her career has combined practical project experience with business management roles and academic research to deliver successful projects that meet stakeholders' expectations.

Lynda Bourne is a member of the International Faculty at EAN University, Colombia, teaching in the Masters of Project Management course and is also visiting International Professor in the Master's program at the Faculty of Exact Sciences and Innovative Technologies, Sholokhov Moscow State. The modules she teaches are focused on stakeholder engagement, communication and leadership.

Dr. Bourne is a Fellow of the Australian Institute of Management and a Fellow of the Australian Computer Society. She was awarded PMI Australia's "Project Manager of the Year," and was included in PMI's inaugural list of the "25 Influential Women in Project Management."

Lynda is a recognized international author, seminar leader, and speaker on the topic of stakeholder engagement and the **Stakeholder** *Circle* visualization tool. Her book *Stakeholder Relationship Management: A Maturity Model for Organisational Implementation* (Gower, 2009, 2011) defines the SRMM® model for stakeholder relationship management maturity.

She has presented and has been a key speaker on stakeholder engagement practices to audiences in the IT, construction, defense, and mining industries at meetings, workshops and conferences in Europe, Russia, Asia, Australasia, South America, and the Middle East. She edited the book *Advising Upwards* (Gower, 2011) containing practical advice for those seeking to influence their senior stakeholders. She presents work-shops regularly in the government sector on stakeholder engagement and project governance.

Dr. Bourne is a member of the Core Committee for PMBOK 6th edition; her contribution is on the stakeholder and communications knowledge areas.

1

Making Projects Work

INTRODUCTION

Projects are performed by people for people; the key determinant of success is the relationships between the project team and other people involved in the project, collectively the project's stakeholders. This web of relationships will enable or obstruct the flow of information between people and, as a consequence, directly affect the ability of the project team to achieve the project's objectives and the organization's outcomes.

Projects do not exist in isolation; the communication ecosystem that supports the project is developed by the organization and extends beyond its boundaries to the wider community. A constructive ecosystem is formed by the combination of the organization's support framework and the development of a collaborative culture that recognizes that project success is everybody's business. This chapter focuses attention on successful project delivery through development and expansion of this communication ecosystem.

In a perfect communication ecosystem, the "right" messages will be communicated upwards, downwards, and across the organization to provide people with the information needed to make the right decisions at the right time. The design of the organization's culture and structures to support the communication ecosystem should encourage open and authentic exchange of information within a supportive framework. Within this structure and culture, the ability of people to collaborate effectively for project success is defined by their relationships and their ability to communicate effectively with each other.

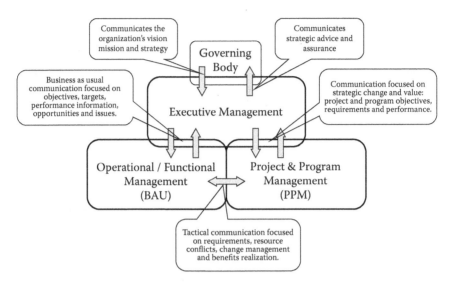

FIGURE 1.1
The communication ecosystem.

THE COMMUNICATION ECOSYSTEM

Figure 1.1 illustrates the communication roles necessary for the effective functioning of the ecosystem. First, the governing body—the executive of the organization or the "governors"—develop the vision, mission, and strategy of the organization and communicate it to the people in the organization. These strategic messages include processes and instructions that assist compliance and reporting mechanisms that provide direction for the organization's management. The various layers of management will then communicate the appropriate strategic advice to the levels below and provide assurance back to the governing body that the vision, mission, and strategy are understood and receive compliance.

Management provides oversight and directs the activities of those working in the operational areas (business as usual, BAU) or project and program management (PPM). It is through the funded and approved project management activities that changes to BAU are performed. Communication downwards to the PPM is in the form of requirements, objectives, and performance standards needed to implement the strategic changes necessary to realize value to the organization. The communication downwards to BAU management will be in the form of objectives, targets, performance information, issues, and opportunities. Communication from both these groups upwards will consist of progress information against the project objectives and requirements and any other information necessary to provide assurance that the work is proceeding according to the expectations of the executive and management groups. Communication between the PPM area and the BAU area will be focused on efficient working relationships and transition from PPM to BAU operations. Information about stakeholder requirements, resource conflicts, change management actions and reporting, and benefits realization will be essential communication in this area. Understanding how the ecosystem operates for effective delivery of the organization's vision, mission, and strategy and operating effectively within it is essential for project success.

In today's organization and communication environments, there are often gaps in the structures and culture needed to build the communication ecosystem described. To close these gaps, organizations need to continue to enhance their ecosystem through improvements in the structures and processes of corporate governance and the strategic management of projects (project governance). Further improvements can be achieved through redrawing the boundaries of the project itself and thereby redefining the responsibilities of the project manager.

This chapter lays the foundation for the more detailed analysis of effective practices of stakeholder engagement and communication covered in subsequent chapters. These practices provide the foundation for delivering successful project outcomes by creating an effective communication ecosystem.

The first section of this chapter defines terms used to describe the outputs of the project and its connection to the processes and practices that provide value to the organization. The second section describes the framework that can deliver the communication ecosystem. These are the structures and communication systems of corporate governance, strategic project management (project governance), and the project itself. The next section proposes that project success is everybody's business, with descriptions of how project managers can create an atmosphere of high performance through using communication strategies specifically designed to create the most appropriate communication ecosystem for project people to work in. The final section is a reality check: what the state of project management is today and what needs to occur to expand or modify the accepted view of project management to move toward the perfect communication ecosystem.

DEFINITIONS

When considering approaches to more effective management of projects, the starting point must be a clear understanding of the essential terms that form the basis for communication within the ecosystem. Effective communication in any setting requires a shared understanding of the language being used, never more so than in the development of the ecosystem where different cultures must merge to form the culture of the communication ecosystem. These terms are *value* (as it applies to organizations), project *objectives*, project *outputs*, project *deliverables*, and organizational *outcomes*.

Value is contextual: The same "benefit" can have different values, depending on the circumstances at any given time or place—an umbrella is far more valuable if it is raining. It can be defined as "worth" and therefore must be "assessed" or "calculated." In an organizational context, value is

- Monetary or material worth, as in commerce or trade: increase in value.
- Equivalent worth or return in money, material, services: to give value for value received.
- Estimated or assigned worth; valuation: a painting with a current value of $500,000.

Value can also be more intrinsic or intangible—less able to be "calculated":

- Meaning or significance: the value of a word.

In the corporate world tangible value is known and understood; these definitions are applied to financial balance sheets and often focus on "shareholder value," which can lead to a culture of short-term decision making to maximize share price and investor return. The intangible definitions of value are less easy to measure. It is about the human element—stakeholders such as the customer, employees, the public, users of a product, organizational reputation. Most thinking and reporting within an organization are focused on the tangibles. However, organizations all depend ultimately on people for their continued existence, whether the efforts are directed toward maintaining and building the organization structurally or working to create relationships within the organization or external to the organization.* From a project perspective, value will be the *tangible* value in the form of

- The product or service that will deliver the benefits that have been claimed in the business case.
- Any additional tangible organizational asset produced and retained.
- Any additional source of revenue.
- Any new customer base or repeat business acquired through the outputs of the project.

Significant *intangible* value for both the organization and the participants in the ecosystem will be realized through

- Additional knowledge and experience for all the stakeholders who have been involved in the work of the project, particularly those who contributed through work on the team.
- Increase of personal or organizational knowledge achieved by stakeholders both within (sponsor, subject matter experts) and outside the organization (suppliers, government representatives, potential users of the outputs).
- Possible improved perception of the organization by involvement of these stakeholders, enhancing the organization's reputation as an organization that is easy to do business with and potentially improving its revenue flow.

Objectives define the boundaries of what will be achieved and guide its planning and execution. They need to be specific and measurable, according to the acronym SMART:

- *Specific*: a clear statement of what will be delivered or achieved.
- *Measurable*: quantifiable and measurable so that everyone is clear about what will be achieved.
- *Achievable*: not too ambitious, but able to be achieved in the approved time frame and budget as well as to the expectations of stakeholders.
- *Realistic*: can be achieved within the time frame and budget.

---

* There has recently been an improvement in recognition of the importance of people to project success (Phillips, 2014; Morris, 2013).

- *Time constrained*: within the specific time frame that has been esti-mated, approved, and funded.

There are two types of *outputs* of a project:

- *The deliverables*: tangible outputs such as the product or service, sup-porting documents, processes, manuals, training documentation.
- *Knowledge* (and *experience*) that has been developed in the process of realizing the project's deliverables, perhaps in the form of a project report that includes "lessons learned": what was successful, what needed improvement, and descriptions of how project issues of all types were resolved. This report will become part of the organiza-tion's knowledge assets.

Outcomes are the means by which value will be gained for the organiza-tion. They are defined in the business case and other early documentation. They will specify how the deliverables will contribute to the organization's success, whether from a business or profit perspective or via enhancement of reputation through improved customer service or corporate social responsibility (CSR) activities.

In summary, value is achieved when the project's output (product, service, or result) is used by the organization to generate the intended outcomes. The outcomes enable the realization of a range of expected and other benefits. Value is created when

- The tangible and intangible benefits are greater than the costs associ-ated with both the project and the change associated with its imple-mentation.
- The final organizational outcomes deliver strategic, tactical, or revenue advantage to the organization (Jenner, 2012). This is stra-tegic alignment—aligning the strategic objectives of the organization with the outputs of the project.

GOVERNANCE

The governance structure is central to the organization's capacity to satisfy regulatory, economic, and reputational requirements. Good governance is fundamental to the long-term viability of the organization itself. The various definitions of (good) corporate governance, including those of the Organization for Economic Cooperation and Development (2004), the Chartered Institute of Internal Auditors (2004), Association of Project Management (APM) (n.d.), and Samphire (2014), have a number of elements in common, even though they vary in content and intent:

- Corporate governance is about decision making and managing an organization according to accepted guidelines, whether imposed by regulatory bodies or by the organization itself. The decisions are made at the board level.
- Management must manage the organization according to the decisions made at the board level.
- These decisions must be made to ensure that the organization achieves its strategic objectives.
- The decisions must be made in the best interests of *all* of an organization's stakeholders—not just its shareholders.
- Honesty, integrity, transparency, openness, responsibility, accountability, and ethical standards are all essential qualities for good governance of organizations.

Key questions of governance are the following (Jenner, 2012:39):

- Is the organization doing the right things?
- Is it doing them the right way?
- Is it getting them done well?
- Is it receiving the benefit?

To deliver answers to these four strategic questions, there must be a clear understanding communicated within the *whole* organization of the following:

- Who is responsible for what? Accountable to whom?*

---

* Often, the terms *accountable* and *responsible* are used interchangeably. I use them to mean different things: You are held *accountable* for something, and you take *responsibility* for something. Responsibility for a task can be delegated; accountability cannot. It also implies that you have the necessary authority to complete the accountable task. The project manager is responsible for the successful delivery of outputs (and in some cases, outcomes); the sponsor or other senior stakeholder is accountable to the board or other governing body for ensuring that the expected value of the outcomes will be delivered.

- What decisions are made where, when, and by whom and using what criteria?

Those who are responsible or accountable can only achieve their objectives through communication that includes establishing

- Clear lines of delegated responsibility,
- Rules and escalation paths when there are variances from the plan,
- The willingness and ability to engage in the necessary communication, and
- Reviews of progress, using regular reporting, stage/gate reviews, and portfolio-level reviews.

The communication process facilitated by the structure described in Figure 1.1 is optimal for the communication ecosystem. The second element in the ecosystem is the strategic management of projects: project governance. In many organizations, project governance is believed (in error) to be about controls. It is actually the organizational systems, entities, and culture that translate the strategy of the governing body into requirements and objectives for BAU and PPM as well as act as agents of the governors through the mechanisms of oversight and direction defined by the governing body. The role of project governance is to build the links between the governing body and the work of the PPM or BAU areas in a constructive and relationship-focused manner.

Strategic Management of Projects (Project Governance)

Project governance is defined by (APM, n.d.:4) as concerning:

> Effective governance of project (and program) management ensures that an organization's project portfolio is aligned to the organization's objectives, is delivered efficiently and is sustainable. Governance of project (and program) management also supports the means by which the board, and other major project stakeholders, are provided with timely, relevant and reliable information ... [and] involves aligning the interests of directors, programme and project teams and wider stakeholders.

Project governance is achieved through the strategic management of project management: APM's definition supports the notion of shared information among all areas of the organization concerned with successful delivering of value through the project's outcomes. It is not just about monitoring and controlling the work; it is about ensuring through appropriate and effective communication that everything is in place to provide support and allow the project manager and the team to do their job. Project governance is an accountability of the sponsor and steering committees.

These definitions of governance and project governance provide insights into the accountabilities and responsibilities of management within the organization for ensuring that the conditions are optimal for delivering project outcomes successfully. They indicate a shared responsibility for successful project outcomes. For senior stakeholders, this means continuous and consistent direction, oversight, and support for project work and the project manager. To do otherwise is to have unrealistic expectations of the project manager and team and increase the chances that the project will not deliver the expected value to the organization.

The idea that the project manager can "heroically" and single-handedly manage the issues that inhibit project success has many flaws. Without executive support, the project team will have to work harder just to maintain the necessary level of project planning, execution, and reporting—the "execution" part of the total project. In addition, the project manager is unlikely to have sufficient resources or authority to achieve the necessary level of stakeholder engagement and communication if operating alone.[*] Providing effective support to the project manager and team is the responsibility and accountability of others—the senior stakeholders.

For an organization to create optimal value through its investment in projects, there must be a clear link between the outputs created by the projects and the requirements of the organization's business strategy. Organizations that have a structure that aligns the project deliverables with organizational goals will be better placed to achieve the value defined by their business strategies. What this means for organizations is that the boundaries of projects (and project manager responsibility) may need to be expanded beyond the execution processes specified by the Project Management Institute (PMI) (2012) in its *Guide to the Project Management Body of Knowledge (PMBOK® Guide)*. Expansion of the boundaries of project manager responsibility will be a feature of the perfect communication ecosystem but must be accompanied by recognition of the roles,

---

[*] The actions necessary to engage stakeholders through effective communication are described in further chapters.

responsibilities, and accountabilities of others throughout the organization who also contribute to delivery of value through the project outcomes.

WHAT SHOULD THE BOUNDARIES OF THE PROJECT BE?

The original purpose of the project management Bodies of Knowledge (BOKs) was to differentiate project activities from other organizational activities and to provide guidelines on how to deliver projects "on time, within budget, to agreed scope"—hence the focus on execution.* Paradoxically, few execution processes or actions are identified in research that attempts to define the causes of project failure or the indicators of project success. The following list comes from research conducted since the beginning of this century. Items on this list result primarily from the actions of those outside the current project boundaries that are focused on execution processes:

- Unclear objectives and success criteria, leading to inadequate scope definition and the consequential underestimation of time, cost and risk.
- Changing sponsor strategy and ineffective or unpredictable leadership from all levels of senior stakeholders, leading to inadequate support for the project manager and team when needed.
- Insufficient planning at the front end of the project (before the assignment of the project manager), leading to unrealistic timescales, ineffective controls, and unrealistic stakeholder expectations.
- Poor communication and a lack of stakeholder consultation or engagement, particularly in the early stages of projects.
- Unsupportive political or economic environment, causing additional communication burdens on the project manager, often without the necessary experience or contacts and often without the support of the senior stakeholders.
- Adverse geophysical conditions, which are totally outside the control of the project manager, often the "unknown unknowns" that can either directly or indirectly cause delays or difficulties within the

---

* The *PMBOK® Guide* has adapted to emerging views about the nature of project management with inclusions of more people-oriented "knowledge areas," such as integration and stakeholder management, in recent years.

project deliverables: directly though extreme unexpected weather or political issues that prevent the work being done or indirectly through those environmental or political issues affecting the delivery of resources (Morris, 2013:8).

The list is not definitive but points to problems that are outside the control of the project manager.

What if most of the factors that cause project failure are actually not the currently *accepted responsibility* of the project manager at all? In the United Kingdom, the APM has attempted to expand the boundaries of project manager involvement and responsibility with a focus on the "management of projects" rather than just the execution processes. Redefining the boundaries of projects, this approach advocates the inclusion of

- Setting project goals,
- Working with stakeholders,
- Managing and shaping the emergent front end,
- Managing technical, commercial, control, organizational, and people factors, and
- Emphasizing effectiveness not just efficiency.

Not only do the processes and practices that restrict the boundaries of the project limit the ability of the project manager to influence how the project work is structured, managed, and delivered, but also they limit the perspective of the project manager and project team.* Restricted project boundaries and therefore responsibilities can limit perspectives and the ability to think creatively.

Changing the way the methodologies used in the organization are structured in the short term may take time, but in the short term the project manager can still develop a wider-ranging focus of stakeholder engagement and communication and move beyond the narrow boundaries of the execution phase. This will be part of the progress that an organization makes to cultivate its communication ecosystem.

---

* This is not to say that processes and practices described in the *PMBOK® Guide* are not useful. The descriptions and sequences of project management processes are invaluable for the project team to have clarity on a standard way to complete the tasks necessary for production of project deliverables that fulfill the project's objectives. The roles and responsibilities of the project manager are now being defined in terms of strategic and influencing activities and have begun to appear in recent additions of the *PMBOK® Guide*.

Effective performance is about answers to the questions: Does the project deliver value to the organization? Does it meet the sponsor's business goals? The following actions contribute to the development of the perfect communication ecosystem because they are necessary for effective performance through the involvement of all stakeholders and therefore project success (Morris, 2013):

- Aligning with the organization's strategic intent—its business strategy—and with the sponsor's strategic directions. Every stakeholder of the project must be aware of the strategy that the project is funded to deliver as well as the objectives and intended outcomes of the project. Project reviews, or health checks, conducted from time to time as part of project governance, ensure that the organization's strategy is unchanged and the expected deliverables and outcomes will continue to deliver to requirements of the governance frameworks.*
- Providing a clear focus on capturing requirements and specifications from stakeholders who are affected by the work or outcomes of the project even at its early stage. This early analysis will be the beginning of regular reviews of the stakeholder community.†
- Ensuring that the effect of the "environment"—political, economic, and social—is understood and minimized. This is achieved through ensuring that the project's business case clearly states the best-known estimates of costs and benefits, with risks described in economic terms (tangible) as well as in the context of the organization's reputation and other stakeholder-related terms (intangible).
- Providing flexibility to the design, its current solution, and implementation strategy, taking into account the uncertainty of acquisition of resources within the organization's procurement strategies.
- Planning and monitoring and active decision making as needed to pull everything together and to move the project or program forward, with the emphasis on improving value while managing risk.

---

* If, during the review, it is noted that the strategy has changed and that the project no longer has a connection to any business outcomes, the project should be reviewed to see if it should be modified or discontinued. It certainly should not go on as if nothing has happened. The funding should be diverted to other activities.

† The stakeholder community will change as the project moves through its phases of delivery: In the early phases, the financial community will be prominent and important; in the execution phase, other stakeholders become more prominent and important and the importance of the financial community is reduced.

Even if the boundaries of project manager responsibility are expanded as suggested, many of these essential actions remain beyond the remit of the project manager. They are the accountability of the senior stakeholders of the organization—not only the sponsor and the steering committee but also those executives who are responsible for governing the organization and the functional managers who contribute resources and frequently benefit from successful delivery of the project's outcomes. Creating a successful project starts at corporate governance, not with the project manager at the start of the execution phase.

Even within the current boundaries of responsibility, the project manager can influence the project's outcomes—through communication. This communication not only refers to the understanding of who the project's stakeholders are—at any time within the life of the project—but also offers the choice of communication strategies and design as a means to measure and improve project performance. The remaining chapters describe in more detail the processes for engaging project stakeholders through effective communication. The next section describes some early activities of communication design that can ensure project performance that is more effective.

COMMUNICATION INFLUENCES PROJECT OUTCOMES

Conway's law as described in Phillips's work (2014) provides an interesting and alternative link between communication and a project's outcomes:

> Organizations which design systems ... are constrained to produce designs which are copies of the communication structures of these organizations. ... This kind of a structure-preserving relationship between two sets of things is called *homomorphism*. (Conway, 1968:28)

Conway gave a description of a system as "that kind of intellectual activity which creates a whole from its diverse parts" fits neatly into the proposal of the communication ecosystem as a cultural activity supported by structure where the efforts of many parts of the organization will create value (as described in Figure 1.1).

Phillips (2014:13) extrapolated Conway's law into the communication environment of a project: "Design of the project's communication environment will be mirrored in the project outcome." The structure of the project and the team influence how the communications for that project will be designed. For example, if the deliverables of the project have been shared among a number of different organizations (such as contracting firms or outsourcers), the design of the outputs will have to take into account the different groups involved with their different approaches and cultures. In this case, the design will have as many subsystems as there are groups contributing to delivery of the outputs, adding to the complexity of the work to deliver the outputs. If there are three different groups contributing to the final output, there will be three different subsystems; the work design and therefore communication design will be shaped to the culture and experience of each of the teams.

The corollary is that if one team is solely responsible for delivery of the project's output there will be a unified design whose output is within the responsibility of the project manager.* The difference in management of the project and its performance will be significant: Having sole responsibility for the project's outputs reduces uncertainty and complexity of communication and should logically increase the chances of delivering a successful project. The project manager with sole responsibility will have complete control of designing the project's work relationships through design of communication.

Phillips (2014:14) hypothesized that the project's communication environment is influenced by "the system design reflecting but also forming how people communicate and interact. ... It is about shaping reality on a project." In this interpretation, communication is a flexible process that is shaped, and shapes itself, according to the structures and culture of the organization and the project organization. It is a recognition that stakeholders are influenced by the information about the project that they receive—a similar idea to the communication ecosystem described at the start of this chapter. It is quite different from the traditional view of project communication, which is seen as a separate activity in which predefined information such as project reports or other project artifacts must be delivered to a fixed group of stakeholders who may or may not be interested in the information transmitted.

---

* The concept of integrated teams was central to the success of the construction phase of a £4 billion T5 project at Heathrow in the United Kingdom. Integrated teams were established for each element of the structure; the teams included designers, builders, and suppliers, with all of the key people colocated.

The design elements of the communication environment that Phillips (2014:21) has developed include

- How the team is organized and located,
- How the work is assigned and coordinated,
- Definition of methods for communication and interactions between the team and its stakeholders, and
- The schedule and workflow of communication and its integration with the other parts of the communication design.*

Phillips (2014) shared the recently emerging views of Morris (2013) and Bourne (2012) that people are central to all successful project activities, and the relationships between these people are built and maintained through communication. The communication environment (or ecosystem) and how it is designed through structure and culture determine project outcomes. The insight that Phillips (2014) contributed is the observation that it is possible to track and measure communication through observing behaviors of people who receive the communication and adjusting its delivery as necessary.

THE REALITY CHECK

The approach of Phillips (2014) implies that the project manager must assume the "heroic" role of driving performance within the project through communication design and observations of behavior that can then be used to drive greater efficiency. This is not entirely in accord with the underlying principle of the perfect communication ecosystem that project success is everybody's business, but it does reflect the philosophy of modern (traditional project) management.

Bergstrand (2009) offered a different view of the effect of project and communication design on project outcomes. He stated that projects are designed to fail when traditional processes of training, selection, and assignment of project team members (and presumably project managers) are used. Much of the training and project processes that are described in the traditional project management BOKs still owe their origins to

---

* The elements of communication design are discussed in more detail in Chapter 8.

methods designed by Frederick Taylor in the early 1900s that were developed for the industrial age. These methods with their focus on development and updating project artifacts, numbers, and static plans may have been useful for building bridges or operating an assembly line but ignore the complexity of relationships with people, who have always been the major causes of uncertainty (Phillips, 2014) and the main factors of risk (Bourne, 2012) in any organization or project.

Others suggested that projects and their structures are all illusion (Whitty, 2005:575): "What we call a project and what it is to manage one is an illusion; a human construct … fashioned and conveniently labelled in the human brain." The "traditional approach" based on BOKs arose from military and construction activities, but its origins are based on Western culture and philosophies. More recently Whitty and Schulz (2007) described the roots of the project management "ethos" as based on Puritan memes.[*] This hypothesis is that ideas on project management and project management behavior stem from the Reformation of the fifteenth century that established the roots of capitalism; they were eagerly adopted by Western—mostly English-speaking—cultures. With capitalism came the protestant work ethic (PWE), the importance of rational thinking over irrational thinking, and reductionist approaches that have influenced the ethos of project management: its culture.

These memes (Whitty, 2005) or cognitive illusions (Kahneman, 2011) are most strongly maintained in the company of like-minded individuals.[†] They often appear in the guise of professional "common sense" and may explain myths that take the form of the heroes, symbols, rituals, and values of the culture of project management (Hofstede, Hofstede, and Minkov, 2010).[‡] The constraints that these myths place on individuals and teams are partly responsible for the high level of failure of projects.

---

[*] "Memes can be considered to be recipes or instruction manuals for doing something cultural; behaviors words or sounds that are copied from person to person. All cultural life including PM is driven by the replicating behaviour of memes" (Whitty 2005:575). It has also been referred to as "thought contagion" or social epidemics that spread like viruses (Gladwell, 2000).

[†] Also "normalization of deviance" (Pinto, 2014), by which an organization's tolerance for deviation from the accepted way of doing things becomes accepted within the organization, and those within the organization think that it is normal. Only an outsider's view can help the insiders view the deviation. This concept applies in project management when project proposals or business cases are misrepresented with an understatement of costs and risks to ensure approval or in planning and scheduling when the views of "contingency" in estimates vary depending on the role of the individual—managers will assume that the estimators will add extra "padding" and therefore immediately adjust the estimates.

[‡] Aspects of culture are described in more detail in a further chapter.

Everybody carries some element of delusion in approaches to life and work. *This matters for projects.* Delusions in the form of selection of information to support our beliefs and of fostering hope and optimism will be what sustain us and help us to overcome all adversity.

Some examples of these myths are the following: The project manager is the hero of the project; the schedule and Gantt chart are "truth"; project reports provide essential information to management; operating within the power relationships of an organization is manipulation; and risk can be rationally planned, and decisions can be made through a rational process.

The Project Manager as Superhero: Represents the Hero Component of Project Management Culture

The myth is that the project manager has to be a superhero: the "lone hero" who wrestles with the project and tames it single-handedly despite every difficulty. Depending on the perspective of project management chosen, this can be explained in terms of training, selection, and the reward system of projects and the influence of the BOKs (Bergstrand, 2009) or the influence of the Western capitalist approach that has created the concept of the "profession" of management as consisting of the elevation of leaders that fit into the culture of the West—individualistic, in command and in control.

The Schedule and the Gantt Chart Are Truth: Represents the Symbol Component of Project Management Culture

Schedules and Gantt charts have been adopted by the project management culture as symbols of professionalism and represent the discipline of project management as defined by the BOKs and professional bodies.

- Estimates, schedules, and resourcing plans are not truth—they are just the best estimates of those involved with the estimating and planning process. Depending on the knowledge and experience of those involved with the work, the estimates, schedules, and plans will be different. They cannot predict the future.
- The term *Gantt chart* for a project's bar chart (reporting) view seems to have been popularized by Microsoft Project, which was launched in 1984–1985. It bears no resemblance to the work or reporting tools

developed by Henry Gantt (Weaver, 2013).* The application of the bar chart for project reporting and the almost-universal adoption of the term *Gantt chart* is an unambiguous example of the thought contagion of memes as described by Whitty and Schulz (2007).†

Project Reports Are Clear Representations of Project Progress: Represents the Rituals Component of Project Management Culture

Project reports provide useful information to management. However, recent research has observed that some project managers have adopted these same reporting tools for the purposes of influencing senior management through selection of format, content, and emphasis (Whitty, 2011). This selection may take the form of

- Framing information in the context of senior management's key performance indicators (KPIs), packaging it in a way that can be reused in the same manager's own reporting,
- Postponing sharing of information that reflects poorly on the project, and
- Presenting the information in a way that masks the uncertainty being experienced regarding the project at that time.

Through this framing, the project manager will appear to be organized and in control even if the reality is the project work is about dealing with unpredictability.‡ The senior stakeholder who is the recipient of this information expects to receive the reports. Even if he or she does not read them or act on their contents, it is part of the expectations—the rituals—that go with the standard communication from project to manager.

---

* Weaver's retrospective of Henry Gantt's work can be found with other white papers he has written on the history of project management and scheduling at http://pmworldlibrary.net/wp-content/uploads/2013/04/pmwj9-apr2013-weaver-where-misuse-terms-gantt-PERT-commentary1.pdf

† And, it is possibly the popularity of Microsoft Project and its influence on ways of working adopted by projects today.

‡ These concepts are useful to apply when managing upwards as discussed in a further chapter and include using "business-like terminology" in correspondence such as e-mails and reports; presenting charts or graphs using Microsoft Excel or Microsoft Project and simplifying them for executives; spending time preparing and structuring meetings and briefings; spending time thinking about the content of communication, keeping e-mails short, used only when necessary, and to the point. Following these guidelines will result in senior stakeholders' perceptions of the project being "in control" and enhancing the project manager's reputation of being efficient (and effective), but they need to be applied in an ethical manner.

Operating within the Power Relationships of the Organization Is Manipulation: Represents the Value Component of Project Management Culture

Many inexperienced project managers will reject the advice of the more experienced managers that they (the inexperienced ones) need to understand how the "politics" of the organization really work and use this knowledge for the benefit of the project. Bourne (2012) defined different levels of skills and knowledge that apply within a project, the third* and most mature of which is *flow*, derived from the concept developed by Csikszentmihalyi (1997) of the combination of skill and expertise to produce the occasional perfect outcomes.† Flow has its best organizational application in understanding the power relationships within the organization and working within them for the benefit of the project. This may entail understanding "hidden agendas" or the source of informal power and influence often held by individuals in the organization that may not necessarily match their formal roles (Pinto, 2000).

Risk Management Is a Rational Process: Represents the Value Component of Project Management Culture

Recent behavioral views of risk management have acknowledged the importance of recognizing that a stakeholder's perceptions of risk will be influenced by the stakeholder's culture and social explanations of the environment (Loosemore, 2011). Risk management is more than a series of checklists to comply with risk management standards. It is a process that includes accepting the irrationality of stakeholders and developing processes that include the identification of stakeholders, broad consultation with the stakeholder community, and management of the risks through communication. People do not act rationally to risks on the basis of defined hazards and benefits (the theory of utility) but often act irrationally according to their individual biases or perceptions. The result is significant perceptual differences between the stakeholder community and those working in the organization or on the project. What is also important but

---

* The other two are *craft*, the ability to use project management tools and techniques for monitoring and controlling project progress, and *leadership*, leading the team effectively and engaging the project's stakeholders.
† The best examples come from music (the perfect performance) and sport, such as hitting the "sweet spot" in golf or tennis. But, they can also apply to other endeavors that require a mix of skill, practice, and possibly luck.

currently has been largely ignored by both practitioners and researchers is that *people are the main source of risk* to a project or organization.*

CONCLUSION

The theme of this chapter was the exploration of the question: How do we make projects work? Or, expressed another way, How do we increase the chances for project success? Possible answers fall into two major areas. The first area concerns the development of an organization-wide communication ecosystem in which information is shared among all areas within the organization for the benefit of the whole organization. The second area examines the culture of project management as it is understood today—testing the commonly accepted beliefs about how project management should be performed and how the project manager should conduct the work of the project to deliver value to the organization.

With regard to developing the perfect communication ecosystem, each layer of management within the organization must contribute to achievement of the organizational value expected within the framework and the culture described in this chapter. Contribution varies according to the functions of the different layers of governance, through providing oversight and direction to those they manage or providing information about progress, issues, and delivery to stakeholders' expectations. The perfect communication ecosystem could be best defined by achieving organization-wide acceptance of the proposition that project success is everybody's business.

A potential solution for the second area of inquiry lies in an awareness of the limitations of the rituals, symbols, heroes, and values of project management as we understand them today: "traditional project management." The culture embedded in traditional project management based on the practices and values of the PWE, Taylorism, and the aura of the professional manager may no longer be relevant to today's global practice of project management. In fact, the culture of project management as it exists today may actually be the source of many of the causes of project failure. Awareness is the first

---

* I have conducted informal research over about 20 years of consulting in organizations that do projects or keep risk registers. At least 95% of all risks relate to people: resource skill and availability; decisions made about funding or design; lack of appropriate support; even the behaviors of people both inside the organization and outside—of not meeting the demands of rationality embedded in the risk management processes.

step in seeking alternative approaches to how project work can be done to deliver value to the organization. Talking about better ways for all parts of the organization to contribute to project success can achieve, through dialogue, new ideas that can be introduced through a process of evolution so that eventually project success really *is* everybody's business.

Part of the evolutionary process is thinking in terms of the boundaries of a project manager's responsibilities: Should they be confined to project execution processes, or should they be involved in more strategic activities? What is the role of executives? There was much discussion at the time of writing about the importance of good governance, both corporate and project—different but interrelated and both important to the project's ability to deliver organizational value.

This book is about not only people and their importance to the success of projects but also how people may or may not be involved with its success or may or may not be victims or winners of its outputs. This chapter argued that project success is achieved through communication and stakeholder engagement at all levels of the organization. The remaining chapters focus on understanding who a stakeholder can be, why stakeholders are important, and analysis of ways that the project manager, the project team, or other more senior members of the project organization can identify and engage the project's stakeholders for any particular time in the project. The final chapter on communication discusses how information from the chapters on different types of stakeholders can be incorporated into an effective communication strategy whose implementation will continue to build and maintain strong relationships with the stakeholders for the delivery of value to the organization.

2

Stakeholders and Organizational Value

INTRODUCTION

Project managers have believed that it is up to them—and them alone—to do "whatever it takes" to make the project successful. Sometimes they do not even really know what success looks like, but they know that they have to do it anyway. But, despite their most heroic efforts, most do not succeed in achieving this elusive objective. The project manager *cannot* deliver project outcomes alone. To build success, the project manager has to enlist the support of all the project's stakeholders through the medium of the organization's communication ecosystem (see Chapter 1). Achieving this support requires a thorough understanding of who is in the community and what they want and expect from the project. This chapter focuses on defining the stakeholder community and providing guidance on developing an approach to building the essential, but often unstable, relationships* needed to support the successful delivery of the project. Until the stakeholder community is known and understood, efforts for meeting stakeholder expectations and building relationships with them cannot be effective.

The structure of this chapter is as follows: First, some definitions of stakeholders and stakeholder engagement are given, followed by a brief overview of some theories of stakeholder relationship management. The third section identifies different types of stakeholders and provides brief

---

* The relationships are unstable because membership in the stakeholder community is dynamic, changing when conditions within the organization change or when the project or other activity moves into a new phase.

descriptions of communication approaches to engage them.* The fourth section looks at ways to analyze the stakeholder community (and the potential stakeholder community) and critiquing some of the methods used to analyze and map it. The final section discusses the value of effective stakeholder engagement, with some approaches to assist in identifying both intangible and, to a lesser extent, tangible value.

WHAT IS A STAKEHOLDER?

The concept of *stakeholder* existed long before management writers took up the cause and adapted the word and concept for an organizational purpose. The term *stakeholder* is defined (http://www.dictionary.com) in the following ways:

1. The holder of the stakes of a wager (this was the original meaning of the word).
2. A person or group that has an investment, share, or interest in something, such as a business or industry. (This is now the generally accepted usage in the English-speaking business world.)
3. Law: A person holding money or property for two or more persons making rival claims.

Research and writing about stakeholders has been primarily in English, with the focus on the meaning and concept of stakeholder in the English-speaking world. In interviews with Spanish-speaking managers in countries in South America and then later with managers from other language groups, I discovered that when "stakeholder" is translated into other languages, it acquires subtly different meanings. Often, the focus is on just one attribute rather than the more inclusive definition developed more recently, such as this one from *A Guide to the Project Management Body of Knowledge (PMBOK® Guide)* (Project Management Institute [PMI], 2012:563):

> Stakeholders are individuals, groups, or organizations who may affect, be affected by, or perceive themselves to be affected by a decision, activity, or outcome of a project, program, or portfolio.

---

* There will be more detail in subsequent chapters of suggested approaches for each type of stakeholder: Engaging stakeholders will require the project manager to demonstrate true heroic behavior by ensuring the right information goes to the right stakeholders and at the same time focusing on leadership within the communication ecosystem.

From discussions with colleagues from different language backgrounds, these subtle differences emerge:

- In Spanish: *partes interesadas* (interested parties).
- In French: *des parties prenantes* (involved parties).
- In German: *beteiligten* (involved) and *Anspruchsgruppen* (who have a claim).
- In Dutch: *belanghebbenden* (having a stake).
- In Japan: "related people" or "people sharing risk and profits."[*]
- In China: "participants with related interest.[†]
- In Brasil: Dinsmore (1999) referred to stakeholders as the "ones who have the beef." This seems to be a consistent view of the term *stakeholder* in that country.[‡]

The strength of a definition of stakeholders such as that of PMI (2012) is that it acknowledges the diverse functions of stakeholders, within and outside the project, making it almost impossible to legitimately overlook any stakeholders. An additional strength of the definition is the focus on *perceptions* as a characteristic of a stakeholder. Perceptions and expectations are discussed in detail further in the chapter, but for the moment it is sufficient to emphasize their importance for successful stakeholder engagement and therefore the project's outcomes.

How something is defined and how it is expressed in language provide a good indication of what the word or concept actually *is* in that culture. The various translations of stakeholder in each culture point to specific ideas about stakeholders. For example, the Spanish translations of stakeholder as "interested parties" or "involved parties" emphasize the collectivist characteristics of the South American culture because of their preference for considering groups of stakeholders rather than individuals.[§] The Japanese and Chinese view of stakeholders as "related" is closer to the modern view of stakeholder and possibly a result of a culture with stronger focus on "collectivism" and relationships than the "individualism" of Western cultures, particularly the English-speaking countries (Hofstede, Hofstede, and Minkov, 2010).[¶]

---

[*] I had the opportunity to speak to a group of project managers in Japan in January 2013 and asked the question regarding how the term *stakeholders* was translated in Japanese at that time.

[†] This definition is from e-mail correspondence with Bob Youker in 2003; he previously worked for the World Bank and is now retired.

[‡] I presented at conferences in Brazil in 2009 and 2011; this definition was the basis of all stakeholder discussions with project managers and project management office (PMO) practitioners in that country.

[§] This preference has been confirmed in a number of conversations with both senior managers and students studying for a master's degree in South America.

[¶] Culture and its influence on each of us are discussed in detail in Chapter 6.

A Stakeholder Has a Stake

By definition, a stakeholder has a stake in the activity, project, or program. For successful engagement, it is necessary to understand the nature of a stakeholder's stake in the outcomes of the project. This stake may be an interest (I); rights (legal or moral) (R); ownership (O); or support in the form of knowledge (N) or contribution (C). There are many potential stakes, so a useful way to remember them is to use the mnemonic IRONIC, with an additional (I) for impact/influence added for neatness. This is illustrated in Figure 2.1.

Interest

Interest has many meanings. It can refer to

- Financial advantage or profit,
- Pastimes or a hobby, or
- Significance or relevance.

To be interested is to be attracted to something or to give it full attention. The interest of stakeholders in the definition of *stake* should be specific: a circumstance in which a person or group will be affected by a decision, action or outcome.* Consider a public event being held in a residential area: for the time that event is running and for a period before and after, people living in the vicinity of the event will have an *interest*, even if they do not enjoy or participate in the subject of that event.†

Rights

Rights can be either legal or moral rights:

- Legal rights cover the legal claim of a group or individual to be treated in a certain way or to have a particular right protected. These rights are usually enshrined in a country's legislation; examples include privacy laws and occupational health and safety.

---

* Because *interest* has many definitions, it is not really a suitable category for measuring an aspect of a project's stakeholder community. The more consistently a stakeholder can be understood, the better it will be for understanding how best to communicate for maintaining robust relationships.
† I live within a kilometer of Albert Park in Melbourne, Australia, where the Australian Grand Prix is held every year. Even though the idea of car racing has no appeal for me, and I have no involvement, I am a stakeholder of the Grand Prix because of the noise and inconvenience of this event.

Interest:	A person or group of persons is affected by a decision related to the activity or its outcomes:
	• Effect of street closures for a public event;
	• Support for the creation of a nature park in another country or region.
Rights:	To be treated in a certain way or to have a particular right protected:
	• Legal right:
	• Occupational health and safety; privacy;
	• Moral right:
	• Heritage protection activists; environmentalists.
Ownership:	A circumstance when a person or group of persons has a legal title to an asset or a property:
	• Resumption of personal or business property for road works;
	• Intellectual property;
	• Shareholders' "ownership" in an organization.
kNowledge:	Specialist knowledge or organizational knowledge required to enable the activity.
Impact or influence:	• Impacted by the activity or its outcomes:
	• Staff, customers, shareholders
	• Impact (or influence) on the activity or its outcomes:
	• Sponsor, governments (legislation, regulation), the public
Contribution:	• Supply of resources
	• People, material, funding
	• Advocacy for objectives or activity success, buffer between organization and activity teams or the performance of the activity

FIGURE 2.1
Potential stakes: the IRONIC mnemonic.

- Moral rights cover issues that may affect large groups of people or natural phenomena, such as environmental, heritage, or social issues. Social issues may extend to speaking on behalf of countries or individuals who cannot speak for themselves or defend themselves and encompass both the activists and the "victims." Moral rights are usually not covered by legislation. Organizations may choose to consider such stakeholders through their corporate social responsibility (CSR) activities.

Ownership

Most stakeholders will have an "interest"; many will have rights. Many may also have a stake of ownership, such as

- A worker's right to earn a living from his or her knowledge,
- Shareholders' ownership of a portion of an organization's assets,

- Intellectual property resulting from the exploitation of an idea, or
- Legal title to an asset or a property.

Contribution of Knowledge (or Experience)

A team member or employee who applies experience or knowledge to the production of an asset for an organization will be making a contribution to the organization's activity. This knowledge is important to the organization's, or project's, success, and the employee or team member will also be affected by the success or failure of the activity.

Contribution of Support

The contribution that a stakeholder, such as the sponsor or senior stakeholder, may make to support the project falls into the following categories:

- Allocation of resources—people or materials,
- Provision of funds—either the initial approval or ongoing assurance of continued funding, and
- Provision of "political support" within the organization's hierarchy or the wider community.

Awareness of a stakeholder's stake in the outcome of the project is essential for managing the relationship between the team and the project's stakeholders. Key questions to clarify the nature of this relationship and to further develop the concept are, Who can be stakeholders? Why are they important?

STAKEHOLDER ENGAGEMENT

Definitions for *engagement* indicate multiple approaches[*]:

- Involvement or commitment, both emotional and physical, to a cause or an idea,

---

[*] Definitions are provided at http://www.visualthesaurus.com; http://dictionary1.classic.reference.com.

- Participation in the actions of a group,
- Intervention, intercession, or conflict, such as military battles or fights,
- Obligations or agreements, either social or financial, such as a promise to marry or other types of contractual arrangements, or
- Employment, especially for a specified time.

Based on the diverse approaches to engagement listed, engagement can be defined as practices, processes and actions that an organization (or project) must perform to involve stakeholders and to secure their involvement and commitment, or reduce their indifference or hostility.

The Institute of Social and Ethical Accountability (AccountAbility, 2006, 2011),[*] released a *Standard for Stakeholder Engagement*. The standard covers all areas of an organization's affairs (external, internal, and social) and is useful as an additional source of information about how to engage stakeholders in areas such as the following[†]:

- *Functional (external) engagements*: customer care, public relations, supplier relations, and regulatory and government relations
- *Organization-wide (internal) engagements*: reporting and assurance; management accounting; human resource (HR) management
- *Issue-based engagement*: human rights; heritage and environmental moral rights; and philanthropic activities

In this book and in the **Stakeholder** *Circle®* methodology that is described in this chapter, stakeholder engagement is the rationale for analysis of the stakeholder community. Engagement of the stakeholders is taking the appropriate information exchange (communication) actions to ensure that the expectations of stakeholders are understood and are included in the strategy and implementation activities of the project. The purpose of this focus is to ensure that stakeholders are aware of the project and its outcomes and are prepared to have the necessary involvement, participation, and interest.

---

[*] The *AA1000 Stakeholder Engagement Standard* is available as a free download at http://www. accountability.org/standards/aa1000ses/index.html.

[†] It also supports the idea that stakeholder identification and engagement are complex and based on a wide definition of *stakeholder*.

Implications for Successful Stakeholder Engagement in Projects

If certain groups or individuals can influence the successful delivery of the outcomes of the project through provision (or withholding) of funds, support, or resources such as materials or people with the essential skills, they should be identified by the project team as stakeholders. Others will self-select: protesters, objectors, or authorities. If any of these groups or individuals fits the definition of stakeholders, then an appropriate level of effort should be directed toward engaging them by developing appropriate relationships driven by communication.

Through effective communication, the stakeholder will *perceive* that his or her needs are understood. The stakeholder will then be more effectively engaged in the success of the project, and through this contribution, the project or activity will have an increased chance of success.

Relationships that are appropriate and sustainable are two sided: Both parties gain from participation in this relationship or have expectations of gaining something. The relationship will not flourish unless both parties participate. To make the relationship work, it is essential to understand the *expectations* of each stakeholder, in particular the stakeholders who have been identified as the most important in the stakeholder community for any given time in the life cycle of the project or other organization activity.

Knowing the expectations of important stakeholders will support early identification of potential conflicts between important stakeholders. It will also be the means to develop a useful message to provide the stakeholder with the feeling of confidence that his or her needs are known and understood. Through targeted communication, the stakeholder can also be assured that the team will make every effort to provide these requirements or ensure that the reasons for *not* being able to provide these requirements are explained so that the stakeholder's *new* expectations can be established. By doing these things, the stakeholder will *perceive* that personal needs are understood and from that will be more effectively engaged in contributing to the success of the project.

EXPECTATIONS

Everybody has expectations. These are their conscious or unconscious needs, desires, or wants and are specific to each individual depending on the individual's past experiences. Nobody can assume to know the expectations of others. In developing robust relationships with stakeholders, understanding the expectations of important stakeholders is a difficult and complex task but is essential to the welfare of the project. Some useful approaches to understanding stakeholders' expectations include the following:

- Ask the stakeholder or stakeholder's colleagues,
- Research project documentation, form a perspective of what expectations may be, and offer some ideas to help the stakeholder formulate his or her own, or
- Use surveys.

Asking

Asking is the most logical step and seems like a good idea; it is far more likely to produce results than assuming knowledge of another person's expectations. The traps may be the following:

- The stakeholder may not have given any thought to what he or she expects to gain or lose as a result of involvement with the project. The answer may be anything that he or she believes will satisfy you at that moment.
- The stakeholder may just give the answer that he or she thinks you want to hear or may just talk about being "on time and within budget and delivering approved scope." There is nothing useful about this information. Time, cost, and scope are the measures of each and every project and are business operation expectations rather than relationship-building expectations.*
- On the positive side, because the stakeholder has actually been asked about his or her wants and needs with regard to the project's deliverables, the stakeholder may develop a positive impression of the project and the project manager. This positive outlook may prove useful later if the individual's support is needed in times of trouble.

---

* The types of expectations that are most useful for building strong relationships are about personal, career, or organizational desires or needs. For example, personal expectations may include building a reputation or experience for future job opportunities; career expectations may be about gaining the reputation and profile that enables early promotion to higher (better-paid) levels. Organizational expectations may be about raising the profile of the section or department or achieving better customer satisfaction or other key performance indicators.

Research

Sources for additional information about stakeholders' expectations or requirements can include

- Gathering information in the public record: web pages, Google information,
- Viewing organizational reports: annual reports, business cases, requirements documents,
- Asking others who may have more information, or
- Seeking confirmation of data collected from other sources, such as colleagues.

Surveys

Many projects and organizations now use customer satisfaction surveys (CSSs) as one measure of success of the project or other work. The data collected for CSSs are only valid if a preliminary set of questions to gauge expectations is collected at the beginning of the project. Most stakeholders will be positive about answering such questions, when they may not be keen to respond to other ways of understanding their expectations, such as those described previously. Zeithaml, Parasuraman, and Berry (1990) produced a useful guide to CSSs—still relevant—that provides examples of well-designed surveys for this purpose.

STAKEHOLDER THEORY

I do not intend to cover the diverse history of stakeholder theory here[*]; this discussion is based on the concept of stakeholder as developed by Freeman (1984) and more recently Freeman et al. (2010). What is covered in this section is a discussion of the two opposite views of stakeholder that still exist and is based on a deeper philosophical viewpoint:

> Can business leaders make decisions about the conduct of the business without considering the impact of these decisions on (all) those who will be affected by the decisions? Is it possible to separate "business" decisions from the ethical considerations of their impact? (Freeman et al., 2010:5)

---

[*] A history of the recognition of the term *stakeholder* within an organizational context was provided by Bourne (2012).

R. Edward Freeman is considered to be one of the early proponents of the idea of organizational stakeholders, writing that they could be defined as "any group or individual who can affect or is affected by the achievement of the organization's objectives" (1984:46). This is not so very different from the definition from PMI (2012) quoted previously in this chapter. Freeman et al. (2010) traced the theory's evolution from 1984 when stakeholder theory was originally associated with the idea of business as being concerned with value creation and trade.* Economics at the time assumed that "values and ethics" did not need to be considered in economic theory. The following are some problems with this approach:

- Can we really divide the world into "business realm" and "ethical realm"?
- Can business executives "do the right thing": Can they separate the "business" decisions they make from the impacts of these decisions on everyone else (stakeholders)?
- How can we combine business and ethics conceptually and practically?
- What should be taught in business schools?†

Freeman et al. (2010:6) referred to the artificial separation of business decisions and considerations of their impact as the "separation fallacy," rejecting it by stating there can be no such thing as "value free economics" (2010:7): It makes no sense to talk about business or ethics without talking about human beings. Business is conducted by human beings, decisions are made by human beings, and the purpose of the value creation and trade is for the benefit of human beings.

The starting point for a correct approach to stakeholders is that "most people, most of the time, want to, and do, accept responsibility for the effects of their actions on others" (Freeman et al., 2010:8). If business is separated from ethics, there can be no moral responsibility for business decisions. What this means is that

- People engaged in value creation and trade (in business) are responsible precisely to "those groups and individuals who can affect or be affected by their actions" (Freeman et al., 2010:8).

---

* This definition of value creation and trade is the working definition used by Freeman (1984) and more recently Freeman et al. (2010).
† See the work of Mintzberg (2005) for a critique of the focus, function, and output of modern business schools.

- This means those who are affected are at least customers, employees, suppliers, communities, and financiers (shareholders).

Stakeholder theory, then, is fundamentally a theory about how business could work *at its best*. It is descriptive, prescriptive, and instrumental (a means to an end) at the same time. Stakeholder theory is more than just considering value for shareholders—it is more complex because there are many relationships involved. For any organizational activity, there will be a complex web of human beings and their needs and wants (stakes).

In answering the question, What makes business successful? Freeman et al. (2010:10) attempted to refute Milton Friedman's article in the *New York Times* (Friedman, 1970), which stated that for businesses to become successful, they must focus on maximizing profits—a focus on shareholders and "shareholder value." However, to maximize profits, there must also exist

- Products and services that customers want,
- Good relationships with suppliers to keep operations at the cutting edge,
- Inspired employees to stand for the company's mission and push it to become better, and
- Supportive communities to allow the company to flourish.

A focus on shareholders is counterproductive because it takes away focus on a fundamental driver to value: stakeholder relationships. The only way to maximize profits sustainably is to satisfy all stakeholders (Freeman et al., 2010:12).

Instead of the flawed shareholder value paradigm, developing a "stakeholder mindset" in organizations and by extension in projects and programs is a better way to maximize profits, with the following pertaining:

- Business is a set of relationships among groups that have a stake in the activities that make up the business.
- Business is about how customers; suppliers; employees; financiers (stockholders, bondholders, banks); communities; and managers interact and create value.
- Understanding business results from knowing how these relationships work.
- The executive's job is to manage and shape these relationships (Freeman et al., 2010:15).

Within this framework, the stakes that stakeholders have will be as follows:

- Owners or financiers (shareholders) have a financial stake in the business in the form of stocks or bonds—they expect a financial return.
- Employees have their jobs and their livelihood at stake: They may have specialized skills for which there is only a small market; in return for their labor, they expect security, wages and benefits, and meaningful work.
- Customers and suppliers exchange resources for the products and services of the firm. They expect to receive in return the benefits of the products and services; these relationships are enmeshed in the practice of ethics in business.
- The local community grants the organization the right to build facilities within its boundaries. The community benefits from taxes and the economic and social contributions of the organization back into the community. Organizations are expected to be good citizens—not to expose the community to unreasonable hazards in the form of pollution or toxic waste. The community expects that the organization will inform it if it discovers hazards to the community resulting from production of its goods and services.

There is great value to be gained in examining how the stakes of each stakeholder or stakeholder group contribute, positively or negatively, to the value creation process of a business and what the role of the executive is in stakeholder relationship management. In this context, stakeholders are defined in the following way:

- *Narrowly*: Those groups without whose support the business would cease to be viable were categorized as "primary" by Freeman et al. (2010:28).* Such thinking was also the basis of the categorization of stakeholders as "legitimate" and "salient" (Mitchell, Agle, and Wood,

---

* I do not agree with the categorization of stakeholders as primary and secondary. In my experience, this particular categorization results in consideration only of primary stakeholders, with relationship building with secondary stakeholders viewed as optional. In the frantic environment of modern projects and other organizational activities, this often means that secondary stakeholders will be neglected for lack of time. This is the reason for adding prioritization as a step in the stakeholder analytics of **Stakeholder** *Circle* methodology.

1997), leading to the accepted viewpoint that only the "important primary" stakeholders matter.[*]

- *Widely*: Those who can affect the business or be affected by its activities are categorized as secondary or instrumental (a means to an end).

Therefore, the stakeholder approach preferred by Freeman et al. (2010:28) is this:

> Executives need to understand that business is fully situated in the realms of human beings; stakeholders have names and faces and children AND they are not placeholders for social roles.

Stakeholder theory must address these issues:

- Understanding and managing a business in the twenty-first century—the problem of an organization's value creation and profitable trade.
- Combining thinking about questions of ethics, responsibility, and sustainability with the current economic view that the organizations that operate within a capitalist framework are exempt from considerations beyond the narrow frame of "maximization of shareholder value"—the problem of the ethics of capitalism.
- Understanding what to teach managers and students about what it takes to be successful in the current business world—the problem of managerial mindset.

Approaches to Stakeholder Relationships

The work of Freeman et al. (2010) takes a practical yet ethical approach to stakeholder theory and the practices of stakeholder engagement. In arguing for an inclusive approach, they examined the major categories of stakeholder theory. The work of Stoney and Winstanley (2001) is useful for exploring ways that stakeholder relationships can be defined. The authors were concerned about the lack of agreement within the industry about who stakeholders actually were and how to identify those who were important. From their review of the literature on stakeholders and stakeholder

---

[*] The basis of the **Stakeholder** *Circle* methodology is a consistent approach to defining characteristics of stakeholders. Given that there is no objective way to measure stakeholder engagement, this consistency of definition is vital. The category of "legitimate" used by Mitchell et al. (1997) cannot be defined consistently.

engagement, they identified five different categories to describe the various stakeholder management approaches:

- Political perspectives
- Purpose and objectives of considering stakeholders
- Value of considering stakeholders
- Consideration of stakeholder intervention levels
- Degree of stakeholder enforcement

Dimension 1: Political Perspectives of Stakeholders

At one extreme lies the Marxist view of political struggle between capital and labor; this view rejects the stakeholder concept. At the other end of that continuum lies the *unitarists,* who believe that shareholders, as owners of capital, will be most important in terms of the strength/legitimacy of their claims on the organization. The position adopted during the development of the **Stakeholder** *Circle* methodology is indicated by the triangle symbol in Figure 2.2. This is a pluralist perspective recognizing that there are a diverse range of stakeholders with valid claims to consider. This position and the positions developed in the other dimensions are described in detail by Walker, Bourne, and Shelley (2008) and Bourne (2012).

	Marxist/radical	**Pluralist**	**Unitarist/Neoliberal**
Political perspective	*Rejects: a dualist view of society*	*Supports: accommodates multiple interests*	*Rejects: primacy of shareholders*
	Reform		**Analysis**
Purpose and objective	*Regulations, best practices and standards*		*Mapping influence, power and interest*
	Intrinsic		**Instrumental**
Value of considering stakeholders	*An end in itself*		*A means to an end*
	Regulation	**Organization**	**Individual**
Level of stakeholder interventions	*Treaties and trade laws: local/ regional/ global*	*Corporate governance*	*Individual rights*
	Voluntarism	**Better Practice**	**Coercion**
Engagement enforcement level	*Philosophy/ethos*	*Codes, templates, examples*	*Legal entrenchment of rights*

FIGURE 2.2

Dimension of stakeholder relationships. (Adapted from Stoney, C. and Winstanley, F., *Journal of Management Studies,* 38(5), 603–626, 2001.)

Dimension 2: Purpose and Objectives of Considering Stakeholders

This continuum ranges from reform through regulations on how valid stakeholders should be recognized and treated to analysis of the stakeholder community through a structured, repeatable approach. Mapping of stakeholder interest lies at the analysis end of that continuum, derived from the analysis of stakeholders to understand and manage their power, access, and influence within that community. The *Stakeholder Circle* methodology supports pragmatic intervention in stakeholder relationships to manage the outcomes of an organization's activities most effectively.

Dimension 3: Value of Considering Stakeholders

This dimension derives a continuum with stakeholders at one end as instruments and agents whose power must be harnessed and controlled (instrumentality) and at the other end as having intrinsic moral rights.

Dimension 4: Consideration of the Stakeholder Intervention Level

The continuum spreads from, at one end, the concept of the community's right to intervene through regulations at a local government, regional, national, or global level and at the other end lies the individual's intrinsic right to "be heard." The organization is positioned at the midpoint, where it can benefit from understanding what influence and power stakeholders may have and can plan and negotiate to influence plans and actions of the stakeholder community. This position implies a need for stakeholder engagement and integration into planning, communication planning, and risk management of all organizational activities.

Dimension 5: Consideration of the Degree of Stakeholder Enforcement

This final dimension relates to the way in which stakeholder interests may be institutionalized within an engagement plan. The extreme positions are voluntary actions on the part of stakeholders and team members and coercion by which a plan must be enacted as formulated. The processes and practices supporting increasing maturity in stakeholder management and engagement should be built through communication of the connection between focus on stakeholder engagement and business practice.

The triangles in Figure 2.2 indicate the focus of the **Stakeholder** *Circle* methodology. The intent is to represent a "middle line" or balanced approach:

- There is a pluralist political perspective for dimension 1.
- A balance of reform exists through application of best practices and standards and analytics through a mapping of power and influence (dimension 2).
- There is recognition that effective stakeholder engagement is most useful when stakeholder relationship management is regarded as both "an end in itself"[*] and "a means to an end."[†] Both perspectives will add value to the organization's activities, just as ignoring stakeholders may decrease the value of the outcome.
- Regulations (legal rights), governance, and accountability form within the organization, and the rights of individuals should all be part of considerations regarding stakeholders (dimension 4).
- There is enforcement of stakeholder rights, an organization's voluntary involvement with CSR policies and practices, as well as recognition that compliance with best practice and continuous improvement will be enhanced through the inclusion of stakeholder relationship management practices within the organization (dimension 5).

Recognition of the multiple dimensions of stakeholder relationship management does not mean that everyone should be regarded as a stakeholder and given equal consideration. This would be unwieldy and impractical.[‡] Identification of stakeholders must be performed within the context of the definition of stakeholder; the list must be prioritized; and the attitude of each important stakeholder must be understood for both effective stakeholder engagement and efficiency in building robust relationships through implementation of appropriate communication strategies.[§]

---

[*] Ethical considerations require that the expectations of stakeholders be considered.

[†] It is equally important that stakeholders are effectively engaged for the benefit of the project or organization.

[‡] This is the reason that prioritization (step 2) is an essential part of the *Stakeholder Circle* methodology.

[§] This is in line with the approach developed by Freeman et al. (2010).

ORGANIZATION ACTIVITIES
AND STAKEHOLDER COMMUNITIES

The description of the five dimensions of stakeholder relationship management and engagement provides a foundation for developing views on how to effectively manage stakeholder relationships for each project. It also provides a starting point for recognizing the diverse activities an organization must perform and therefore the diverse stakeholder communities and relationships it must maintain (and a reference point for the communication system). It is not possible to identify a standard set of stakeholders for the organization; every project that an organization undertakes will have its own unique set of stakeholders. It is not appropriate to state that one set of stakeholders is always more important than any other. To always favor the needs of (say) shareholders over customers or employees means that some stakeholders who are important for specific activities or projects may be ignored, to the detriment of the delivery of value to the organization.

Depending on the type of activity and even on the different stages or phases of that activity, there will be variation in the membership of the stakeholder community. Activities that an organization may undertake can include the following,* which are often implemented using the disciplines of project management:

- CSR activities
- Achievement of competitive advantage and improvement of the bottom line
- Business change
- Mergers and acquisitions (M&A)
- Projects and programs of work

How Many Stakeholders?

Some organizational activities are large and complex and may affect many stakeholders. For example, construction of public facilities or national

---

* Even though the focus of this book is stakeholders in projects, numerous organizations today manage many of their activities using project management disciplines. The list of all types of organizational activities has been included in recognition of that. For more information about these activities, refer to my earlier book *Stakeholder Relationship Management* (Bourne, 2012), which focused on stakeholders in organizations.

infrastructure projects will affect private citizens, landowners, and the natural and historical environment. In a case such as this, it is essential to recognize and accept that there will be large numbers of stakeholders to be identified. There is often an unconscious boundary on what a "good number" of stakeholders can be. It is important for the team and for the team's management to understand that although the initial number of stakeholders identified may appear unwieldy or overwhelming, effective prioritization provides a structured and logical means to identify the key stakeholders for the current time. Particularly in the case of large numbers of stakeholders, the application of a structured methodology, such as the *Stakeholder Circle*, is indispensable.

ANALYZING THE STAKEHOLDER COMMUNITY WITH THE *STAKEHOLDER CIRCLE*

The *Stakeholder Circle* methodology is based on the concept that an organization's activities to realize value are central to any consideration of the stakeholder community on which success depends. Figure 2.3 shows the relationships. All decisions or understanding of the relationships are from the perspective of the project manager. Surrounding the work (or project) is the team, often overlooked in many stakeholder engagement processes.

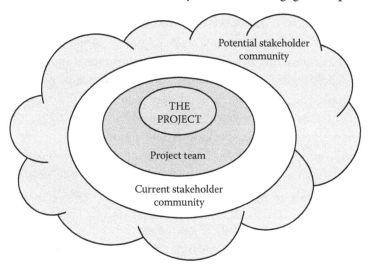

FIGURE 2.3
The circle of stakeholders.

Surrounding the team is the community of stakeholders that has been identified as key to the success of the activity *at the present time.* The outermost circle references potential stakeholders, those who may, or will, be important to the success of the activity at a later stage.

By differentiating current stakeholders and potential stakeholders in this way, confusion about which stakeholders are important at that moment and how best to manage the current relationships will be minimized while ensuring that planning for future relationships is managed effectively. The stakeholders in the outer circle may also be considered in risk management processes because they may cause the work to be at risk of failure in the future, or these stakeholders may need to be considered in marketing plans as potential customers.*

Managing Stakeholder Relationships

The **Stakeholder** Circle is a five-step methodology that provides a flexible approach to understanding and managing relationships within and around the project. It also supports the concept of the dynamic nature of the stakeholder community. The methodology is based on the concept that the project can only exist with the informed consent of its stakeholder community, and that managing the relationships between this community and the project team will increase the chances of success. The stakeholder community consists of individuals and groups, each with a different potential to influence the project's outcome positively or negatively. The potential of important stakeholders to influence the project's success or failure holds the key to targeting communication toward the right stakeholders at the right time during the life of the project. Through this analysis, the team will develop appreciation of the right level of engagement—the information and communication needed to influence stakeholder's perceptions, expectations, and actions.

The **Stakeholder** Circle is a flexible model that can be adjusted to cater for changes in stakeholder community and stakeholder influence throughout the life of the activity. There are five steps to the methodology:

- *Step 1*: identification of all stakeholders.
- *Step 2*: prioritization to determine who is important.
- *Step 3*: visualization to understand the overall stakeholder community.

---

* Remember that people are the main source of risk (Chapter 1).

- *Step 4*: engagement through effective communications.
- *Step 5*: monitoring the effect of the engagement.

Step 1: Identify

Step 1 in the **Stakeholder** *Circle* methodology provides a course of action for

- Knowing who stakeholders are at a particular time.
- Gathering information about each individual or group in anticipation of planning targeted communication.

It consists of three activities: developing a list of stakeholders; defining the nature of the relationship (what is the stake of each stakeholder and the stakeholder's expectations of the project); and describing the spheres of influence as detailed in Figure 2.4. Each stakeholder has directions of influence: upwards, downwards, outwards, and sidewards. *Upwards* stakeholders are senior managers of the organization; *downwards* stakeholders are members of the team; *outwards* stakeholders are stakeholders outside the projects; and *sidewards* stakeholders are peers of the project manager.

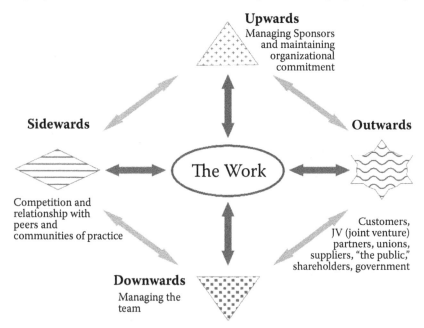

FIGURE 2.4
"Directions" of influence.

Step 2: Prioritize: How to Understand Who Is Important

The results from step 1, identify, are the starting point for *step 2, prioritize.* For complex, high-profile activities, the unranked, unrefined list can be large.* With large numbers of stakeholders, the team must clarify which of these stakeholders are more important at this time in the life of the project.

A system for rating and therefore ranking stakeholders according to their relative importance to the work at a particular time is based on three aspects:

1. *Power:* the power an individual or group may have to permanently change or stop the project.
2. *Proximity:* the degree of involvement that the individual or group has in the work of the team.
3. *Urgency:* the importance of the work or its outcomes, whether positive or negative, to certain stakeholders (their stake) and how prepared they are to act to achieve these outcomes.

Power

Power can be understood as a necessary part of the structure of relationships and neither good nor bad. Power exists in organizations through hierarchical structures; the exercise of power is a political process, and all relationships are power relationships (Stacey, 2001). The definition of power used in step 2, prioritize, describes the relative power to "kill" or "save" the project. It is not necessary to identify the type of power that a stakeholder wields; it is essential only to understand the extent to which this power affects the continuation of the work itself.

Proximity

The rating proximity provides a second way of identifying how a stakeholder may influence the work of the project or its outcomes. Its contribution is the acknowledgment of the importance of regular, close, and often face-to-face relationships developed within the team and how these relationships influence the outcomes of the work. The immediacy

---

* In working with organizations using the **Stakeholder** *Circle* methodology and software for mapping and managing stakeholder relationships, I have assisted in projects that have over 100 stakeholders (both individuals and groups) identified in the first step.

of this relationship contributes to trust among the members of the team and more effective work relationships as the team members understand the strengths and weaknesses of those they work with on a regular basis (Granovetter, 1973). An individual's ability to access independently all other members of the team (Rowley, 1997) develops a stronger team culture and enhances the team's ability to achieve group goals. Groups work best when they have met each other (face to face) at least once, and they work even more effectively if colocated* (McGrath, 1984).

Urgency

Urgency is based on the concept described by Mitchell, Agle, and Wood (1997), whose theory described two conditions that may contribute to the notion of urgency:

1. *Time sensitivity*: work that must be completed in a fixed time, such as a facility for the Olympic Games.
2. *Criticality*: an individual or group feels strongly enough about an issue to act, such as environmental or heritage protection activists.

In the **Stakeholder** *Circle,* urgency is rated through analysis of two subcategories: the *value* that a stakeholder places on an outcome of the work and the *action* that he or she is prepared to take as a consequence of this value or stake. The inclusion of urgency in the prioritization ratings balances the potential distortion of an organizational culture that identifies stakeholder with a high level of hierarchical power as most important. If power and proximity are the only measures, stakeholders with little power but a high sense of urgency, such as the "lone powerless voice," can cause significant damage to the project's outcomes if their stakes are not acknowledged.

The Prioritization Process

The team rates the list of stakeholders against the statements for power, proximity, value, and action, agreeing on the rating and recording it then developing a ranked list of stakeholders. The results of these steps will

---

* This research, conducted in the 1980s, may soon be superseded by research into generation Y's communication preferences for online forms and text messaging. The **Stakeholder** *Circle* simply defines *proximity* by involvement in the work of the teams.

enable teams to develop a better understanding of the unique characteristics of their stakeholder community and the relationships within it.

Step 3: Visualization: Presentation of Complex Data

The objective of every stakeholder mapping process is to present a useful picture of the stakeholder community, in particular which stakeholders are most important.* The brain processes ideas fastest visually (Rock, 2006). Therefore, the complex data collected about stakeholders will be most easily understood by others when presented in several complementary forms, such as the appropriate combination of

- Graphical or pictorial views,
- Tables or sorted lists,
- Written explanations, or
- Discussions.

Designing visual aids that convey useful information about stakeholders is not straightforward. A two-dimensional, flat sheet of paper cannot easily present the multifaceted relationship likely to exist between the team and their stakeholders. Some of the dimensions that may need to be considered include:

- *Attitude*: Will the person help or hinder the work?
- *Hierarchy*: Where is the person in the organization's structure compared to the activity manager: higher/lower, internal/external, colleague or competitor?
- *Influence*: How well connected is the person?
- *Interest*: Does the person have an active interest, passive interest, or no interest?
- *Legitimacy*: Does the person have some level of entitlement to be consulted?
- *Power*: What is the person's ability to cause change?
- *Proximity*: How involved is the person in the work?
- *Receptiveness*: How easy is it to communicate with this person?

---

* The **Stakeholder** *Circle* software produces a unique map of every stakeholder community and shows the power, proximity, and influence of each important stakeholder through graphic representations of the data collected in the stakeholder analysis process defined previously. More information and access to a trial version of the software are available online (http://www.stakeholder-management.com).

- *Supportiveness*: Does the person support or oppose the work?
- *Urgency*: Does the person perceive the work to be important to them?

This list is far from exhaustive but serves to demonstrate the challenges of indicating which stakeholders matter and the nature of the relationship between each stakeholder (individual or group) and the team.

Step 4: Engage

Any relationship requires constant work to maintain it; this applies to family relationships, friendships, management of staff, and maintenance of professional networks. Relationships between an organization or project and its stakeholders are no different. The team must understand the expectations of all of the important stakeholders and how they can be managed through targeted communication to maintain supportive relationships and to moderate the consequences of unsupportive stakeholders for the benefit of the organization and its activities. Step 4 defines the *attitude* of a stakeholder—how supportive each one is of the project and how receptive the stakeholder is to information about the project.

Attitude is defined as follows:

- *Emotional*: a state of mind or feeling; a positive or negative approach to life; a result of perception, learning, and experience; and
- *Behavioral (either personal preferences or related to culture)*: tolerance; opinion; manner.

Receptiveness is a key part of defining attitude. It is defined as willingness to engage; sympathetic and accessible nature; and openness to, and interest in, information about the activity and its progress, issues, and outcomes.

Application of Attitude in Organizations Today

A stakeholder's attitude toward an organization or a project can be driven by many factors, including

- Whether involvement is voluntary or involuntary.
- Whether involvement is beneficial personally or organizationally.
- The level of a stakeholder's investment either financially or emotionally in the activity.

If the individual or group perceives that the project outcomes will be beneficial, the individual or group is more likely to be prepared to contribute to the successful outcomes of the project. If, on the other hand, the individual or group sees themselves as victims or losers, they will be more likely to hold a negative attitude regarding that activity. Part of the assessment of the stakeholder's attitude will be a review of the stake the stakeholder has and his or her expectations and requirements for success or failure of the activity. The assessment will need to take into account the following elements that shape attitude:

- Culture: organizational, team, or individual,
- Identification with the activity and its outcomes,
- Perceived importance of the activity and its outcomes, and
- Personal attributes, such as personality and role.

The engagement profiles are developed by

- Assessing the actual attitude of selected stakeholders,
- Describing a realistic target attitude of these stakeholders necessary for success of the activity, and
- The level of support and receptiveness that would best* meet the needs of both the project and the stakeholder. If an important stakeholder is both actively opposed and will not receive messages about the activity, he or she will need to have a different engagement approach compared to stakeholders who are highly supportive and encourage personal delivery of messages.

Examples of Engagement Profiles

Figure 2.5 shows some engagement profiles. Stakeholder 1† has been assessed as ambivalent about the activity, neither supportive nor unsupportive (3), and not really interested in receiving any information about the activity (2). These results are shown by X in the appropriate boxes in the matrix. However, the team has decided that the target attitude *should be* neutral (3) and ambivalent about information (3); this is shown with a bold

---

* *Best* involves balancing what is realistically achievable against the importance of the stakeholder moderated by the amount of effort that the team can allocate to the communication process.

† The vertical dimension of the matrix allows assessment from 1–5 for levels of support where 1 = totally unsupportive and 5 = very supportive. The horizontal dimension allows assessment of receptiveness to information about the project, where 1 = has no interest in any information and 5 = openness to all information about the project.

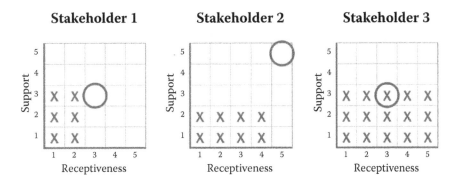

FIGURE 2.5
Engagement profiles.

circle. In this assessment, there is only a small gap between the stakeholder's current attitude and the attitude the team has agreed is essential for the success of the activity: The engagement profile is shown as close to optimal.*

Stakeholder 2 has been assessed as passive unsupportive (2) and at a medium level of interest in receiving information about the activity (4). For project success, the engagement profile *should be* actively supportive (5) and eager to receive information at any time (5). In this case, the gap between the current engagement profile and the optimal profile indicates that a high level of effort will be required to develop communication strategies for this stakeholder to encourage the stakeholder's support and interest in information about the activity; generally, this level of support is only sought from key stakeholders, such as the sponsor, steering committee, or a member of the steering committee.

Stakeholder 3 in Figure 2.5 has been assessed as neither supportive nor unsupportive (3) but eager to receive information any time (5). The team has assessed that this stakeholder *should be* at a level of receptiveness of ambivalent: neither supportive nor nonsupportive (3). This is a situation in which the current profile is significantly different from the optimal profile and will require careful handling from the team to avoid alienating the stakeholder.

Step 5: Monitor the Effectiveness of the Communication

The work of step 5 includes implementing the planned communication action and then monitoring and evaluating the results to understand the

---

* It is not essential that all stakeholders have a high level of support and receptiveness toward the activity; part of the key decision the team has to make is whether the stakeholder in question is important enough to warrant any work that is necessary to achieve this high level of support. This information has been gathered through the analysis in steps 1–3.

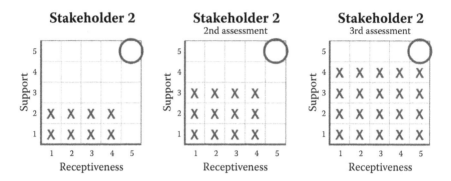

FIGURE 2.6

Measuring the effectiveness of communication using engagement profiles.

effects of the implementation and derive learning. The communication plan is developed based on the information gathered through the four previous steps of the *Stakeholder Circle* methodology. Step 5, monitor, is focused on processes to ensure the plan is implemented, the results of the communication activities are monitored and evaluated, and the plan is revised where appropriate. This is the Deming cycle of *plan, do, check, act* (Tague, 2004): the basis of the doctrine of continuous improvement, a powerful concept that contributes to organizational learning and successful implementation of organizational activities. The communication plan will be structured within the communication ecosystem for that organization.

Figure 2.6 illustrates how it is possible to measure the effectiveness of communication, in this case to stakeholder 2. It shows the results of regular monitoring of changes in a stakeholder's level of support and receptiveness (*attitude* and how the new measures of attitude are changing through implementation of the communication plan.

Stakeholder 2 fits the profile of a senior manager in the organization, perhaps the sponsor or a group such as the senior leadership team. It may also describe a stakeholder outside the organization, such as a government leader or a powerful lobby group. For stakeholder 2, the first assessment shows that *heroic** communication efforts are required to close the gap between current and target attitude. In this case, the intention of any communication must be to increase the stakeholder's level of support

---

* *Heroic* communication has been described in the previous chapter as the highest level of communication activity required when there is a large gap between the current attitude and the target attitude of a key stakeholder.

and receptiveness to information about the activity and its progress and issues. The second assessment reveals that some progress had been made, but more work is necessary to achieve the desired level of engagement. The decision the team needs to make at this point is whether to continue at the same level of communication expecting steady growth in this stakeholder's attitude or to include additional techniques and messages to raise the levels of support and receptiveness to the desired level.

In the case of stakeholder 2, whatever the team decided to do, their efforts were moderately successful: In the third set of measures, the stakeholder was rated as passively supportive, with the target defined as actively supportive. The decision the team must make at this stage is whether to aim for the highest level of support or be satisfied with the result achieved to date. This decision must be made in the context of the needs of the project, the amount of available time and personnel allocated to this task, and whether the team can actually gain any more of the stakeholder's time and attention. The team may need to

- Seek advice from other stakeholders with more knowledge and experience of the politics of the organization or the expectations of the stakeholder under consideration.
- Draw on the combined knowledge and experience of its members to support decisions about whether to continue as planned or modify the communication plan or the target attitude.

The time and effort required to develop and maintain robust stakeholder relationships impose higher overhead than many projects or organizations believe can be allocated. Even when project managers and teams recognize the need to spend more time and effort on stakeholder engagement activities, often tight budgets and unreasonable demands mean that more focus on stakeholder engagement may mean less time for other project work. Senior managers in particular do not recognize the importance of stakeholder engagement and may not be interested in supporting any initiatives to improve stakeholder engagement. The final section provides some guidelines for defining the value of stakeholder engagement to organizations, although the concept of measuring the costs and benefits of improved stakeholder engagement processes and practices is relatively new and with few useful data.

THE VALUE OF EFFECTIVE STAKEHOLDER ENGAGEMENT

Financial measures of value, primarily "shareholder value," have been the source of decisions made by organizations without understanding (or heeding) the impact that such actions will have on other stakeholders—employees, customers, the public. The best way for organizations to survive and prosper is to focus on wants and needs of all stakeholders and try to deliver appropriate value to each one. "Value" will be different for each stakeholder group and will be linked to their expectations and requirements.

One definition of *value* is "worth": It must be "assessed," "calculated," or given a material association. *Value* can also be more intrinsic or intangible—less able to be calculated, such as significance: the value of a word or the value of corporate reputation.

In the corporate world, tangible value is known and understood; these definitions are applied to financial balance sheets and often focus on "shareholder value"—driving a culture of short-term decisions to maximize share price, investor return, and executive bonuses. The intangible definitions of value are less easy to measure. This is the contribution of the human element: stakeholders such as the customer, employees, the public, users of a product, or organizational reputation. Failure to consider how these other stakeholders perceive organizational value and to enhance organizational value is failure of the organization to be as effective as it can be. An organization's assets and structures—tangible and intangible—are *all* the result of human actions. The assets of the organization related to human competencies are in the form of knowledge, skills, experience, and social networks of the stakeholders within the framework of the communication ecosystem (Sveiby, 1997).

Zero Cost of Quality

The concepts of the "zero cost of quality" can be useful in assisting organizations to monitor and measure investment in people through a focus on what happens when this investment is missing. Quality is free (Crosby, 1979:1)—what really costs an organization is failure to do things right the first time. The best way to illustrate how this concept might be used is to describe the program of an organization that has successfully done so.

CRC Industries first started tracking the cost of quality in 1997, considering it an essential measure for improving business results and the foundation of its continuous improvement efforts (Donovan, 2006). The company measured "failure dollars" (money spent because of product and services that did not meet customer requirements). Using this approach, CRC reported that failure dollars were reduced from 0.7% of sales to 0.21% of sales from 1997 to 2005. In this organization, cost of quality means the expense of failing to provide a quality product or service and requires the measurement of the costs of

- Materials and labor for rework,
- Correct shipping and customer service errors, and
- Product replacement and waste.

When organizations focus on reducing costs, they will usually do this at the expense of customer and employee satisfaction: "The costs of poor quality make up as much as 15% to 30% of all costs" (DeFeo, 2001). On the other hand, when organizations focus on eliminating "poor quality" by elimination of waste, reduction in inaccurate orders or billings, or reduced allowances to customers for late delivery, they can reach their targets for cost reduction in ways that result in improved relationships with customers, employees, and other stakeholders.

It is possible to extend this concept to stakeholder engagement processes and practices. Stakeholder engagement is free—making it more relevant to today's organizations. The cost of *not* understanding and engaging *all* stakeholders is tangible[*]:

- Substantial costs in compensation to affected stakeholders or product recall,
- Loss of assets, and
- Loss of share value.

More important, costs are also intangible:

- Loss of reputation,
- Reduced morale of staff, and
- Loss of valuable corporate knowledge when many experienced technical and managerial staff are forced to leave the organization through "right sizing"—reduction of staff numbers.

---

[*] A case study of BP's disaster in the Gulf of Mexico in 2012 was presented (Bourne, 2012). It is the thesis of this case study that too much focus on cost cutting for "shareholder value" resulted in the failures of the Macondo Well and the subsequent oil spill and loss of life and livelihood.

Value to the Organization

Successful projects are those whose important stakeholders perceive them to be successful and of value to the organization. The identification of the right stakeholders and the development of targeted communication to meet the needs of the project and the expectations of stakeholders will lead to a higher level of commitment and support from these stakeholders. Stakeholders are more likely to support projects that they think will succeed and are more likely to withdraw support from activities that they perceive are not succeeding. Therefore, it is essential to communicate relevant information to important stakeholders to provide them with the perception the activity is well managed. This can be achieved through targeted communication that is aligned with their expectations and their information requirements and includes the full spectrum of the communication ecosystem (discussed in Chapter 8).

On Time/On Budget Delivery

Delays to implementation of projects on time and on budget usually occur through

- Delay in essential senior management approvals,
- Sponsor advocacy not provided when it is needed,
- Promised resources not supplied when needed,
- Supplier delivery promises not met, and
- Other people-related issues.

The result will often be that the project's progress is delayed. If stakeholders are more engaged and committed and their communication needs are met, there is less chance that any issues will have a negative impact on the progress of the activity. Delays to the work will incur additional expenditure and have an impact on the budget.

Value to Stakeholders

People (stakeholders) are essential to the successful delivery of the project and its outcomes. Building and maintaining robust relationships and maintaining an appropriate level of communication to stakeholders will ensure that they are engaged, supportive, and involved when

- They receive information they require,
- They are consulted, and
- Their needs and requirements are "heard" and, if possible, acted on.

Value to the Project or the Organization

Alignment of risk management practices and stakeholder relationship management practices highlight the significance of managing relationships for success, bringing value to the project or the organization. Engagement can be achieved through

- Understanding who is important in a dynamic environment and how best to deliver essential information to engage the stakeholders,
- Feedback on work that is being done or should be done to successfully deliver the project outcomes—communication *from* the stakeholder,
- Early warning about impending events or decisions that may affect the success of the project—also communication *from* stakeholders, and
- Effective handling of (people) risk through targeted communication.

Value to the Team

Both the team and the team's manager will benefit from the application of stakeholder relationship management processes and practices in the following ways:

- They learn about operating more effectively as a team.
- They gain a sense of achievement through more successful communication and stakeholder engagement.
- They learn more from each other through discussion and consultation and through working with stakeholders who know more about the subject, the politics, and the environment.

CONCLUSION

The debate over who can be stakeholders of a project or an organization has been going on for over 30 years. In that time, the landscape has moved from stakeholders as a restricted group and there was indecision about whether stakeholders other than those who directly contributed to the creation of value within a business (owners and shareholders) should be considered (had legitimacy) to the broader view of stakeholders advocated by Freeman et al. (2010). Debates about ethical considerations, about who actually contributed to the creation of value, and how to deal with conflicting stakeholder interests have not really abated. But, what has happened is that stakeholders are now seen to be essential to the success of a project or organization. Questions remain: Who? How many? What to do to engage them?

The following chapters provide further information that leads to an effective process for communication strategies and implementations based on the needs of the project as well as the needs and expectations of the stakeholders, covering specific guidelines for dealing with the directions of the stakeholder community: upwards, downwards, sidewards, and outwards. Before moving to cover these important aspects of a project's stakeholder community, it is necessary to devote some time to the most relevant theories of leadership. This chapter recognized that the primary task of the project manager is leadership: leadership in the form of working with all stakeholders within the communication ecosystem. Leadership, not heroism, is the key to acknowledgment from all the project's stakeholders that project success is everybody's business.

3

Focus on Leadership: Theories for Leading and Managing

INTRODUCTION

The team is often overlooked when considering the stakeholder community and how to engage them. Downwards stakeholders working on the project (the team) can be staff (employees) or contractors and full time, part time, or for a specified period of time. The team members, whether individuals or groups, may contribute through roles such as planners, technical specialists, business analysts, or team leads. Many perform temporary specialist tasks, joining the project team when their work is scheduled and leaving when it is completed. This affects the dynamics of the team, sometimes disturbing the balance of personalities and roles within the project team and therefore the performance of those who remain. To ensure the best use of these resources, the project manager must understand how to lead and motivate the team when this happens. Leadership is an essential competence, particularly within the environment of the team but also for other areas of stakeholder engagement.

This chapter is organized as follows: First, a discussion of the definition of *team* is given, followed by a brief history of management: how researchers and practitioners sought to understand what motivated workers and how to use that information to motivate them. The next section touches on the history of leadership theory and the evolution of leadership approaches to creating the best environment for individuals and teams to work effectively. The fourth section addresses the fundamental leadership task of making and taking decisions.

WHAT IS A TEAM?

Thompson (2011) defines *team* as a group of interdependent individuals sharing the responsibility of achieving objectives and results. Characteristics of high-performing teams are

- *Interdependence*: Success requires the combination of both individual and team effort with mutual responsibility.
- *Authority*: Each member of the team reflects the authority of the team toward delivering its objectives.
- *A social context*: The group will be inspired and more effective because of the social nature of the relationships built within the team.

A team's effective performance includes both individual results and collective work products (Katzenbach and Smith, 1993). This means that successful teams are clear on the need for both individual accountability as well as *mutual* accountability. Successful teams develop a shared purpose, measured by specific performance goals. The essence of such a team is common commitment.

The team's leader can support good performance through

- Helping to set performance standards and direction,
- Having early "kick-off" meetings and establishing clear rules of behavior,
- Selecting members for skill or potential (as possible),
- Ensuring the team receives essential and timely information through regular meetings, both formal and informal, and
- Providing reinforcement through positive feedback, reward, and recognition.

Effective (high-performing) teams do not happen by accident. They need

- Clear and agreed purpose and objectives,
- Measures of progress and success,
- Feedback as acknowledgment for success but also counseling and coaching when necessary, and
- Recognition that they are a group of individuals who must deliver the outcome through working together.

For the development of successful and high-performing teams, project managers must understand that there is *no one best way* to be a leader. This may explain why there are so many different and sometimes contradictory theoretical approaches to management and leadership: these theories and theoretical approaches are attempts to assist managers and leaders to do what is necessary to attain high performance.

A HISTORY OF MANAGEMENT

Theories of management that still have an impact on the development of successful teams today are:

- Fayol's functions of management: theory of business administration
- Scientific management (Frederick Taylor)
- Hawthorne experiment and its findings
- Maslow's hierarchy of needs
- Herzberg's hygiene theory
- McGregor's theory X and theory Y

Henri Fayol: Functions of Management

The contributions of Fayol's ideas to (administrative) management theory are twofold (Crainer, 2003). His ideas arose from these two principles:

1. Management processes and practices are universal—applicable to any endeavor that requires a structured, planned approach.
2. Management is a discipline that can be defined in a rational way (and taught to others).*

Fayol defined five functions of management: forecast and plan, organize, command or direct, coordinate, and control (in the sense that a manager must receive feedback about a process in order to analyze the cause of the deviations and make necessary adjustments).

---

* Crainer (2003) attributed Fayol's ideas as the basis for legitimacy of the modern manager of business administration (MBA) degree.

His 14 principles of management are still the focus of management efforts today:

1. *Division of work*: Work specialization is the best way to use the organization's resources.
2. *Authority*: Managers must be able to give orders. Authority and responsibility are closely connected.
3. *Discipline*: Effective leadership leads to good discipline, encouraging both adherence to the organization's rules and the ability to enforce them.
4. *Unity of command*: Every employee should receive orders from only one superior.
5. *Unity of direction*: Each group working to the same objective should be led by one manager and one plan.
6. *Subordination* of individual interests to the general interest.
7. *Remuneration*: Workers must be paid a fair wage for their services.
8. *Centralization*: Decision making can be centralized (to management) or decentralized (to subordinates). The leader must decide on the best mix for success of the work.
9. *Scalar chain*: Authority moves downwards from top management to the lowest ranks. Communications should generally follow this chain.
10. *Order*: People and materials should be in the right place at the right time.
11. *Equity*: Managers should be fair to their subordinates.
12. *Stability of tenure of personnel*: High employee turnover is inefficient. Management must ensure effective resource planning.
13. *Initiative*: Employees should be encouraged to originate and carry out their creative ideas.
14. *Esprit de corps*: Promoting team spirit will build harmony and unity within the organization.

Scientific Management (Frederick Taylor)

Fayol's ideas are now central to thinking and teaching of management principles even though his actual writing is relatively unknown. The work of Frederick Taylor, on the other hand, is well known and frequently referenced. Taylor was a self-styled "consultant to management," developing the *Principles of Scientific Management** in 1911. These were based on a search

---

* Taylor described scientific management as "75% science and 25% common sense" (Crainer, 2003).

for the "one best way" to achieve efficiency through the development of repetitive "decomposed" actions.*

Central to scientific management was decomposition: breaking down every task into its smallest components, measuring the time each component takes, and improving the work processes and instructions to reduce production or development time.

> This meant that workers knew exactly what was expected of them and that managers knew exactly how much should be produced. It also meant more accurate piece work rates could be set with more reliable bonuses and penalties. (Crainer, 2003:45)

Taylor's other significant contribution to modern organizations, and project management, was the introduction of the English-speaking world's obsession with time, with time marked for the workers by the factory clock or siren that set the start and finish times of a workday. Taylor's ideas, along with their focus on producing more products or results more efficiently and more cheaply, permeate much of our modern work environment as well as being one of the core components for success in projects.† Henry Ford's assembly line process for efficiently producing cheap automobiles was one of the many applications developed from Taylor's scientific management principles.

The Hawthorne Experiments and Their Findings

Taylor's work established the role of management as measurement and through that control and supervision—soon to become the realm of middle management, even today. This focus on efficiency led to the depersonalization of workers, denying them their individuality and disallowing flexibility in the workplace (Crainer, 2003). The human relations model emerged in reaction to this perceived dehumanization. The Hawthorne experiments of Elton Mayo and his colleagues were an attempt to develop an understanding of the human aspects of work and to balance the "machine" view resulting from Taylor's theories and their application.

---

* This reductionist approach is still evident in project management practices. One clear example of this reductionist approach in project management is the work breakdown structure (WBS), a structured approach for decomposition of project scope into smaller, more convenient "work packages" that enable more effective (and efficient) planning, resourcing, costing, and reporting.

† Taylor's influence on the symbols, rituals, heroes, and values of project management was described in Chapter 1.

Mayo's Hawthorne experiments were conducted at the Hawthorne Works of the General Electric Company in Chicago between 1924 and 1932 and examined the effects on productivity of changes to the physical environment (Crainer, 2003). Through this research, Mayo sought to understand the effects of fatigue and monotony on job productivity.[*] He changed the working conditions of the women volunteers, removing them from the general factory area in a special area that they could identify as theirs alone. He varied the length and frequency of rest breaks and work hours and modified the temperature and humidity of their work environment, consulting his volunteers before each change. The increased productivity that resulted led him to develop his theory about human motivation.

There was one other unexpected outcome of the experiments: The control group also produced higher output than before the start of the experiments. These data have been interpreted as the result of the additional attention also paid to the control group during the conduct of the experiments.

The conclusions supported by the data collected during the experiments were that

- Teamwork is social. Informal groupings at work influence the habits and attitudes of the worker.
- Acknowledgment and recognition, security, and a sense of belonging contribute more to worker's morale and productivity than the physical environment.
- Collaboration must be planned and encouraged to take advantage of the power of team culture and teamwork.
- When people realize that they are being observed, they modify how they act (often in terms of what they believe to be socially acceptable behavior[†])—the "Hawthorne effect."

Maslow's Hierarchy of Needs

The Hawthorne experiments emphasized the importance of teamwork and the need to ensure that the goals and objectives of staff aligned with the goals and objectives of the organization. Continuing the search for understanding what really motivates workers, Maslow developed the concept of the hierarchy

---

[*] He had actually been commissioned by GE to find ways to increase the productivity of the workers through improvements in lighting.

[†] The Hawthorne effect can be clearly seen in the behaviors of individuals on TV reality shows.

of needs (Paloma Vadillo, 2012:92–94). He proposed that people have basic needs, and the drive achieving these needs was what motivated them. He proposed five levels, from lowest (physical) to highest (philosophical):

1. Physiological (food, health, and clothing)
2. Safety (personal safety and security)
3. Belongingness and love (the need to belong to a group)
4. Esteem (the need to be valued by oneself and others)
5. Self-actualization (the need to be all that one can be)

Owen (2012) has adapted this model to the work environment so that the levels will read as follows:

1. Physiological (pay and conditions)
2. Safety (job security)
3. Belongingness and love (the need to belong to a group and to leave a legacy)
4. Esteem (recognition and acknowledgment)
5. Self-actualization (reaching one's full potential). This can be achieved through seeking and succeeding at intellectual challenges—stretch assignments—and working to improve communication and political awareness.

Figure 3.1 illustrates Maslow's hierarchy and Owen's (2012) adaption to the project environment.

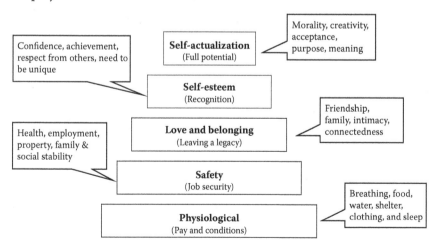

FIGURE 3.1

Maslow's hierarchy of needs. (Adapted from Maslow, A., *Psychological Review*, 1943, and Owen, J., *The Leadership Skills Handbook.* 2nd ed. London: Kogan Page, 2012.)

Herzberg's Hygiene Theory

Herzberg's hygiene theory of motivation proposed two sets of factors that can influence the motivation of workers:

- Intrinsic factors or "motivating factors," such as interesting or challenging work and the opportunity to develop new skills and experiences.
- Extrinsic factors or "hygiene factors," such as pay and conditions or comfortable work environment.

The essence of Herzberg's theory is that individuals will be initially satisfied with additional pay or benefits, but this satisfaction is not sustainable for long: The worker could soon become dissatisfied with the current situation. The factors that motivate are factors that encourage increased contribution or a sense of achievement. A motivated worker who feels that he or she is making a contribution (to the team as well as personally) will often work longer hours to finish a challenging task because of this motivation and sense of achievement (Herzberg, 1987). Figure 3.2 illustrates these concepts, adding the revised list of motivators and factors for dissatisfaction avoidance (hygiene factors) that resulted from additional investigations and, with the data collected, ranked each of the factors in importance (Herzberg, 2003).

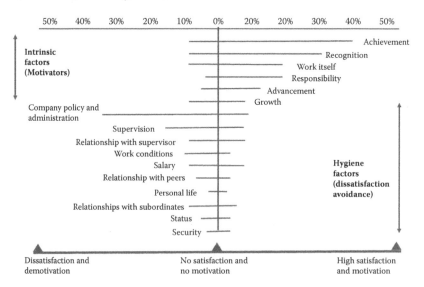

FIGURE 3.2

Herzberg's hygiene theory. (Adapted from Herzberg (1968) and Herzberg, F., *Harvard Business Review,* January 2003, 87–96.)

This "employee-centered" style of management will not be achieved by "command-and-control" management or coercion but through changing the nature of the work being done, offering continuous challenging work, and acknowledgment of achievement. Motivators will have a much greater impact on long-term satisfaction and motivation of employees.

McGregor's Theory X and Theory Y

In the search for the secret of motivating workers, McGregor developed theories X and Y, which describe different management styles. Theory X managers believe that workers will avoid work whenever possible and that

- People will only work if they are controlled and threatened.
- The worker will not readily assume responsibility.
- Workers have little ambition and must be closely supervised at all times.

Theory Y managers assume, on the other hand, that employees want to be creative and self-directed and are generally enthusiastic about their work. Theory Y has the following alternative assumptions:

- Physical and mental work can be as stimulating as play or rest.
- Command and control are not the only way to manage the output of workers.
- Organizational aims and objectives can result in worker self-direction through the design of satisfying activities.
- With the proper leadership, a worker can learn not only how to take responsibility but also seek responsibility.

Table 3.1 summarizes the difference between the management styles of theory X and Y.

At some time in the late twentieth century, there was a shift in emphasis that led to distinct differentiation between the roles of management and leadership. The best description of this difference is that managers "do things right" and focus on efficiency and leaders "do the right things" and focus on effectiveness. This now widely accepted split between management practice and leadership does not mean that a leader does not need to be involved in management activities within the team or a manager does not need to develop leadership skills to be more effective. Many theories of leadership have been developed, some contradicting others, some defining

TABLE 3.1

Comparison between Theory X and Y Management Styles

Management Criteria	X-Type Manager	Y-Type Manager
Power	Authority through control and position in the organization	Authority through respect
Control	Process compliance	Outcomes, achievement
Communication style	One way: tell and do	Two way: tell and listen
Measures of success	Make no mistakes	Beat targets, satisfy stakeholders
Attention to detail	High	Moderate
Tolerance for ambiguity	Minimal	Moderate
Political willingness and ability	Moderate	High
Preferred management structure	Hierarchy	Network

leadership from different perspectives than others. This gives the project manager the opportunity to select a theory or style that best fits personal preferences or suits the situation, and taking into account the needs of the project and its stakeholders, for the purpose of motivating team members to increase the effectiveness of the individual as well as the team. The next section describes the core theories of leadership from the perspective of helping project managers know how to act and lead their team.

THEORIES OF LEADERSHIP

Literature about leadership is plentiful; a simple search on amazon.com provides over 100,000 results. The sheer volume of information about leadership could be an indicator that the search for how to motivate workers through providing the most optimal conditions* for effective work output continues. Research continues as part of a quest for the answer on "how to be a good leader." My contribution to this quest is twofold: first to discuss the example of an individual who is recognized by many (including me) as a good leader and second to discuss the evolution of theories of leadership and how they apply to motivating individuals and teams effectively.

---

* Current trends are "humanistic"—ensuring that all best psychological conditions are in place and that the worker has flexibility, consultation, and acknowledgment. Last century, the trend favored command and control; there is no guarantee that if the current theories are not effective that the theories will not swing back.

The Leadership of Ernest Shackleton

Sir Ernest Shackleton led an expedition to Antarctica in 1914 in the ship *Endurance*. The *Endurance* was trapped in ice for almost 2 years, more than 1,200 miles from civilization and with no means of communication. The crew was forced to camp on the ice and to eat penguins, seals, and their dogs to survive. When the ice began to break up, finally destroying the *Endurance*, Shackleton led his men in three small lifeboats to land on Elephant Island after nearly a week in the freezing seas. Leaving most of the men sheltering in two lifeboats on the island, Shackleton, with a crew of five men, sailed the third lifeboat to a whaling station on the island of South Georgia to seek help. On arrival at the whaling station, Shackleton organized the rescue effort for his crew waiting on Elephant Island and made the return journey as soon as possible: Everybody was saved (Morrell and Capparell, 2001).

Shackleton exhibited many of the skills that Fayol defined as the domain of management. He meticulously planned the expedition, organized and coordinated the provisioning of the expedition and acquisition of crew members, and directed them in their tasks throughout the expedition. The leadership themes related in this story emphasize how

- He cared for his crew's physical well-being.
- He ensured that their emotional needs were met—as much as he was able to in the constraints of the environment where he found them.
- He was both persistent and resilient at all times.

These themes are echoed throughout this chapter.

In the preface to the work of Morrell and Capparell (2001), Shackleton's daughter, Alexandra Shackleton, lists the keys to his success as

- Learning from bad experiences, having diverse interests, reading widely.
- Hiring the best people: He looked for qualities of optimism and cheerfulness. In return, he gave them the best compensation and equipment that he could provide.
- Creating a strong team spirit: He established routines, ensured everyone knew their own and others' roles and responsibilities, removed hierarchies that were not relevant, and used informal gatherings and activities to build the team culture.
- Ensuring that each member gave their best: He led by example. Shackleton knew the capabilities and weaknesses of his crew; he

worked with individual crew members to help them meet their full potential and helped them be successful.

- Using effectiveness in a crisis: He took control in the crisis and inspired optimism in everyone; he worked closely with those who were not happy and created a model for intellectual leadership.
- Forming special teams for special activities: With regard to balance of expertise and knowledge, he encouraged the teams to work together.
- Overcoming obstacles always with the objective in mind: He took responsibility for achieving the objectives and kept sight of the big picture while focusing on the details and the people.
- Leaving a legacy of successful leadership even when the "project actually failed."

The characteristics of Shackleton's leadership provide a useful guideline to answer the questions, Is there a set of characteristics that determine a good leader? Could it be a personality? Is it charisma? Behavior? Or, are they chosen by followers because of their achievements? Are leaders born with innate leadership capabilities? Or, is it possible to develop leadership skills?

The source of Ernest Shackleton's leadership abilities seems to be both inherent (genetically and from the approach to life of his own family) and learned (from his own experiences and approaches): He was able to match his leadership styles to the needs of his team and their situations.

Are good leaders born or made? The next section explores the following leadership theories:

- Goleman's (2000) six leadership styles
- Trait theory
- Transactional leadership
- Charismatic leadership
- Situational leadership
- Transformational leadership
- Authentic leadership
- Vroom's theory of expectancy

Goleman's Leadership Styles

Research conducted around 1997 in partnership with the consulting firm Hay/McBer resulted in the formulation of six different styles of leadership (Goleman, 2000). Data collected in this research from 20,000 executives also led to the conclusion that the most effective leaders did not rely on only one leadership style but adapted their leadership to suit the situation, sometimes automatically and sometimes after careful consideration. "The styles, taken individually appear to have a direct and unique impact on the working atmosphere of a company, division, or team, and in turn on its financial performance" (78). The research also found that most of the qualities that separate average manager/leaders from the best leaders lies within their grasp of emotional competencies (i.e., self-awareness, self-management, social awareness, and social skill).* Table 3.2 summarizes the six styles qualitatively and how they may affect the work environment.

The importance of these results are that they

- Provide some more robust analysis of leadership characteristics, moving away from speculation based on inference, experience, and instinct. Born leaders have these instincts; the question was, How can we teach leadership to others?
- Provide a detailed understanding of how different leadership styles affect performance and results.
- Offer clear guidance on when a manager should switch between them for most effective results.

Goleman, in pursuit of measures that were more quantitative to support this theory, combined these leadership styles with six categories developed by McClelland and Burnham (2003) to understand what influences the organization's working environment—its "climate." The six categories are

- *Flexibility*: Employees feel free to innovate, unencumbered by red tape. They are stimulated to come up with better ways to do their jobs.
- *Responsibility*: This is a sense of responsibility toward the organization. Employees are encouraged to take calculated risks.
- *Standards*: The quality level (a high level) that managers and employees set is guided by standards.
- *Rewards*: Employees' sense of cooperation to a common purpose offers rewards.
- *Clarity*: Accuracy in expressing the company's mission and values provides clarity.
- *Commitment*: Employees' sense of cooperation to a common purpose shows commitment.

---

* Emotional intelligence (EI) is discussed in Chapter 4.

TABLE 3.2

Leadership Styles

	Leader Modus Operandi	The Style in a Phrase	Basic Emotional Intelligence Competencies	When the Style Works Best	Overall Impact on Climate
Coercive	Demands immediate attention	"Do what I tell you"	Drive to achieve, initiative, and self-control	In a crisis, to kick-start a turnaround or with problem employees	Negative
Authoritative	Mobilizes people toward the vision	"Come with me"	Self-confidence, empathy, change catalyst	When changes require a new vision or when a clear direction is needed	Most strongly positive
Affiliative	Creates harmony and builds emotional bonds	"People come first"	Empathy, building relationships, communication	To heal rifts in a team or to motivate people during stressful circumstances	Positive
Democratic	Forges consensus through participation	"What do you think?"	Collaboration, team leadership, communication	To build buy-in or consensus or to get input from valuable employees	Positive
Pace setting	Sets high standards for performance	"Do as I do, now"	Conscientious, drive to achieve, initiative	To obtain quick results from a highly motivated and competent team	Negative
Coaching	Develops people for the future	"Try this"	Developing others, empathy, self-awareness	To help an employee to improve performance or develop long-term strengths	Positive

Source: Goleman, D. (2000). *Harvard Business Review, 78*(2), 78–90.

Table 3.3 shows the connection between the leadership style and the organization's climate. The data in Table 3.3 show that the authoritative leadership style has the most positive effect on "climate," with affiliative, democratic, and coaching styles close behind and the coercive style the least effective. Although in general terms some styles are more effective than others, as is shown in Table 3.3, even the coercive style is useful in a crisis or when dealing with a difficult team member.

The point of the six leadership styles of Goleman is that flexibility is important in a leader.* Inexperienced leaders may not be able to adapt easily to this level of flexibility, but a starting point is to recognize the styles you currently use and work toward developing the others through conscious application of them in the situations that warrant their use.

Trait Theory

Leaders today have to work in the shadow of the "greats": those outstanding individuals who have been universally recognized as great leaders. The ranks of great leaders include Gandhi, Abraham Lincoln, Dr. Martin Luther King, Napoleon, Steve Jobs, and of course, Sir Ernest Shackleton. These leaders have "done great things." The following are the major traits that they all seem to have in common (Northouse, 2013):

- *Intelligence*: strong verbal and reasoning skills
- *Self-confidence*: certainty about one's own skills and competencies
- *Determination*: desire to achieve the goals, which includes persistence, drive, resilience
- *Integrity*: credibility, honesty, and trustworthiness
- *Sociability*: ability to form relationships, good interpersonal skills, and ability to create cooperative relationships with their followers

Trait theory has a focus on personality. McCrae and Costa (1997) described five traits. With conscious effort, a leader can improve on personal raw personality traits, much in the same way that an emotionally intelligent leader strives to improve

- *Extraversion*: sociable, assertive, and emotionally expressive
- *Conscientiousness*: thoughtful, with good impulse control and goal-directed behaviors, organized, and mindful of details

---

* In reference to Shackleton's leadership style, he was predominantly an authoritative leader but was able to assume other styles when necessary.

TABLE 3.3

Measures of Effectiveness of Leadership Styles

	"Climate"					
	Coercive	Authoritative	Affiliative	Democratic	Pace Setting	Coaching
Flexibility	-.28	.32	.27	.28	-.07	.17
Responsibility	-.37	.21	.16	.23	.04	.08
Standards	-.02	.38	.31	.22	-.27	.39
Rewards	-18	.54	.48	.42	-.29	.43
Clarity	-.11	.44	.37	.35	-.28	.38
Commitment	-.13	.35	.34	.26	-.20	.27
Overall impact on "climate"	-.26	.54	.46	.43	-.25	.42

Source: Goleman, D. (2000). *Harvard Business Review*, 78(2), 78–90.

- *Openness*: imagination and insight with a broad range of interests
- *(Low) neuroticism*: decreased tendency to experience emotional instability, anxiety, moodiness, irritability, and sadness
- *Agreeableness*: includes attributes such as trust, altruism, kindness, affection (Goldman, 1990)

These traits fit the "great leader" approach to understanding leadership. They focus on what a leader needs to "have" or "be" to become a "good leader." Trait theory ignores the situations when individuals feel compelled to step into leadership roles temporarily for a single event or situation, even though the individual does not display the leadership traits just described. This is the theory of "situation leadership," discussed later in the chapter.

Transactional Leadership

Transactional leadership is based on expectation of reward, such as meeting followers' emotional and material needs in return for contracted services or support or involvement in certain activities (Bass, 1985). Generally, the transactional leader will have a focus on

- Procedures and efficiency
- Working to rules and contracts
- Managing current issues and problems
- Using reward and coercive power bases

Some followers require this leadership approach and will often gravitate to leaders exhibiting these behaviors; the transactional leader tries to deliver what followers want (Yukl, 2002). The effective leader will develop more flexibility: sometimes a task-oriented approach and in other circumstances a more relationship-oriented approach.

Charismatic Leadership

Charismatic leaders are, or become, the embodiment of the values and beliefs of their followers. They often appear in difficult times when followers will expect these leaders to help them make sense of a situation and resolve the issues (Northouse, 2013). In the world of projects, it is unusual for the project manager or members of the project team to exhibit charismatic leadership, but possibly a senior stakeholder will, potentially causing issues for the project manager and for the team.

Transformational Leadership

Transformational leaders will lead in a way that empowers their followers, seeking to enhance self-sufficiency and to change their values and attitudes.* It requires

- Long-term strategic planning
- Clear objectives and vision
- Leading by example—walk the talk
- Efficiency of systems and processes

This type of leadership goes beyond satisfying existing needs in the followers: It seeks to engage the "heart and mind" of followers (Bass, 1985).

The leadership/management grid developed by Blake and Mouton (1964) summarizes the potential mix of leadership and management behaviors or the possible combinations of results orientation and people orientation. Figure 3.3 is adapted from the original description.

The result is five styles of leadership that relate to whether the leader has more concern for results or more concern for people:

- *Authority/compliance*: The emphasis is on results. Communication to the team or other stakeholders may be limited to instructions on how to complete the assigned task. This style can be perceived as overpowering and controlling.
- *Country club*: The emphasis is on relationships within the team or stakeholder community, rather than a focus on reaching objectives. This type of leader will focus on minimizing conflict and developing an environment of support and care for the needs of the team. The team will feel nurtured but may be frustrated at never achieving results.
- *Impoverished*: There is minimal concern for either results or the welfare of the team. This leader is uninvolved and indifferent, resigned and apathetic.
- *Middle of the road*: A balance exists between concern for results and concern for people.

---

* Shackleton's leadership, although mostly focused on transformation of his crew, could include transactional behavior when necessary.

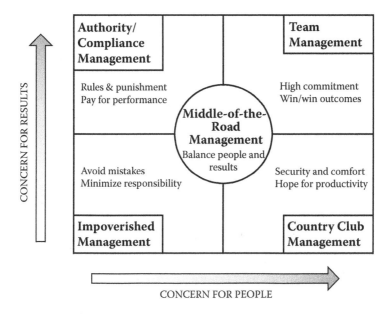

FIGURE 3.3

Leadership/management grid. (Adapted from Blake, R. R. and Mouton, J. S., *The Managerial Grid: The Key to Leadership Excellence*. Houston, TX: Gulf, 2003.)

- *Team management*: There is strong emphasis on achieving results and within an environment that encourages teamwork as well as the involvement of each team member (Northouse, 2013).

The preferred style for most effective leadership will be team management because it demonstrates high concerns for both results and people, but there will be occasions that require other behaviors. Complex, high-profile, or urgent projects may require more focus on tasks and less on relationships, whereas other more sensitive projects may respond better to a greater emphasis on relationships than on results. The leader needs to have made the assessment at planning and through continuous monitoring ensure that whatever approach is selected has the agreement and ongoing support of the appropriate stakeholders.

Situational Leadership

Selection of leadership style (or leader) may need to vary depending on various factors[*]:

---

[*] Once again, Shackleton's story illustrates his application of aspects of the leadership theories discussed here.

- Maturity of the team or individuals in the team.
- Risk profile of the project or the organization where decision making and change initiatives are based on degree of risk involved.
- Type of business: Is it a creative business or supply driven?
- How important and complex the change is: The organizational culture may be long embedded and difficult to change.
- Nature of the task: Will success require a cooperative approach or a directive approach? Do the team members and stakeholders require structure or flexibility (Yukl, 2002)?

Leaders may have to vary styles of team leadership throughout the development of project objectives depending on the level of skills and motivation of the team. This also takes into consideration the changing nature of the team structure and how a team forms and adapts.*

The behaviors defined in situational leadership are also a combination of task (directing) and relationship (supporting) behaviors. Directing behaviors help the team through the provision of instructions, detail, clear roles, and responsibilities. Supporting behaviors encourage team contributions in decision making and completion of the more complex tasks within the project through praise, listening, and helping the team solve problems related to the work. The behaviors are applied according to the leader's assessment of the team's competency and commitment and often the assessment of each individual in the team. The assumption built into this theory is that as the team (and the leader) matures the styles will change, cycling from directing, through coaching and supporting, finally to delegating. The behaviors of situational leadership are classified as follows (Yukl, 2002):

- *Directing (telling)*: There are clear instructions for the team or others.
- *Coaching (selling)*: Talking and listening help the team build confidence and motivation.
- *Supporting (participating)*: Team members still need active assistance for shared decisions.
- *Delegating (autonomous)*: Team members have some responsibilities for planning and decisions.

Effective leaders understand that they will need to vary their leadership behaviors to meet the needs of their followers and the needs of the project.

---

* Theories of team formation are discussed in Chapter 4.

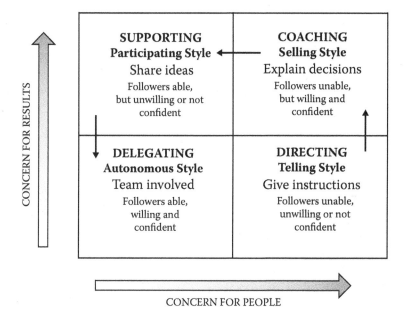

FIGURE 3.4
Situational leadership. (Adapted from Hersey, P., Blanchard, K., and Johnson, D. E., *Management of Organizational Behaviour.* 7th ed. London: Prentice Hall International, 1996.)

The Blake and Mouton leadership/management grid and the Hersey and Blanchard leadership style grid (Figure 3.4) provide guidance for leaders who wish to improve the effectiveness of their teams. They are both focused on the recognition that a leader's role will need to be both task oriented and relationship oriented at different times or for different teams. Ultimately, the message is that there is *no one best way* to be a leader, and effectiveness depends on so many aspects from personality to a focus on specific leadership styles and behaviors.

Authentic Leadership

In reaction to loss of trust in political and business leaders and the perception of absence of ethical decision making, the concept of authenticity in leadership is emerging in the literature. An authentic leader is one who is

- Self-aware
- Compassionate, honorable
- Ethical and authentic

This type of leader behaves ethically and exhibits strong positive personal values, with courage to lead and do the right thing.* While recognizing that sometimes difficult decisions must be made regarding the success of the project, the authentic leader acts with compassion and with regard to the emotional well-being of followers and other stakeholders (George, 2003; Terry, 1993).

Vroom's Expectancy Theory and Decision Model

The contribution that Vroom (Vroom and Jago, 1988) has made with expectancy theory is the analysis of how people are motivated, rather than what motivates them, which has been the major theme of most of the theories discussed in previous sections of this chapter. By understanding the mechanisms by which people are motivated, it is possible to develop an action plan to ensure that the motivators that have been provided are exploited appropriately. There are three basic elements of expectancy theory:

- *Expectancy*: an individual's belief that by making an effort he or she will produce significant and quality output. Expectancy plays a key role in the individual's behavior. If, on the other hand, the individual believes that he or she will not be acknowledged for any work he or she does, the person will not make much effort.
- *Instrumentality*: the belief that a person will receive a reward if the performance expectation is met. This reward may come in the form of a pay increase, promotion, recognition, or sense of accomplishment. Instrumentality is low when the reward is the same for all performances given.
- *Valence*: the value an individual places on the rewards of an outcome, which is based on their needs, goals, values, and sources of motivation. Influential factors include one's values, needs, goals, preferences, and sources that strengthen their motivation for a particular outcome. Valence is characterized by the extent to which a person values a given outcome or reward. This is not an actual level of satisfaction but rather the expected satisfaction of a particular outcome.

These steps for an action plan should entail the following:

- Determine what type of rewards the team member would value.
- Agree with the employee's desired performance standards.

---

* See Shackleton's story.

- Ensure that those standards can be achieved.
- Guarantee that the agreed performance level will be rewarded as agreed.
- Be certain that the reward is considered adequate and appropriate.

For the action plan to be effective, the team member must have a high degree of trust that the reward will be granted if the desired level of performance is reached. The more authentic the leader is, the more likely this theory will be effectively implemented.

MAKING DECISIONS

Leadership implies making and taking decisions (see the sidebar on page 86). Decisions are core to effective problem solving, planning and scheduling, resource allocation, and conflict resolution and to actions necessary for effective engagement of stakeholders. Effective leadership includes motivating, inspiring, and developing the team and its individual members. It also requires making decisions about how much control needs to be applied to the work and the workers and decisions about the best way to engage stakeholders throughout the communication ecosystem.

We make decisions every day, sometimes consciously and sometimes unconsciously, about every aspect of our lives. Sometimes, we make them alone; sometimes we need the help of another or others. And, we know that some of the decisions will be sound, some not so sound, and some will have negative consequences. Often, we make decisions from an emotional basis, without any of the rational step-by-step processes advocated for business decisions.

Decision making, conflict management, and problem solving are frequently treated as separate topics; however, they are interrelated, and all focus on achieving the best possible result for the project or organization. Ideally, there would always be enough of the right information and rational maturity to treat everything as a problem and reach a sound solution, but this is rarely the case.

Most decision-making processes are more complicated than the standard process described in textbooks (e.g., Thompson, 2011), which assume a predictable and ordered universe. The following is a description of the logical rational approach to decision making, which theoretically forms the basis for making any decision* (Thompson, 2011).

1. Define the problem and agree on some acceptable outcomes.
2. Gather information to assist in understanding the background and ensure that all parties have access to this information.
3. Create alternative options and prioritize them.
4. Choose the decision-making process.
5. Make the decision.
6. Implement the agreed solution.

The complications are these:

- *The type of problem*: What if the problem is not easy to define? Or, what if a solution is not easily developed or agreed?
- *Personal preferences and values*: Who should be involved in the decision-making process? How can we minimize the effect of personal preference and bias?
- *Information*: How much information can realistically be gathered to assist in the decision making? Who should be involved in the information collection process? How will you know if you have enough information or the right sort of information?
- *Alternatives*: How do you prioritize alternatives? How will you reduce the uncertainty about whether you have chosen the best alternative?
- *Implementation*: How do you prepare for implementation?

The next section provides answers to these questions.

Define the Problem

There is more than one type of problem; sometimes, a solution is not obvious or even possible. Most problem-solving processes assume there is a best answer, that the information needed to determine the answer is available, and that people involved in the process are acting rationally. Many of the problems that arise in the project environment have at their basis conflicts between team members or other stakeholders, based on their emotional responses, which may not be able to be resolved through rational processes.

---

* The devil is in the details. So, although the high-level process is useful, it is only a guideline.

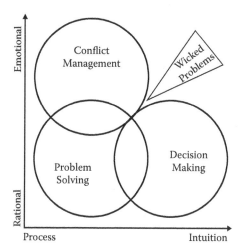

FIGURE 3.5
Problems, conflict, and decisions.

Problem solving and decision making are closely aligned (Figure 3.5). There is always a problem, issue, or dilemma that requires a decision in the best solution to implement. The weakness of the "problem-solving" concept is the assumption that there will be sufficient information to make the "right decision" if a rational process is followed. Unfortunately, many decisions are not that straightforward. The types of decision that may need to be addressed in the project environment range from "wicked problems" to "simple problems"; they all require different approaches:

- *Wicked problems* are problems that do not have a single convergent solution set (Phillips, 2014). Many problems that arise in projects fall into this category, made more complex because of the involvement of people in every element of the project. The definition of the problem and its decision/solution keep changing as its complexity is uncovered. There is no amount of expertise or information that can deliver a solution that everyone will agree on. Wicked problems do not allow for the step-by-step approach of the decision-making formula defined. A single solution or decision proposal cannot be broken down into smaller components. It has to be dealt with as a whole, using iteration to learn from experience and ensure that as many stakeholders as possible are in agreement with the decision.
- *Dilemmas* have no "right" answer; intuition and background experience may be the only paths to choosing the "least-bad" option.

Often, dilemmas have an ethical component; this is what makes it difficult to deal with them. For ethical dilemmas, this set of questions can often be helpful*: Is the solution legal (according to the laws of this country)? Is it fair (will anybody be unfairly disadvantaged)? How will I feel if my mother (or the media) hears about this decision I have made?

- For *conundrums*, in the modern business context, the meaning has shifted to mean a complex or perplexing problem that has no clear solution and is difficult or impossible to resolve based on current knowledge. The challenge is to determine what sort of decision you are being asked to make and how to acquire additional knowledge† (Reeson and Dunstall, 2009). "Hindsight does not always lead to foresight" (Snowden and Boone, 2007:71).

- *Mysteries* lack adequate information for resolution, and it is not possible to know if or when better information will "appear"; any decision must be based on the options understood "at this time."

- *Puzzles* have one right answer that may be resolved in one correct way or may be achieved through several different routes. Solving a Rubik's cube is a puzzle to most people; in the first instance, we lack adequate information to easily solve it. Experts in Rubik's cubes know the processes needed to reach the "one right solution" and can apply them in a few seconds. The way to solve a puzzle is to obtain the skills and information you need. If you do not know, find someone who does. Once you have the information and know-how, the puzzle is reduced to a problem, and making a correct decision is straightforward.

- *Problems* just require hard work and the application of "problem-solving processes" to reach the best decision.

The Decision-Making Process: Who Should Be Involved?

Choosing the best method for making the decision will usually be the decision of the leader of the team, taking into account the problem or issue that requires a decision. And, of course, it will depend on the leadership

---

* It will not be easy to answer these questions either, but they have proven useful to me for making and implementing decisions when working in other cultures.

† The concept of complex problem solving touches conundrums, mysteries, and puzzles. All three may involve a large number of diverse, dynamic, and interdependent elements in a novel situation for which it is difficult or impossible to receive good quantitative data. An interactive model to assist this process and improve outcomes is available online (http://www.idiagram.com/CP/cpprocess.html).

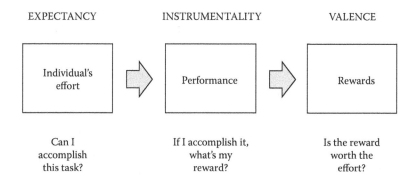

EXPECTANCY   INSTRUMENTALITY   VALENCE

Individual's
effort

Performance

Rewards

Can I
accomplish
this task?

If I accomplish it,
what's my
reward?

Is the reward
worth the
effort?

FIGURE 3.6
Vroom's expectancy theory. (Adapted from Vroom, V. and Jago, A., *The New Leadership: Managing Participants in Organizations.* Englewood Cliffs, NJ: Prentice Hall, 1988.)

style and personality of the leader: A coercive or autocratic leader will be more likely to choose the autocratic path, whereas those with styles that are more consultative will choose one of the other options. The maturity, experience, and knowledge of the team; the nature of the problem; and the time available to the leader will all influence the decision-making process and its outcome. Anything that involves participation of others will naturally take longer than one that does not require any consultation. However, additional participants can provide different points of view and offer knowledge and experience that may not be available to the individual or small group of experts, improving the quality of the decision.

Vroom and Jago (1988) (Figure 3.6) defined five decision methods:

- *Autocratic*: The leader makes the decisions with little or no involvement of other team members. The decision is made quickly, but it may not be the best option, and it may not be accepted by those who were not consulted but will be affected by its implementation. If the situation is "chaotic,"[*] such as dealing with the urgent aftermath of a tornado or earthquake, this style of leadership is most appropriate.
- *Inquiry*: The leader asks for information from the team but will make the decision independently. There is some consultation with team members or other stakeholders, but the leader still makes the decision. This is most useful when expert advice is needed because the problem is "complicated."

---

[*] The description of problems as "chaotic," "complex," "complicated," and "simple" developed by Snowden and Boone (2007) combines leadership and decision making aligned to different types of problems.

- *Consultation*: There are different degrees of consultation with team members, but the leader is the final decision maker. More people are consulted and may feel that they have had some input regarding the final decision. This method also allows for input from experts.
- *Consensus building*: This involves extensive consultation and consensus building within the team. The leaders share the problem with the team members, and together they work to reach a consensus. The leader in this case has theoretically no more influence than anyone else. This process is the most time consuming—consensus takes time and there is no guarantee regarding the quality of the decision. This is a good approach if the problem is "complex"; it requires definition of multiple alternatives and prioritization.
- *Delegation*: The leader delegates the decision-making process to the team members, who make the decisions without the leader's involvement. If the problem is "simple," this is the best approach.

How Can We Minimize the Effect of Personal Preference and Bias?

The actions of defining the problem and gathering information to enhance the decision-making process are subject to biases supported by how each one of us interprets "reality." Biases are ways of thinking and acting that are habitual, often unconscious. They are part of how our individual brains have interpreted our experiences and how our culture (national, generational, gender) drives attitudes and actions and makes them seem ordinary and acceptable to us but perhaps unacceptable to others.

The brain has an extraordinary capacity to develop connections.* Different people look at, interpret, and describe the same situation in different ways; this is the basis of our bias. Some of the biases that affect projects and their organization and the decision-making process are as follows:

- *Framing bias*: How the topic is "framed" will influence the decision. Depending on the words selected, the importance given to certain parts, what is included, and what is not included, it is possible to draw different conclusions from what appears to be the same information.

---

* For example, the way that jazz musicians can play extraordinary music by extemporizing around the basic theme of the harmony in an original way is different from the work of another musician who is also "jamming."

- *Confirmation bias*: This bias reflects a tendency to consider evidence that supports a position, hypothesis, beliefs, or desires and to disregard or discount equally valid evidence that refutes them. For example, risk experts will be focusing more strongly on their knowledge of risk or leadership experts on leadership theories.
- *Attentional bias*: How we perceive and analyze a situation is affected by whatever is in our minds at that time; it is also called the *bandwagon effect*. It is our tendency to do (or believe) things because many other people in our networks also believe them; this is shown in team decision making as *groupthink*.
- *Optimism bias*: The tendency to be overoptimistic, overestimating favorable and pleasing outcomes and playing down the less-pleasing ones, leads to this bias.
- *Planning fallacy*: With a planning fallacy, the tendency is to underestimate task completion times.
- *Availability heuristic*: An availability heuristic estimates what is more likely using what is more available in memory. The events we remember best are the unusual ones, events that made us happy or sad, or events that caused us to experience other strong emotions.

Alternatives: How Do You Prioritize Alternatives? Reduce Uncertainty?

Generate options through group creative processes such as brainstorming, using facilitators, perhaps planning for a negotiation, or individual reflection.

- If it is possible, choose a solution that solves the problem in the simplest way, remembering that not all problems that a project will encounter can be readily processed in this way.
- Conduct a risk assessment on selected decision options and the planned implementation process, particularly if the problems or issues are complicated or complex.

Implement the Solution and Review the Effectiveness of the Implementation

As with any implementation process, a strategy and plan will need to consider impacts on other work and on stakeholders. A review should be conducted after a suitable interval, depending on the problem or issue and the decision solution.

COLLECTING AND INTERPRETING
INFORMATION FOR DECISION MAKING

Biases are rooted in how we perceive the world based on our own experiences and knowledge, our cultural background, and the basic processes of our brain. The illusions that the brain constructs profoundly influence our lives and how we work—and how the decision-making process is influenced (Chabris and Simons, 2009). These are the illusions of

- Attention: looking without seeing. If our attention is directed to certain aspects, we may not "see" other important things, even when we are looking directly at them. In project work, we may miss important clues to the behavior of our stakeholders because our attention is directed elsewhere.
- Memory: in particular, the difference between how we think memory works and how it actually works. Memory depends not only on recalling what happened but also on how we make sense of what happened. The longer the gap between the event and its recall, the greater the distortion will be.
- Confidence: The confidence that people project is often an illusion. It causes us to overestimate our own qualities, especially relative to the abilities of other people, and to interpret the confidence (or otherwise) that other people exhibit as a signal of their abilities or knowledge.
- Knowledge: We tend to confuse ability to operate with knowledge of how it works. Believing that we understand things at a deeper level than we really do sometimes causes us to make dangerous and misguided decisions.
- Cause: Our minds are built to detect meaning in patterns, to infer causal relationships from coincidences, and to believe that earlier events caused later ones. We can even perceive patterns where none exist. Our understanding of the world is systematically biased to perceive meaning rather than randomness and to infer causes rather than coincidence. We are usually unaware of these biases. Experts are primed to see patterns that match their well-established area of knowledge—their knowledge and experience have formed how they see. Their brains will use a

process of selective matching, ignoring what does not fit and selecting what does.

- Potential: We think that vast reservoirs of untapped mental ability exist in our brains, just waiting to be accessed—if only we knew how. This illusion combines two beliefs: The first is that the human mind and brain harbor the potential to perform at much higher levels in a wide range of situations and contexts than they typically do. Second, this potential can be released with simple techniques that are easily and rapidly implemented.*

Examples of these illusions exist in the world of organizations and projects, from the focus on certain aspects of project information (attention) or false memory of promises made by senior stakeholders and then forgotten (memory), the respect that confidence and knowledge bring, to the biases that we bring to decisions. We cannot eliminate these biases, but if we have some awareness of them, we will be able to at least question "irrefutable facts" or the ability to be "objective" in making decisions. This means that the decision-making process, however it is managed, must also take into account the other factors that affect decision making (Frame, 2013), such as biases and experiences of those who are involved in making the decision and presenting the information on which the decision is made.

---

* An example is the industry built around the statement that "most people only use 10% of their brain capacity": This "10% myth" has been reinforced with the introduction of brain scans using functional magnetic resonance imaging where only small portions of the brain light up in any experiment, but although the bright spots indicate areas of increased activity, this does not mean that the dark spots have no activity.

CONCLUSION

In this chapter, the foundation theories of management and leadership were discussed. Although it is not intended to be a complete survey of all theories, there is a significant representative sample included to provide the project manager, or any potential leader, with enough information to develop a personal management and leadership style and a habit of life-long learning and development. The most important theme of leadership is that there is no one best way to lead or manage; by understanding the origin and the application of the various theories, a project manager can adapt the information to suit his or her own way of working and that of the team. The common theme of this chapter was about motivating team members and not only doing what is necessary to build the most effective team but also about applying the same motivations to other stakeholders within the communication ecosystem for the benefit of the project and the organization. Decision making, an essential part of the leader's role, is also described. The next chapter discusses aspects of leading teams that are more practical: the essential leadership skills of motivation, managing conflict, and giving feedback, all of which depend on an understanding of the theories of managing and leading discussed in this chapter.

4

Focus on Downwards: The Practicalities of Leading the Project Team

INTRODUCTION

As defined in Chapter 2, the project's team members are stakeholders—in many ways the most important stakeholders. They contribute to the success of the project through their knowledge, skills, and contribution to the work. For optimal contribution, they need an effective work environment. This is the leadership role and responsibility of the project manager. The theories of leadership described in the previous chapter are intended to assist project managers seeking to lead their teams and to motivate them by providing the best possible environment to facilitate project success.

The leadership theories provide the project manager with access to different perspectives of successful leadership. A flexible leadership style will best meet different circumstances within the project and within the team. The leader's actions and behaviors support the team and its individual members through fostering collaboration and cooperation and minimizing the distractions of conflict or other negative reactions.

This chapter discusses the more practical aspects of leading and managing downwards. The first section establishes a framework in the form of the theory of emotional intelligence (EI) of individuals and teams and the benefits of such techniques for managing teams with members from diverse backgrounds.* The second section discusses some relevant theories of team formation and practical interventions in the process of team formation that may reduce conflict and may increase the effectiveness of the team's work. The final section analyzes the essential skills that form the tool kit of a leader for most successfully engaging downwards stakeholders: motivation, giving feedback, managing conflict, and coaching.

EMOTIONAL INTELLIGENCE

Emotional intelligence was defined by Salovey and Mayer (1990:189) as

> the ability to monitor one's own and others' feelings and emotions, to *discriminate among them and to use this information to guide one's thinking and action.*

EI is a useful tool and relationship development concept that will assist project and program managers in managing and leading their team. The emotionally intelligent leader will understand the need to build strong stakeholder relationships and have the tools to do so through more effective communication to this group of stakeholders. Other examples of the outputs of an EI leader are as follows:

- A positive work environment focused on sustaining team morale,
- Awareness of the need to recognize situations that may lead to conflict in the team or with stakeholders and work to intervene early to resolve them,
- Approaches to developing each team member through understanding the individual's needs, including the emotional components, and
- Developing with the team, by working with them to produce a project vision and way of achieving it that inspires everyone (Mersino, 2007).

---

* The application of EI concepts as an effective leadership style does not imply that EI is the only technique to achieve an effective working environment for the team. EI has the advantage of being familiar to most people working in a project and organizational environment and of being sufficiently self-contained to provide a practical application of the necessary actions and behaviors to foster team success. There is also a direct link between many of the theories of leadership described in the previous chapter and the focus on people as described in the methodology of stakeholder engagement: the **Stakeholder** Circle.

Goleman (2011) based his earlier work on these ideas and extended them significantly to four characteristics of emotionally intelligent leaders or managers. Project managers can assess themselves on the extent to which they exhibit these characteristics* and from that assessment develop an improved emotional quotient (EQ). These four aspects are

- *Self-awareness*: knowing one's strengths and weaknesses and level of self-confidence,
- *Self-management*: emotional self-control, optimism, and adaptability,
- *Social awareness*: empathy, organizational awareness, recognizing follower and stakeholder needs, and
- *Relationship management*: inspirational leadership, being a catalyst for change, developing others.

The sidebar provides more details about how to improve EQ.

It is possible to test the level of EI through questions such as those developed by Thompson (2011), summarized next.

To gauge the level of *self-awareness*:

- As a leader, can you identify and share your emotions† with team members?
- In a team context, is each team member comfortable with sharing emotions with others?

For understanding *self-management*:

- How do you manage your emotions?
- Do you seek the opinions of others before making decisions on conflict caused through appropriate actions?
- Can each team member identify with the emotions, personalities, or decision-making processes of others in the team?

---

* There are many online EQ tests. Some examples are found at the following sites: http://psychology. about.com; http://testyourself.psychtests.com; http://www.helpself.com; http://www.mindtools.com.
† Emotions include feelings, passions, and doubts—in fact, all our qualities that represent the part of us that is irrational. It is not really possible to be rational about our emotions. At the very least, the basic human emotions of fear, surprise, happiness, anxiety, sadness, anger, and disgust can be shared within the team environment (with care). Sharing emotions does not mean letting those emotions take over all conversations. Interestingly, with these basic emotional responses, our facial and verbal expressions will tend to provide clues that are easy for most other people to interpret. The leader can begin the process of sharing emotions by asking the question: "How do you feel about ... ?"

For understanding *social awareness*:

- Can the leader understand and describe the emotions of team members (without making assumptions about those emotions)?
- Can each team member understand the emotional states of other team members?

Finally, there are some questions to understand the level of *relationship management*:

- Can the leader inspire others through enthusiasm, optimism, and genuine concern for the team and for the team's success?
- Can each team member inspire, or be inspired, through optimism and general concern for the team?

EI can be learned, and an individual's EQ can be improved with the appropriate training.

Questions such as those listed and their answers can provide an indication of a leader's (or a team's) strengths and weaknesses and act as a starting point for any improvement activities.

For maximum effectiveness, leaders must learn to balance their own emotions, striving to reduce the effects of worry, anxiety, fear, or anger to think clearly and effectively. Balancing emotions is not about suppressing them or denying their presence. It is about understanding your own emotions and using that understanding to manage situations effectively. By recognizing the emotional part of our being and accepting that we can never operate entirely rationally, we are more realistic about how we think and make decisions. That knowledge makes available more options for effective leadership.

The emotional state of the leader affects the entire team, department, or organization. Everyone will recognize situations for which the strong emotions of one individual can affect the mood of the whole group: We can "catch" emotions from others. If one of the team members has strong feelings of happiness or of sadness, these emotions can change the mood of the whole group. This is *emotional contagion* (Hatfield, Cacioppo, and Rapson, 1993). It means that if leaders are positive and motivated, they can motivate and inspire their followers (or other stakeholders). Empathy with the team motivates, inspires, and creates feelings of unity and team spirit.

Research has suggested that EI can be developed as a *team* competency and not just an individual competency. That is, teams themselves—not just

SOME IDEAS ABOUT HOW TO IMPROVE EQ

Self-awareness can be achieved through keeping a journal, writing down your experiences and how you felt at those times. Having a mentor or a confidante to talk through issues can help increase awareness and understanding of other ways to deal with difficult situations.

Self-management of emotions can be improved through simple breathing exercises; these will not only provide some time for your emotions to moderate themselves but also provide the increased oxygen to your brain that has been known to reduce the effect of the "fight-or-flight" mechanism that anger or anxiety may generate.

Social awareness can be improved through trying to be more observant of the actions of others; body language and tone of voice can often provide clues to the emotional state of others. Above all, do not assume you know the other person's emotional state; it is better to ask the person than to make assumptions about what the person is feeling.

Relationship management is embedded in the theories and methodologies described in Chapter 2:

- Know who your stakeholders are at any time in the project;
- Understand their expectations of the team or the project or you as leader;
- Develop ways to build and maintain that relationship through appropriate communication; and
- Monitor and measure the effectiveness of that communication.

The methodology described in Chapter 2 provides guidelines to assist the improvement of relationship management—and through this increasing the EQ of an individual or the team. Additional ways to improve relationship management skills as a leader are covered in other parts of this chapter and the following chapter: motivation, conflict management, and acknowledgment.

their individual members—can increase their EQ. Leaders build the EQ of teams by building an environment that supports emotional development in constructive ways. An EI-focused team culture creates a strong group identity, builds trust among members, and instills a belief among members that they can be effective and succeed as a team. A team with a high EQ does not consist only of individuals with high EQs; an emotionally intelligent team is aware of the emotions of each member of the team, the emotions of the group as a whole, and even the emotions of individuals or groups (stakeholders) outside the team itself.

Improving the EQ of a team may require specific team-building activities. Team building, whether it is a big-budget adventure or something of a smaller scale, is about developing ways for the team to work together that

- Help members work with emotions, building an EI culture through a common language in which certain words have specific meanings within the group and the team can accept members' emotional states or there are more physical ways to vent their emotions.*
- Favor optimism or provide ways to discuss potential risks of actions without seeming negative.
- Encourage proactive problem solving, giving the team members control over situations because they have the means to identify problems, jointly develop solutions, and work together to achieve positive outcomes.

The gains from team building or other programs that build the team culture need to be sustained. This can only occur through the formal and informal support of the organization and through the efforts of the team's leaders, coaches, and each other. Above all, leaders, organizations, and the team members themselves need to recognize the benefits of emotionally intelligent leaders, individuals, and team members, in particular the strong connection to improved team performance. In the absence of support from the organization or management, the project manager can still develop EQ within the culture of the team in ways that have already been discussed. The result will be a strong team culture in which members are clearly identified with the group. This clear identity will forge a supportive and strong team culture.

THE NATURE OF TEAMS

A team is a group of individuals whose focus is on achievement of a shared goal: the project outcomes. The members of the team must work individually and collectively to achieve this goal. Project teams are

---

* In the 1980s, some Japanese companies provided their employees with a room full of blow-up dolls representing management. The employees were encouraged to "vent" their frustrations by punching these dolls.

temporary because of the nature of a project: an entity with defined beginning and end assembled to produce value for the organization. An effective project team has identifiable membership and through the organization's approval process has authority to acquire resources and expend approved funds to deliver the outcomes that satisfy the needs of the project's and organization's stakeholders. The team is a network of relationships, a social system, in which everyone within that social system is committed to the successful delivery of project outcomes and has tapped into the communication ecosystem* to build and maintain those relationships.

Successful teams have the following characteristics:

- They understand the expectations of their stakeholders, ensuring that these expectations are satisfied, and the stakeholders also perceive that their expectations are met.
- They have a clear team identity defined by the relationship between members of the team and recognized by those both within the team and outside it.
- They have clear objectives and work together to achieve them to satisfy their stakeholders' expectations through the support structure of the organization and its leaders.
- They promote individual growth and learning, encouraged by each other and their leader.

Toxic teams, on the other hand, have the following characteristics (Robbins and Finlay, 2000):

- The team members are too competitive with each other—there is no such thing as "friendly competition."
- They are too collaborative or conforming, exhibiting a lack of diversity, perhaps even groupthink.†
- They are too focused internally (ignoring anything outside the team) or intolerant of those who do not conform.

---

* This is described in Chapter 1.
† *Groupthink* is defined as follows: When a team's members are similar in background and insulated from outside opinions and when there are no clear rules for decision making, faulty decisions may be made through pressure to conform or through an inability to accept alternative options.

- There is team tyranny, by which the only acceptable social grouping is the team and everything must be done as a team—really believing that "there is no *I* in team."[*]

Toxic teams can improve. The leader can take specific action to reduce toxicity through

- Reducing the size of the team: Robbins and Finlay (2000) suggest that any group should have somewhere between five and ten people working together[†] to enable good communication among all the individuals within the team.
- Training for all the team: It does not matter whether the training is technical, behavior change, or awareness programs for cultural diversity or conflict resolution. The act of learning new skills together can help introduce new ideas and new ways of working and strengthen the team relations.
- Reviewing the purpose and objectives of the work and outcomes of the project jointly, led by the project manager.
- Focusing on team and individual performance as well as reinforcing standards of behavior through reporting.

TEAM FORMATION AND CONSTRUCTION

Effective teams do not happen accidentally. They need

- A clear purpose and objectives,
- Reinforcement of standards through measures of progress and success,
- Feedback, both positive and negative, and
- Recognition that success is achieved through both individual achievement and working together.

---

[*] The idea that "there is no *I* in team" has been replaced by the understanding that successful teams are an interdependent combination of relationships providing satisfaction to the individual working both independently and interdependently within the group. Interestingly, most European languages do have an *I* in team—only English and German do not. French, Spanish, Portuguese, and Italian translate *team* as a form similar to the Spanish *equipo*, so for the Romance languages there actually is an *I* in *team*.

[†] My own experience indicates that work teams of between three and five are ideal. This supports working closely without developing cliques; it also means that decisions can be made and implemented more effectively. To develop working teams of this size will require organizing the full project team into groups with common roles, responsibilities, working patterns, knowledge, or experience.

Every effective leader recognizes that proactive interventions will be necessary from time to time to assist the team to continue to work together successfully. In this section, leadership of Agile teams and virtual teams is discussed, followed by two theories of team formation, on the premise that knowledge of these theories can assist the team's more effective working and supplement the leadership theories discussed previously with additional practical applications of the art of leadership. These theories are Tuckman's model of Team Formation (Tuckman and Jensen, 1977) and Swift Trust (Meyerson, Weick, and Kramer, 1996).

Agile Teams

In urgent projects, temporary groups of experts may be gathered to solve unique but essential problems for the organization. Team members are motivated when they feel "special" and know that what they are doing is seen by their leaders and the organization as important.[*] It gives them a chance to do exciting and important work. Sometimes, these projects will be managed through Agile processes. The Agile method of product development was originally conceived for software development.[†] It has sometimes been adopted (and adapted) for project work. The technique involves short iterative cycles, by which the work is "time boxed"—broken into planned "chunks" of work according to specified time frames, such as fortnightly intervals. Another feature is prototyping: iterative development of functionality, screens, or reports that allow stakeholders to review the prototype and provide feedback on whether this prototype actually meets their needs and expectations. With these regular reviews, the outcome of the project will be more likely to meet stakeholders' expectations rather than developing an excellent technical solution that does not meet stakeholders' needs.

The Agile process can deliver good results, particularly if the end result and the execution methods are uncertain, but use of the Agile method does not mean that all important project processes can be ignored. Essential documentation, such as plans, risk and issues registers, communication plans, and progress reports must still be maintained but perhaps delivered in a different way. However, successful Agile projects will rely on the

---

[*] This is identified in the Hawthorne experiments described in Chapter 3.
[†] The Agile Manifesto can be found online (http://agilemanifesto.org/).

team's "tacit knowledge"[*] and experience as well as willingness to adapt (Adkins, 2010).

The most effective members of Agile teams will be comfortable with complex change and the uncertainty that comes with such complexity; often, this will require a culture change within the team and its stakeholders. The best of these teams will thrive on chaos, enjoying the freedom that comes with such a process. An Agile team will need to recognize the importance of frequent but brief regular communication. Adkins (2010) emphasizes the importance of a high degree of ongoing stakeholder involvement and high degrees of flexibility. Short daily meetings that include stakeholder involvement (particularly user representatives and senior management), that include reports on today's plan, yesterday's progress, and issues that will slow progress, are also recommended actions.

The Leaders' Role in Successful Agile Projects

Regular communication, flexibility, and cooperation are keys to success in Agile projects. It is the role of the leader to manage the environment and encourage the team to help this occur. In particular, the encouragement of constructive feedback between stakeholders and team members is essential. High levels of motivation, loyalty, and respect for all stakeholders involved are catalysts to successful outcomes.[†]

It is the leader's role to develop and sustain this working environment (Adkins, 2010). It is also the leader's role to work through the dilemmas of Agile projects and to balance the often-conflicting needs of a successful Agile team. Agile's dilemmas center on how to build and maintain the right mix of agility and discipline. Discipline will take the form of maintaining current essential documentation, reporting, and information exchange between stakeholders. If discipline is missing, the enthusiasm of the team soon dissipates, but too much discipline leads to excessive bureaucracy and reduced agility. The balance is important because well-organized teams and individuals need some discipline to maintain purpose and strengthen resolve. On the other hand, the Agile mindset helps develop adaptability. Balance is essential because a mix of discipline and flexibility have been recognized as essential to the most effective way to work and motivate individuals.

---

[*] This is defined as "knowledge held by practically every normal human being, based on his or her emotions, experiences, insights, intuition, observations and internalized information" (http://www.businessdictionary.com).

[†] A team with high EQ will be more likely to be successful in this environment.

Boehm and Turner (2004) make the following observations:

- Agile methods handle flexibility by building a shared set of objectives and strategies and providing the means through daily updates for making necessary adjustments in response to reality.
- Agile methods do not always scale up to complicated or longer-term projects.
- Traditional (or plan-driven) projects manage complexity through extensive documentation.

This is an evolving area of management knowledge and understanding. In the next few years, techniques for successfully applying Agile approaches to large complicated projects may emerge.

Virtual Teams

Salas, Cooke, and Rosen (2008) identified effective practices for managing virtual teams. Although these strategies could apply to practically every team, the challenge that managers face is how to implement them effectively in a virtual work environment, where members rarely have the opportunity to work in the same location.* Leaders of virtual teams must possess strong written and oral communication skills. They also must understand that managing such teams requires conscious and concentrated effort. Salas, Cooke, and Rosen (2008) recommend that leaders

- Define team members' roles and responsibilities in the first meeting and "ground rules."
- Develop a culture of teamwork through setting challenging but achievable goals to motivate team members to build strong and productive relationships with each other.
- Set the standard for frequent information exchange (communication) to stakeholders outside the team (at all locations) and within the team.
- Set an example for all team members by following the communication guidelines and supporting the team's goals and objectives.

---

* Teams have worked in this format for many years before the term *virtual* was invented. In my early project management days, many Australian national projects required input from team members in other parts of the country and overseas. Telecommunications was primitive by today's standards and face-to-face meetings more common, but the basic principles were the same as today.

- Track progress and productivity: Improved software tools and virtual private networks give leaders effective and accurate ways to track information, to gauge team performance and individual contributions, and to ensure that everyone is aware of progress and productivity (Gray and Larson, 2008).
- Provide frequent, regular, structured communication of the essential information to engender trust. This includes ensuring that, for multizone teams, meeting times are rotated to ensure that no team member is unfairly disadvantaged.

THEORIES OF TEAM DEVELOPMENT

The process of evolution of the working relationships within the team will be different for every team; the work is different each time, and the people in the team and the dynamics of the relationships they form are different. Knowledge of the way that teams form can assist the leader in ensuring that potential for conflict can be minimized.

Tuckman's Model of Team Formation

Tuckman and Jensen (1977) developed a model of team formation that consists of four stages: forming, storming, norming, and performing. A fifth stage, *adjourning*, was included in the model later. Figure 4.1 shows how the relationship within the team matures over time, each stage beginning its development before the preceding stage reaches its full maturity. It also shows how the team may cycle between storming and norming stages as team members join or leave the team. Each stage is described in more detail in the following sections.

Forming

The team is focused on getting to know each other and understanding the scope of the project. The team members will be excited and enthusiastic and perhaps anxious and overwhelmed. There will be a focus on not only avoidance of conflict but also perhaps some competition for "position" within the team. The leader's role in this stage is to establish ground rules describing the team structure, standards of behavior, and performance

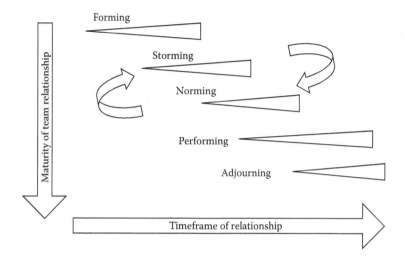

FIGURE 4.1

The stages of team formation. (Adapted from Tuckman, B. W. and Jensen, M. A., *Group and Organisation Studies, 2*, 419–427, 1977.)

expectations. Forming will be complete when the group has established a group identity and begins to think of themselves within that team identity.

Storming

The storming phase is marked by internal conflict; members accept that they are part of a group but resent the constraints on how they work as individuals. There may be power struggles and conflict over roles and responsibilities or how decisions are made. When conflict is resolved and the project manager's leadership is accepted, the group will move on to the next stage. The role of the leader will be that of "circuit breaker," only resorting to intervention if the power struggle or conflict prevents progress of the project's work.

Norming

In the norming stage, close relationships develop, and the group demonstrates team cohesiveness. Recognition of shared responsibility for the project has developed, and the team culture has formed around support networks within the team and willingness to explore ways to develop stronger team spirit and alternative options for doing the work. When the team has established its own culture, there will be agreement on team norms, behaviors, and commitments. The role of the leader will be that of an observer—the team is often "self-managing" to the extent that leadership is shared within the team and many decisions can be made within the team.

Performing

At the performing stage, the team is fully functional and in many ways self-directed. The group focus will be on how to accomplish the project objectives through maximizing joint and individual strengths and minimizing joint and individual weaknesses. The relationships within the team are strong, and there is a willingness to work through any problems or conflicts without intervention from the leader. The role of the leader will be that of coach.

Adjourning

A fifth stage, not in Tuckman's (1965) original work, is included in the work of Tuckman and Jensen (1977). This is the stage of celebration of accomplishments, recognition of the efforts of all those involved, and preparing to leave this group and the relationships that have been developed over the course of the project. Team members may feel conflicting emotions, ranging from depression that relationships will be dissolved to pleasure and a sense of accomplishment. The role of the leader is important at this stage. He or she must help the team members move on from this relationship and focus effort on moving on to the next assignment.

How This Model Is Useful

The leader can help progression with interventions specific to each stage through the following:

- Selection of team members who can work together combined with team-building exercises that fit the needs of the team but are within the constraints of the budget.*
- Awareness of potential conflict and appropriate interventions and assistance in resolving any conflict that does occur.

---

* Selection of members of the team may not be possible. This means that the project manager's leadership role will also involve extensive coaching of individuals or early intervention with conflict management of the issues that may occur.

- Acknowledgment of both individual and group achievements through a variety of rewards and recognition.
- Celebrations at achievement of milestones and ensuring that team members are encouraged to develop new skills through motivating challenges.

How Good Is This Model?

When the model was developed, it described the prevailing employment arrangement that supported continuous membership within the team. Generally, the team consisted of mainly staff members who stayed in the team throughout most of the life cycle of the project. This model best fits occasions when the members of the team do not vary. *Every time someone joins or leaves the team, the dynamics of the team will change;* this may result in the team regressing to a previous stage—from norming back to storming, for example. If, as in modern technology projects, specialists join the team for short periods of time and then leave, there will be a constant cycling of the team through norming back to storming and then to norming again, as shown in Figure 4.1.

Swift Trust

Swift trust (Meyerson, Weick, and Kramer, 1996) was developed in an attempt to explain how groups of people work together in situations when the outcome is urgent and there is no time for team building. The team does not have the luxury of developing according to the model described by Tuckman. They are forced to find ways to work together. The "glue" is the focus on a shared deliverable supported by the leadership of the project manager in providing an environment of "trust" that each team member is capable, skilled, and willing to work with the other team members to achieve the expected outcome. Trust is the "attitude" of the team in this situation, and trustworthiness is the "behavior" that each member needs to exhibit to ensure that the team can continue to work until the urgent objective has been achieved.

Swift Trust Works When

- Participants can produce the expected result using their existing skills and capabilities.

- There is a limited history of working together, and it is unlikely that they will work together again.
- These projects are usually required to operate with limited resources and overlapping networks, and the tasks are often complex, requiring interdependent work and an urgent deadline.
- The work is not routine and not well understood and requires constant interplay.
- Team members assume that everyone can be trusted to work together for the good of the project, and each person knows that the others are trustworthy and acts as if trust is already present.

To develop confidence quickly, the project manager or leader must include only those with recognized expertise and ensure that there are clear and agreed roles and responsibilities within the team. Leaders can build and maintain an atmosphere of *swift trust* in the following ways[*]:

- Dealing with problems and conflicts as soon as they occur,
- Promoting team communication, frequent but brief,
- Encouraging team communication,
- Addressing performance issues in private, and
- Recognizing and celebrating the achievements.

THE TOOL KIT OF A LEADER

In this chapter, the discussion has centered on teams, how they form and ways that the leader can intervene or act to reduce conflict and increase effective performance through encouraging the growth of effective relationships. However, the team will not be able to operate to maximum effectiveness without ensuring that each member is operating to maximum effectiveness. Three leadership tools in particular are essential to ensure each individual contributes to the fullest extent: motivation, giving feedback, and managing conflict.

----

[*] In other words, operating in an environment of EI, or recognizing that the only way to fulfill all the expectations of the project's stakeholders (including team members), is to construct an environment of trust and interdependence to maximize chances of successful delivery of project outcomes to the satisfaction of *all* important stakeholders.

Motivation

In my opinion, the principal focus of the management and leadership theories described in the previous chapter was understanding motivation—building the optimal environment for workers or teams to operate as effectively as possible. Embedded in those theories was the assumption that the organization could provide the conditions* or that the leader could employ the appropriate level of support or intervention to foster motivation. That perfect world does not yet exist, so part of the project manager's job is to recognize what needs to be done to motivate the project team members. Motivation is defined by dictionary.com as

- The act of providing someone with a reason to act in a certain way, or
- An inducement or incentive—something that motivates.

According to Thompson (2011:27): "It is not enough for members of a team to be skilled; they must also be motivated to use their knowledge and skills to achieve shared goals. Motivation comes both from within a person and from external factors." Even when the organization has provided a genial environment, a dysfunctional, or toxic, team will cause the relationships within the team to deteriorate and can dilute the goodwill and enthusiasm carefully developed in the process of team formation. Team members may feel that their work does not contribute to project success and that they are not making any progress or that their input is no longer seen to be important. This situation can lead to team members feeling they have no influence over their environment or cannot rely on others. The belief the team members have in themselves affects actual performance (Thompson, 2011).

There are both motivation gains and motivation losses. Motivation gains refer to circumstances that increase effort by team, such as the following:

- The less-capable member will work harder to keep up with others. This is known as the Kohler effect—social comparison when one feels that their efforts are indispensable.
- Weaker members will work harder when they expect their work to count, especially when everyone receives feedback about performance in a timely way, and they value the outcome personally.

---

* Herzberg's hygiene theory, described in Chapter 3, provided a ranked list of factors that motivated or demotivated.

- The motivation gains are more effective when they work in each other's presence.

Motivation losses refer to two main effects: social loafing and free riders. Social loafing is an effect of large groups in which the larger the group is, the lower each individual's effort will be; each person feels that his or her efforts (or lack of effort) will not be noticed.* So, there is little motivation to work hard. The free-riders' effect can occur in large teams. The larger the team is, the less likely an individual will work hard. The result is that often a few people will do most of the work, while others who believe that their contributions will not have much impact may work less. If this situation is allowed to continue, other members of the group may stop working hard because they may want to reduce the rewards of the free riders. The key aspects of the concept of free riders are:

- Diffusion of responsibility: An individual's efforts are less identifiable, leading to "deindividuation," by which the individual has no responsibility.
- Reduced sense of self-efficacy: Individuals feel that their contributions will not make a difference. This is different from "social striving," a situation that occurs when the least-capable member feels indispensable, causing everyone to work harder.
- Sucker aversion: Team members feel they are being taken advantage of unfairly. This will cause them to wait to see how hard others will work.†

Counteracting Social Loafing

The leader has a responsibility to counteract the toxic effects of social loafing—both to strengthen a positive team culture and to motivate team members. Some ways to reduce social loafing and its effects are to

- Increase individual accountability and clarify each team member's personal responsibility for the outcomes and for improving the team spirit. This is achieved through frequent reports on member contributions and team performance reviews and feedback.

---

* Vroom's theory of expectancy described this situation.
† The only exceptions to sucker aversion will be baby boomers or individuals driven by the Protestant work ethic. Members of these cohorts may view work itself as ennobling or essential and continue regardless of what others in the team are doing.

- Promote individual involvement through more challenging individual tasks and rewarding team members for outstanding work.
- Reduce size of teams. Restructure to ensure that the working groups are smaller, generally between five and ten.

The free-riders' effect and social loafing are only two potential team demotivators. Social relations within the team can deteriorate to the level that members do not respect others in the team or there are other instances of incivility in the form of gossip, rudeness, unconstructive criticism, or personal remarks; these are other causes of demotivation for individuals. Once again, the leader has the responsibility to correct this situation. The leader must "walk the talk" and model good behavior in the following ways:

- Respect everyone on the team.
- Acknowledge good work and encourage those who are struggling.
- Treat mistakes as learning experiences.
- Seek feedback about individual behavior.
- Refuse to take sides in arguments and encourage conflicting team members to resolve the conflict.
- Discourage gossip about people.

Other Demotivators

Porath and Pearson (2013) emphasize the importance of the leader's behavior in building and maintaining a highly motivated team. They list some leader behaviors to avoid:

- Sending or reading e-mails during a presentation.
- Taking credit for the work of the team but blaming the team for mistakes.
- Reacting with anger when the news is bad.
- Allowing a culture of disrespect to form in the team.
- Being insensitive to the cultures of others in the team.

Delegation and Motivation

In the previous chapter on theories of leadership, Herzberg's hygiene theory described the difference between leadership actions that satisfy but are not sustainable, such as pay and conditions, and the more effective long-term

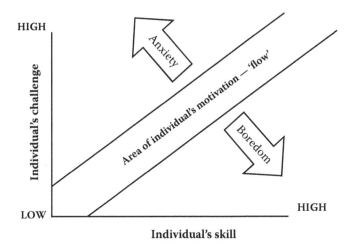

FIGURE 4.2

The motivation balance in delegating work. (Adapted from Thompson, L. *Making the Team: A Guide for Managers.* Englewood Cliffs, NJ: Prentice Hall, 2011.)

motivators, such as challenging work and acknowledgment of individual achievement. To sustain motivation within the team, the leader must recognize the necessity of delegating interesting, challenging tasks to team members to allow them to gain experience and to overcome new challenges.

Figure 4.2 illustrates the balance necessary to consider when leaders attempt to motivate team members through the allocation of challenging tasks. The ideal is the line between work that is too challenging and work that is not challenging enough. This has been termed *flow* from the concepts of Csikszentmihalyi (1997) who described flow as that combination of talent and practice by which both come together to provide an experience of success or happiness.* From the point of view of motivational challenges, flow is a challenging task that is still within the capabilities of the team member to achieve success, not so easy that boredom occurs and not so difficult that the challenge is abandoned as "too hard." It is a fine line to achieve this balance, but it is achievable when the leader knows the team member's skills, capabilities, and disposition well enough to make that judgment. And, an essential additional ingredient is assistance with

---

* Common illustrations of flow are in ball sports such as tennis or golf: The ball hits the "sweet spot" and soars precisely where it was intended to go—a rare occasion but satisfying. There are other examples in the field of music, such as that moment when the instrument produces a most beautiful sound or in dance. Other examples in the world of business may be when the team works together to produce a joint strategy or an outcome, and everyone is in accord.

goal setting and regular reporting to assist the team member to continue to work toward achieving the agreed objective.

Delegation

Delegation is an essential aspect of leadership; it provides the opportunity for challenging and motivating roles for team members, and it also lightens the load of the leader through transferring tasks and activities from the leader to others. Delegation is often not easy for the leader; many leaders do not want to delegate. They fear

- Loss of personal control through unexpected outcomes in the achievement of the objectives of the work, leading to personal stress,
- The perception of time wasted in explaining, coaching, and correcting the work or direction of the team member to whom the work has been delegated, and
- Dilution of personal standards. There is often a perception that no one else will produce outcomes that match the standard of the leader.

The Benefits of Delegation

It is a leader's responsibility to help team members develop additional skills and experience. Delegation is one method to use. Other benefits of planned and managed delegation are:

- It shares the workload of the project, particularly that of the leader.
- It allows the leader to focus on what he or she is best at doing and enables the team member to learn new skills beyond normal team roles.
- It shows that the leader trusts the team member to take on the challenge and "stretches" the team member, encouraging him or her to seek new stimulation through accepting challenges, thus building new skills that will benefit the individual as well as the team as a whole (Owen, 2012).

A leader should consider delegating tasks that

- Can be done better by a subordinate,
- Are urgent but not high priority,
- Are relevant to a subordinate's career,

- Are of appropriate difficulty,
- Are both pleasant and unpleasant, and
- Are not central to the manager's role.

Delegation requires planning and careful preparation before handover and regular support and attention afterward, until the task is complete. The leader must

- Specify responsibilities and reporting requirements,
- Provide adequate authority and specify limits of discretion and inform others,
- Ensure subordinate acceptance of responsibilities,
- Monitor progress in appropriate ways,
- Arrange for the subordinate to receive necessary information,
- Provide support and assistance, avoid reverse delegation, and
- Make mistakes a learning experience.

Feedback

At times when a team member makes a mistake or is exhibiting behavioral problems, when good behavior needs acknowledgment or poor behavior needs counseling, the leader must provide feedback. Giving feedback, positive or negative, is hard even for the most experienced leader, and the team member who is the subject of feedback (particularly negative feedback) will often not react positively. Common responses are:

- *Deny all wrongdoing*: "That is not what happened."
- *Spread the blame*: "I was told to do this," or "I thought someone else was doing this, but they let me down."
- *Change the subject*: "There are more important issues to focus on than this!"

It may be necessary to rehearse the feedback process and be prepared for the defensive responses. This is a time when access to a coach or confidante will be most valuable; the opportunity to try out different approaches and to be prepared for negative responses will be useful.

Giving Negative Feedback

Unacceptable behaviors, such as being disrespectful of others on the team, not working with the team, or causing conflict of any sort, are strong demotivators for the rest of the team. This behavior cannot be ignored; if allowed to continue without check, it will affect the morale and high performance of the rest of the team. The effort the leader invests into preparation and delivery of feedback, particularly negative feedback, benefits both the person whose behavior is unacceptable and the rest of the team, particularly those who are directly affected by this behavior. The individual behaving unacceptably benefits through direct action clarifying how this behavior is affecting the rest of the team and coaching on how to improve it, and the morale of the team is reinforced through observing that the leader will act to ensure the team's continued success. Negative feedback is an essential aspect of team leadership and necessary for the effectiveness of the team as a whole.

Never say "But." Some leadership courses teach that when giving negative feedback, starting with a positive statement acknowledging the strengths or achievements of the person who is to receive negative feedback softens the impact of the negative feedback to follow.[*] However, it is not effective to give praise and follow that with "But" and the negative feedback. *Everything is forgotten except what comes after the "But." But* is a word of exclusion, whereas *and* is inclusive. So, *and* is a better joining word if you feel you need to praise first. It is important to practice this technique to be clear and certain not only about what has to be said and how it has to be said but, even more important, the use of *and* and not *but*.

Preparing to Give Feedback

An approach such as the one that follows is useful because it provides the necessary information for the team member and allows the leader to be fully prepared[†]:

1. *Situation*: Choose a time when both you and the team member are stress free; often, the first thing in the morning is good. Ensure the time is blocked out in the diary of both so there can be no interruptions. Choose a venue that is quiet and private.
2. *Specifics*: If you choose to give praise first and then move on to the situation that requires negative feedback, be sure that you practice

---

[*] This is often referred to as the "sandwich" approach.

[†] Feedback should be mainly positive; acknowledgment is a strong motivator. A good rule of thumb is a 5:1 ratio of positive to negative feedback. Some recent research has shown, however, that people actually seek negative feedback, particularly if a process such as described here is used.

a smooth transition from positive to negative without the "But." Be clear in the description of the circumstances and event that you want to focus on,[*] for example: "I want to talk to you about your behavior in our team meetings over the last 6 months. You have been interrupting other team members when they are speaking, constantly checking your e-mails, and arriving late. This is disruptive behavior. It is not acceptable to me or your fellow team members."

3. *Personal impact*: Describe how this behavior affects those working with the team member.

4. *Insight and inquiry*: The team member may become defensive and respond with some of the responses listed previously—spreading the blame, denying all wrongdoing, and becoming emotional. Unless the issue has been caused by a strong personal problem, it is essential to move the conversation from the emotional[†] to the team member accepting that the behavior needs improvement and beginning to develop solutions to resolve the issue.

5. *Ask questions* to assist *the team member* to work out the best options for resolution: "What do you think is the best way to improve these behaviors? Is there something that I or your team members can do to assist?" Remember: *Do not tell them what to do.*[‡] The power of the solution comes when the person exhibiting the negative behavior articulates and agrees to it.

6. *Next steps*: It may take more than one conversation to develop acceptance of the need to resolve the behavior and to develop an approach for its implementation. Once an improvement or development path has been agreed, the leader must summarize the agreed actions and a time frame and set up a series of meetings for reporting on progress.

Managing Conflict

It is often the actions or behaviors of other team members that cause conflict within the team. Giving feedback is useful when the isolated actions or behaviors of one individual are the source of the conflict, but more

---

[*] It is important to have the conversation clearly focusing on the behavior *not* the person.

[†] The emotional component has been described as "drama" in the work of Rock (2006) based on neuroscience. The implications of the neuroscience approach in communication are discussed in more detail in a further chapter.

[‡] The chapter on communication has some suggestions for coaching conversations that might be useful in this situation.

often, it will be a set of circumstances that will lead to conflict within the team. No matter what the source of the conflict, it must be dealt with as soon as possible—conflict will not "go away" no matter how much the leader tries to ignore the situation or its consequences.

Thompson (2011) defined three major types of conflict:

- *Relationship conflict*: This is caused by personality conflicts, resentful behavior, or rival "cliques" within the team. Even if the conflict is isolated to a few individuals, it can affect the performance of the team. At its worst, it can cause team members such stress that they will leave.
- *Task conflict*: There may be disagreement about ideas, plans, or project strategies. Sometimes, discussions will lead to further creativity if channeled correctly, but more often these disagreements will lead to further conflict and even polarization of the conflicting sides.
- *Process conflict*: This is similar to task conflict but focuses on how to do a task and *who* should do it.

Managing any of these types of conflict requires preparation and fearless implementation. If the conflict stems from behaviors of individuals, the approach for giving negative feedback may be the most useful tool. If the conflict stems from dysfunction between groups, it may be necessary to assist these groups in developing their own solutions through an approach that enables each group to work together to define the problem and then the best resolution, followed by an implementation plan and success measures. The process is as follows:

1. *Together* agree on what the problem really is or if there actually is a problem. The problem needs to be stated in the same manner as the project's scope statement: In one (short) sentence, state the problem and not the cause or the consequences.
2. *Together* agree on some optimal outcomes. There may be more than one outcome or resolution that is acceptable to all parties. These also have to be stated as clearly and succinctly as possible.*

---

* It is often the process of working together on these definitions that paves the way to a successful outcome. Often, conflict is based on misunderstandings of the actions or words of others; by working together on the definitions, in many cases the misunderstandings can be resolved with only minimal further work.

3. *Only then* should the group identify potential solutions.*
4. *Agree* on the best course of action and develop an implementation plan.
5. *Set a date* for the next meeting to report on progress.

Blake and Mouton's Approach

Blake and Mouton (1964) developed an approach to conflict resolution that is still the basis of approaches used today. The methods for conflict resolutions are

- Forcing or competing
- Smoothing or accommodating
- Compromise
- Problem solving/confronting
- Withdrawal or avoiding
- Facilitated (binding or nonbinding)

Table 4.1 provides a summary of options and their consequences for maintaining a relationship afterward. There is no "one best way" to resolve conflict. It is essential to select the method best suited to the problem and its importance to the team, the person and his or her personality, and the situation.

Interventions to Minimize Potential Conflict

Some options for leaders to minimize potential for conflict within the team (Thompson, 2011) are given next:

- Team redesign to reduce adverse team dynamics. This should ensure that cliques are dispersed or that individuals with conflicting personalities do not work together. Sometimes, it will be necessary to reduce the size of the work groups within the team to encourage improved and more effective communication.
- Conflict coaching to build trust and to encourage constructive debate.
- Behavioral training for the individual may provide the individual with tools and techniques to assist in modifying behaviors.

---

* It is only human to want to go straight to "solution mode"; imposing the discipline of points 1 and 2 will ensure that everyone is working to solve the same problem, not multiple individuals creating interpretations of the problem.

TABLE 4.1

Options for Conflict Resolution

Approach	When to Use It	Effect on the Relationship
Forcing: "Just do as I tell you."	When you know you are right; in emergencies; when the stakes are high; when you have power over the others.	*Low*: Does not provide any incentive for a continued relationship.
Smoothing: "I don't want to argue. What do you think is the best way?" May not be a satisfactory outcome.	When the stakes are low; to maintain harmony; when any solution will do; when you need a trade-off at a later date.	*Medium*: The side that gives in too easily may also not necessarily keep to the agreed action; passive-aggressive behaviors may result.
Compromise: Both sides must give up something to reach a resolution.	When the problem is complex; when you need a temporary solution; to maintain a relationship; when you will not get anything if you do not; when both parties need to be "winners."	*Medium*: Compromise is often a "lose-lose" outcome.
Problem solving: Both sides agree on the actual problem and some acceptable outcomes and then work together to resolve the issue within those parameters.	When you have the time and the skills; when there is mutual trust and respect; when you need to gain commitment.	*High*: But it may take longer than other options to reach an agreed outcome.
Withdrawal: Walking out in the middle of the meeting.	When the stakes are low; when the stakes are high but you are not ready (there is no chance of gain); a strategic withdrawal to gain time; to maintain neutrality.	*Low*: But often just a strategic part of a longer resolution process; often used in negotiation.
Mediation or conciliation	When an impartial third party can build trust and help break down barriers.	*Low to high*: Depends on how much input the disputing parties have to the solution and the skills of the mediator.
Arbitration or litigation	When all other options have failed and there is no relationship left to manage (a final and binding resolution has to be enforced by an external authority).	*Low*: Does not provide any incentive for a continued relationship.

Coaching

Counseling and coaching team members—dealing with the negative behaviors or performance issues of team members—are important leadership roles. Coaching can help a team member discover *personal* potential and resolve *personal* problems. It is not about telling the individual what to do or giving advice (Owen, 2012). Coaching can be in the form of

- Helping solve problems through listening and asking questions to aid understanding and "unblock" thought processes;
- Listening, summarizing, and encouraging reflection;
- Guiding the individual to reach personal solutions;
- Giving feedback (positive or negative); and
- Encouraging action.

Many books on leadership have a section on coaching the team (Owen, 2012; Paloma Vadillo, 2012; Rock, 2006).* The processes vary, but the fundamentals are the same and are summarized in the sidebar.

There are some fundamentals that must not be ignored:

- *Accentuate the positive*: It is not the coach's job to criticize. Table 4.2 compares positive questions with unacceptable negative questions.
- *Challenge the team member* to act on the discoveries made in the coaching session. For example, if the individual has decided to gather

TABLE 4.2

Effective Questions for Coaching

Problem Focus	Solutions Focus
Why didn't you achieve your goals?	What do you need to do next time to hit your targets?
Why did this happen?	What do you want to achieve here?
Where did it all start to go wrong?	What do you need to do to move forward?
Why do you think you are not good at this?	How can you develop in this area?
What is wrong with your team?	What does your team need to do to win?
Why did you do that?	What do you want to do next?
Who is responsible for this?	Who can achieve this?
Why is this not working?	What do we need to do to make this work?

Source: Adapted from Rock, D. (2006). *Quiet Leadership: Six Steps to Transforming Performance at Work*. New York: HarperCollins.

---

* Any of these texts will be useful to provide a structure for and assistance in coaching techniques.

FUNDAMENTALS OF COACHING

- Define the *objectives* of the coaching session (or sessions)*:
  "What do you want to focus on today?" "What do you want to
  achieve in this coaching conversation?"
- *Plan* for the coaching conversation: "How are you going to proceed?" Perhaps some guidance questions, such as "What is the
  situation?" If you have found a coaching structure that you are
  comfortable with, stay with that process; it will help you with
  the coaching work.
- Put *process* before content; it is not useful to allow the coaching
  conversation to move to interesting but unrelated discussions
  or to encourage the individual to use emotional language in
  the coaching conversation. A coaching structure based on neuroscience has identified that encouraging the team member to
  "think" about the problem discussed will produce a better outcome than allowing the conversation to stay at the emotions or
  "feelings" level (Rock, 2006). Questions such as, "What do you
  think is the best way to achieve this?" Or "What do you think is
  the next step?" *rather than* "How do you feel about this?"
- Help the individual explore *alternative* actions with questions
  such as, "What alternatives do you have?" "What are the benefits
  of this approach?" What are the risks?"

Finish every session with action, but ensure that the team member
understands that you are still available to assist: "What are the
next steps?" "Do you want to meet next week to discuss progress?"
"When would you like to have the next coaching session?"

---

* There may need to be a series of coaching conversations to help the team member and team
resolve the issue.

more information before making a final decision, the challenge will
be to help the person commit to a practical realistic course of action.
- *Focus on solutions*: It is helpful to continue to focus on how this
  problem occurred. A problem focus often causes regression to emotions. The most productive approach is to encourage thinking about
  the future and concentrating on actions that will produce solutions
  to the problem.

- *Most important of all, do not give advice*: Help the person *think* through personal issues.

Ultimately, the objective of coaching and the most positive contribution a leader can make is to help the team member develop new habits of working and thinking so that this problem, or similar ones, will not recur. This is best achieved through coaching conversations that

- Focus on facts
- Move from the emotional to thinking processes
- Encourage different thinking through seeking alternatives
- Provide new goals

Finally, Paloma Vadillo (2012) defined conditions for successful coaching:

1. Do not judge. Coaching is about providing a collaborative and safe environment so that the "coachee" can find his or her own solution.
2. In the first session, as part of agreeing to the objectives of this coaching relationship and defining what success looks like, build a "contract" that the conversations will not "go backward" and revisit the cause of the issue. The only way is forward.
3. The outcome is an action plan and implementation of the solution.
4. It is important to create a climate of trust and open dialogue.
5. Know when the coaching has achieved its objectives. Apart from offering assistance in the future, there is no need to have further coaching sessions.
6. The coaching will have succeeded not only if the coachee achieves personal objectives but also if there remains a longer-term relationship.

CONCLUSION

The focus of this chapter was on some practical aspects of engaging the project team. This was through a focus on each team member as well as the team as a whole to help them perform to their maximum capability for the success of the project. This encourages the growth and development of individuals within the team and ultimately the team as an entity.

Teams are often overlooked as important stakeholders of projects or programs but clearly are essential for successful delivery of project outcomes. Without the involvement of a committed team, the project will not be successful. We began with the theory of EI as an essential tool and attitude for the leader, the team members, and the team as a whole. This was followed by discussions of theories of team formation and interventions to reduce conflict. The ensuing theme of this chapter was what the leader (or project or program manager) must do to ensure effectiveness of the team's work and the skills that form the leader's tool kit: motivation, conflict prevention and management, and development of approaches for development and growth of individuals, such as feedback and motivation. Senior stakeholders are also stakeholders whose involvement in the project is essential to its success. Managing upwards is the focus for a project manager seeking to be successful in the realm of projects and programs. It is discussed in the next chapter.

5

Focus on Managing Upwards

INTRODUCTION

This chapter offers a perspective, and some guidelines, for understanding the expectations of the project's senior stakeholders and developing relationships with them for the benefit of the project and the project team members. Chapter 3 focused on the theoretical aspects of leadership from the perspective of the project manager leading the team. Those theories will prove useful in helping the project manager understand the roles, responsibilities, and motivations of their senior stakeholders.

This chapter is loosely organized to answer the following questions:

- What does the project (and the team) need from senior stakeholders to be successful?
- What can the project manager do to ensure that senior stakeholders are appropriately engaged and focused on doing whatever is necessary to help the project (and therefore the organization) succeed in an environment of uncertainty and change?

The chapter is organized as follows: First, an analysis of the dilemma faced by the senior leadership team in performing their leadership roles in the organization is provided. Understanding the pressure of the roles of senior stakeholders can help build empathy between the project manager and the senior stakeholder.* This is followed by a focus on a specific senior stakeholder role, that of the sponsor, not only recognizing the importance

---

* In Chapter 4, the importance of emotional intelligence (EI) in relationships was discussed.

of that role but also recognizing that the project manager must build strong relationships with other senior stakeholders. The final section analyzes some common problems facing the project team with regard to senior stakeholders: building a reputation of credibility, dealing with difficult people (bosses), and learning to say no to senior stakeholders.

THE MANAGERS' DILEMMA

Talbot (2003) proposed that the development and creation of industrial and postindustrial organizational forms derives from military models, traced back to military organizational innovations of Napoleon in the early nineteenth century. Later in the nineteenth century, infrastructure projects such as the Western Railroad of the United States were the catalyst for the hierarchical and bureaucratic line and staff management structure and soon became the dominant management structure: the traditional functional structure. The language and culture of management as we practice it today has direct links to the Napoleonic military connection through its organizing principle of hierarchies and inclusion of the metaphors of war in the language of business: the battle for market share, prioritizing and allocating resources, campaigning, killer strategies, captive markets, unity of command, or war chest. The military metaphor is the dominant paradigm driving the organizational culture by which senior management still believes that it must remain "in command" and "in control."

Senior functional managers in an organization have usually attained those positions by displaying aptitude for operating within the corporate "jungle." This aptitude covers the ability to quickly recognize "potential enemies" and use the precepts of command and control to manage their people and the output of their people. However, once these managers reach the highest levels of an organization, the requirements of the executive role change from command and control to leading and motivating: from competition to collaboration. Many executives find changing the habits of a working lifetime difficult.

Making the Transition to the Executive Level

To understand more about what it means to be an executive in a large organization, it is important to explore the nature and culture of organizational leadership: what it takes to reach an executive position and the demands of decision making in today's competitive environment. Newly appointed executives struggle to make the transition to the ranks of the senior leadership team from their previous position, often an operational role. The Watkins (2003) study of Fortune 500 organizations identified four broad categories of challenges for new executives:

- Letting go of "hands-on" detail and thinking/acting more strategically (the big picture),
- Developing new and unfamiliar skills and behaviors in an environment with new rules (learning on the job),
- Managing upwards (they also have to do it), and
- Balancing early wins with realistic goals (getting "runs on the board").

The transition strategies reported as successful included

- Managing upwards through clarifying expectations of key stakeholders on objectives, goals, and leadership styles,
- Building alliances and support structures through establishing personal credibility with stakeholders and understanding the culture (not only of the organization but also of the leadership team—the peers of the executive), and
- Focusing on personal reinvention, substituting skills, values, and behaviors not appropriate to the new role with those now appropriate.*

The issues that new leaders face are in conflict with the temptations that come with the new positions of power (Lencioni, 2002):

- *Choosing status over results*: The chief executive officer (CEO) must judge success by the results of the organization the CEO leads, not the trappings of status or the advantages of power.
- *Choosing popularity over accountability*: The individual may be reluctant to give negative feedback so that people who report directly to the individual "like" them.
- *Choosing certainty over clarity*: This involves waiting too long for more information rather than making a decision without all the "facts."

---

* It is interesting to note that the challenges and transition strategies that the new executives recognized they needed to address for success in the new role are exactly the same as the challenges and strategies that project managers within the organization must use to manage the relationships with these same executives (senior stakeholders).

- *Choosing harmony over productive conflict*: The individual is uncomfortable with the confrontation of direct reports.
- *Choosing invulnerability over trust*: The leader cannot admit to being wrong. Great leaders admit that they do not know everything and use the full strength and resources of the team to help with decision making.

Five Levels of Leadership

The cult* of leadership has emphasized (or developed) the concept of the CEO as *hero*. Jim Collins (2001) describes a different way of thinking about leadership. From his research into the leadership of long-term sustainable organizations ("What makes an organization go from good to great?") he developed a hierarchy of leadership qualities and characteristics culminating in level 5 leadership, which he defined as a blend of humility and will that moves a company to sustainable greatness The idea of CEO as hero equates to Collins's level 4 leadership. This is the paradox of leadership: The qualities that Collins identified for most effective leadership do not necessarily result in the CEO or other executives as being the "front man" of the organization or the one who must "lead the troops into battle." The level 5 leader is a strategist and not only recognizes the path that an organization must take for success but also empowers the management team to meet the challenges. Table 5.1 describes the five levels and their characteristics.

THE SPONSOR

Uncertainty, ambiguity, and turbulence affect everyone in the organization, through all levels. To succeed, project managers need to be flexible, to deal with unexpected problems, and to build credibility with the project's senior stakeholders. The sponsor can provide useful assistance through ensuring that the project has adequate funding and resources and through providing a buffer between the politics of the organization and the work of the project.

---

* The CEO is not only the spokesperson and "brand" but also the embodiment of the organization, paid according to the results of the short-term share market, rather than any strategic perspective or long-term view of organizational sustainability. Shareholder value was discussed in more detail in Chapter 2.

TABLE 5.1

Five-Level Model of Leadership

1. Highly capable individual	• Contributes through talent, knowledge, skills, and good work habits.
	• An effective team member.
2. Contributing team member	• Contributes to the achievement of group objectives; works effectively with others in a group setting.
	• Able to take on team leader roles with supervision.
3. Competent manager	• Organizes people and resources toward the effective and efficient pursuit of predetermined objectives.
	• An efficient manager of resources, finance, reporting.
4. Effective leader	• Promotes and encourages commitment to and vigorous pursuit of a clear and compelling vision; stimulates the group to high performance standards.
	• A leader who takes on a "hero" persona; "hands on"; often takes the "spokesman" role.
5. Executive	• Builds enduring greatness through a paradoxical combination of personal humility plus professional will.
	• Is clear on what success really looks like, understands and operates well within the power relationships of the organization, and is willing to mentor others.

Source: Collins, J., *Harvard Business Review, 79*(1), 66–77, 2001.

The supportive involvement of senior stakeholders, particularly the sponsor, is key to project success. In far too many projects, the sponsor is not involved, leading to failure of communication within the communication ecosystem and failure to engage important stakeholders. In many cases, the sponsor does not even realize that he should be involved with a project as he or she is often nominated through a governance process that fails to communicate adequately to all those who should be involved.* One of the most important communication activities of the project manager and team will be to ensure that the sponsor is aware of the project, knows what to do to assist, and is willing to assist when necessary.

When the relationship with the sponsor does fail, as indicated by unwillingness to assist when necessary, it is most likely to be caused by the following:

---

* The era of the "accidental project manager" has largely passed, but we are still in the age of the "accidental sponsor."

- Ineffective communication between the project team and the sponsor,
- Poor relationships and lack of understanding of the role of the sponsor and the objectives and benefits of the project,
- Poor understanding of expectations, both the sponsor's expectations and the project's needs and expectations, and
- The maturity and experience of the project manager in working within the power relations of the organization and unwillingness to "advise upwards."[*]

The Office of Government Commerce UK (OGC) (2008) defines the sponsor role as the interface between ownership of the project and delivery of its outcomes. Characteristics of this sponsor role are

- Having knowledge about the business and sufficient information about the work of the project and its outcomes to be able to make informed decisions for the benefit of the project and the organization.
- The ability to network effectively, negotiate well, influence people, and build and maintain robust relationships with stakeholders within and outside the project for the benefit of the project and the organization.

As well as essential governance and strategic involvement,[†] the responsibilities of the sponsor role include (Crawford and Brent, 2008)

- Project and program budget allocation,
- Provision of a buffer between the political forces of the organization and the project at all levels of the organization,
- Assistance with major problems,
- Approval of the project plan, project charter and project baselines, and any major changes, and
- Assistance in resourcing the project; issue and risk management.

Managers who are still locked in the "command-and-control" era will blame the project manager for any failure and will continue to intervene

---

[*] I have chosen to use the term *advise up* instead of *manage up* for two reasons: The first is to be clear that the relationship between the project and the sponsor is one of colleagues working together for the benefit of the project and the organization. Second, this is to distinguish between this type of healthy relationship and the relationships of dysfunctional organizations, where managing up often describes the actions of subordinates expecting their managers to solve all problems.

[†] These actions were discussed in Chapter 1.

by imposing more controls when they perceive that the project is "out of control." Enlightened sponsors realize they are the senior partner in a collaborative relationship and are aware of the project and clear about how they can assist the project manager in delivering project outcomes to stakeholder satisfaction. There is no certainty that the sponsor will understand the nature of this role; one of the essential roles of the project manager is to ensure that the sponsor, and other important senior stakeholders, understands how they can help the project. Often, they want to assist but are unsure how to go about it; one of the important communication roles for the project manager is providing information to help the senior stakeholders assist.

The most important tool for building support is sustained communication: communication whose purpose is clear, whose format and content are appropriate to the requirements of the sponsor, and whose effectiveness is monitored and modified as necessary to meet the needs of the project and the expectations of the sponsor (also a stakeholder). The most successful communication will come from teams who have established credibility through a sustained campaign to develop a reputation for delivery of results and fearless good advice (see Chapter 8 on communication).

Three Important Rules for Sponsor Engagement

There are three important rules for developing a strong supportive relationship with senior stakeholders, in particular with the sponsor:

1. Always communicate in business language: The sponsor may not know much about the discipline and language of project management and may not care. To brief the sponsor (or any other important senior stakeholder) efficiently, it is necessary to provide information that is appropriate—concise, clear, and in business terminology—*not* project management terminology. Communicating in this way reduces barriers of mismatched language; the sponsor will also recognize that the project manager is making an effort to ensure the clearest possible information exchange and therefore may be more inclined to listen and act on this information.

2. If there are problems, offer recommendations: The sponsor (or any other senior stakeholder) does not want to be given more problems to handle. The nature of the role of a senior manager is onerous and full of urgent issues. At times when the project needs support, or

there are decisions to be made that affect the future of the project or the team, the best way to achieve the optimal result and build credibility with the sponsor is to present an analysis of the problem and some recommendations on how to solve it with information to help the sponsor make the right decision.

3. Make the sponsor, or any senior stakeholder, "look good": This means *no surprises* ever. It is essential to support the sponsor by ensuring that there are no surprises in the work that is the sponsor's responsibility.* Early warnings may also allow the sponsor to act to minimize the impact or reduce the liability of a problem that can escalate further out of control. It is also important to brief the sponsor about the progress and issues of the project as frequently as possible, particularly if the project is complex or high profile or the outcome is important to the success of the organization. The briefing does not have to be long; if the information flow is brief and concise, the sponsor will always make time to hear what is happening.

Power within Organizations

Understanding how to work within the power structures of the organization is important because access to resources (financial, human, material, and informational) must be negotiated with or through senior stakeholders. The team rarely has the organizational authority, or status, needed to "require" cooperation and so must rely on other attributes to achieve the organization's outcomes. These attributes are the ability to

- Build credibility through the reputation for successful management and leadership,
- Develop and maintain networks as a source of influence and access to power,
- Be willing to operate within the power structures of the organization,
- Understand the expectations of the project's senior stakeholders and use language that matches their own roles and experience,

---

* This includes your project. Be prepared to give bad news as soon as you are aware of it and have analyzed the cause and consequences. By doing this, you may prevent the sponsor from being embarrassed by lack of information.

- Recognize that the groundwork must be laid *before* a crisis occurs through targeted communication of progress, including fearless but fully analyzed reporting of issues or risks, and
- Help the sponsor assist the manager and team deliver success to the organization.

Some aspects that project managers and their teams need to consider are the following:

- The drivers for management "deadlines": What does the stakeholder expect to achieve through meeting these deadlines?[*]
- Being heard: Managers and teams should act with a long-term focus to build credibility in the eyes of the senior stakeholder as insurance for when the project really needs the intervention of the sponsor.[†]
- The project manager may also need to develop a network of allies: influential stakeholders who are supportive of the work and are prepared to be an advocate for the work and the team[‡] (influence networks).
- The approach of a methodology such as the **Stakeholder** *Circle* is used to understand who all the important stakeholders are and how best to engage them through purposeful, targeted, and appropriate communication.[§]

Dealing with Difficult Stakeholders

Although the relationships with stakeholders involve all types of groups and individuals, relationships with senior stakeholders seem most difficult. With this group of stakeholders, the stakes are high; they have the most to lose if things go wrong and often see things differently from those who are below them in the organization's hierarchy. Anyone—everyone—who has ever worked in an organization (of any type) will have encountered at least one "difficult" senior stakeholder. They can be recognized because they

- Set aggressive deadlines or impossible tasks,
- Have unrealistic expectations of the outcomes but are not being prepared to discuss or modify these expectations, and

---

[*] This is discussed further in the next section regarding saying no.
[†] Building credibility is discussed further in this chapter.
[‡] The importance of networks is discussed in the next chapter.
[§] Chapter 2 described actions to engage stakeholders.

- Are "too busy" to discuss details or issues or are not interested in progress reports but become angry when things go wrong.

Inevitably, "rogue" stakeholders* will cause problems within the project's stakeholder community. This trouble can come in the form of

- Seeking to cancel the work or change its scope or technical direction,
- Attempting to reduce the funding, and
- Requiring additional or different reporting.

Helping the Sponsor Help You (and Your Project)

The *techniques* for managing the expectations of senior stakeholders and managing the behaviors of difficult colleagues (who are also stakeholders) are in part based on *building credibility* so that when support is needed, it is readily given. The process is about building credibility through following the three "rules" previously listed. Building credibility will take time, but when assistance is needed from the sponsor or another senior stakeholder, help will be more readily given because the sponsor or senior stakeholder is aware of the project, trusts the project manager, and knows that any call for help will also provide recommendations about how the help is best given. It is worthwhile remembering that the sponsor's reputation is now attached to the success of this project, and the sponsor should welcome the opportunity to act to ensure its continuing success.

Understanding how, and having the willingness, to work within the power structures of the organization is an important skill to acquire because access to resources (financial, human, material, and informational) must be negotiated. Without organizational authority or status, project managers must rely on the abilities outlined previously in this chapter to achieve the organization's outcomes, including

- *Building credibility* through the reputation for successful management and leadership,
- Developing and *maintaining networks* as a source of influence and access to power,

---

* These are recognizable instantly because they support one of the conflicting parties or seek to demonstrate their power and control in the environment surrounding the project. Their actions or activities will be a cause of conflict within the project's stakeholder community.

- Understanding the *expectations of stakeholders* and communicating in the language that matches their own roles and experience,
- Recognizing that the *groundwork must be laid before* a crisis occurs through targeted communication of progress, including fearless but fully analyzed reporting of issues or risks, and
- *Helping the sponsor* assist the manager and team deliver success to the organization.

When the Sponsor Leaves the Project

It often happens that the sponsor or other important project stakeholder moves away from involvement with the project because of a promotion, resignation, or a focus on other organizational activities within the organization. All the work invested into building the profile for the project and building a trusting relationship between the project team and this stakeholder has been undone by this one action. Often, there is no option but just to start again, working to build credibility and trust with the new sponsor. Project managers, who are aware of the risk, will have built other relationships with other important senior stakeholders.* This investment is worthwhile—it means that the project will still have protection during the time that a new relationship is being developed between the project and the new sponsor.

MANAGING RELATIONS WITH SENIOR STAKEHOLDERS

Developing a relationship with senior stakeholders requires a great deal of personal effort from the project manager.† Baldoni (2010) lists seven different styles that can be used, alone or in combination, to influence others:

1. *Information*: Dissemination of information (communication) is the key to building relationships and influencing others.

---

* Senior stakeholders on a project steering committee (if one exists) are good candidates for this type of insurance, provided that care is taken to avoid undermining the sponsor.

† Modern project management is moving toward the idea that success in projects is more about management of people than technical expertise. This is the theme of this book: understanding who the stakeholders are at any time in the life cycle of the project and managing these relationships is the pathway to successful delivery of project value.

2. *Charisma*: Leadership "presence" is built from confidence, mutual respect, and recognizing the importance of taking others' needs and expectations into account.

3. *Participation*: The person recognizes that people who are invited to participate in something that they consider to be worthwhile and interesting will become more involved and passionate than if they are just bystanders.

4. *Compromise*: Different points of view are worked through to achieve an outcome that is acceptable to all. Built into this concept are willingness to listen to the perspectives of others and recognition that an outcome that has majority support is more likely to be successful.

5. *Reason*: Appeals are made to the intellect rather than emotions.

6. *Emotional appeal*: Appeals are made to the issues that individuals believe in—a type of WIIFM: "What's in it for me?"

7. *Coercion*: This involves application of force and ensures compliance to ethical codes or law. Taken to extremes, it becomes bullying.

Influence can be applied in many ways and for many purposes, but like so many other important communications, it must be adapted to the situation and to the people who the project manager seeks to influence.

Building Trust

Trust is a two-sided relationship: One person trusts, and the other person is trusted (Green and Howe, 2012). The "trust equation" is about trustworthiness. The four aspects of trustworthiness are as follows:

- *Credibility*: This is achieved through being recognized as having expertise in your profession: recognized as having experience and past successes (in this case, in previous projects) as well as being current with the industry and business environment in which you are working, clearly enjoying what you do, having passion for project management, and working to build robust relationships; and finally recognizing that you do not have all the answers (having an inquiring mind, ensuring that all necessary information can be obtained and is obtained).

- *Reliability*: Acting in a consistent and predictable fashion—your word is your bond (what you say you will or can do is what you will or can do). Setting expectations with all stakeholders through making realistic promises, communicating in stakeholder's language, and ensuring that if promises are not being met that the stakeholder knows as soon as possible, along with some remedies.

- *Intimacy*: This is about really listening to the stakeholder and doing what is possible to bridge the gap between the two parties to try to reduce misunderstandings. This can be achieved by really listening to both the words and the context. Just because the sponsor is powerful does not mean that everything is easy for the sponsor. The investment in maintaining relationships in any part of the organization takes time and effort. It is important to use this chance to build the relationship further by getting to know the sponsor as a person, not just someone who is essential to the project. Often, the relationship is enhanced by the sharing of small personal details; it is not necessary to cultivate the friendship of the sponsor, but building a little personal connection into the work relationship will increase intimacy and build trust. Having started this, it is important to be consistent; otherwise, the sponsor will be suspicious of your motives.

- *Self-orientation* (it is not always about you): This is about recognizing that your deadlines and your issues should not be the primary reason for building relationships with senior stakeholders, particularly the sponsor. It is better not to focus on seeking acknowledgment for your efforts instead of the team or to talk more than you listen; this is an important leadership skill as well as an important point in building robust relationships. *Instead*, it is better to work with the team or the sponsor to seek joint solutions to issues or conflict; to ensure that credit is given to all those who worked to deliver success; and more important, to be truthful about knowledge and acknowledgment.[*]

Honesty is the key to building and maintaining trustful relationships with all stakeholders; this honesty is also key to being able to influence your senior stakeholders. With credibility and the reputation for trustworthiness, you will have earned the right to be heard. Remember that reciprocity is essential as well: If you listen, seek advice, and recognize the importance of building a robust relationship with important stakeholders, when you need them they will step in to assist.

---

[*] This is the concept of EI as discussed in the previous chapter: self-awareness, self-management, social awareness, and relationship management. The project manager with a high EQ will be more adept at building and managing the relationships and having the maturity and self-confidence to advise upwards—even to give feedback to the boss and to say no.

Dealing with Difficult Bosses

Everyone who has been involved in delivering organizational outcomes has a horror story about working with difficult stakeholders. These stories usually involve:

- The difficulty and frustration of working in the command-and-control management culture and unsuccessful attempts at "being heard" by senior management,
- How lack of experience can cause the manager and team to try desperate measures or just give up and provide the senior stakeholder with whatever the stakeholder wants even if it is not in the best interests of the organization or the current work,
- How focus on one stakeholder can lead to neglect of other equally important but less vocal stakeholders and subsequent perception of failure of the activity, and
- How everyone reacts (not necessarily logically) to uncertainty.

The stress and anxiety experienced in coping with change is borne by everyone in an organization, not only the managers, but also all members of the organization's community. To reduce the stress and manage the anxiety, it is essential to

- Identify stakeholders for each phase of the project. Who is important will change as the project moves through each of its phases.
- Be clear on what a successful outcome means for each of the important stakeholders. Knowing these expectations means that the manager can target messages to gain the support and influence of each stakeholder within the framework of what was considered "successful" (Bourne, 2012).
- Understand that there will inevitably be conflicts regarding the expectations between important senior stakeholders. The conflicts must be resolved as soon as possible.
- Know that, with experience, operating within the power structures of the organization, and learning from mistakes, *advising upwards* becomes less complicated.
- Build credibility within the organization through a reputation in the industry and utilize the influence networks developed and sustained over time.

- Recognize that it takes time and continuous effort to analyze and review the stakeholder community, understand the expectations of the important stakeholders, develop targeted communication strategies, and negotiate with the stakeholders who had conflicting expectations.

Dealing with difficult senior stakeholders is a significant part of the role and responsibilities of the project manager. There is no single solution; every circumstance is different, so any approach will need to be a balance of different actions. Above all, it will take time to build the necessary relationship with these key stakeholders. It may be helpful to look at these types,[*] discussed by Scott (2006), in more detail:

- The incompetent boss
- The micromanager
- The boss who gives unclear instructions or is disorganized
- The boss who blames others or takes undue credit
- The boss who acts like a tyrant or is a "game player"

The Incompetent Boss

The incompetent boss stakeholder may represent a textbook case of the manager who is relatively new to the position, has risen to this higher level from middle management, and is still trying to grasp the different responsibilities and requirements of the new role. He or she may be looking to other managers at this new level to provide examples on how to best cope with the new role and responsibilities and relying on them to help find the way. The profile of this manager is of one who does not make decisions, postponing action until someone else must make the decision. He or she does not know what to do or what is going on and depends on others in the team, or colleagues, to manage the situation. This stakeholder may be a technical person or an operational manager who has been rewarded for success in the previous job with a promotion to a management position and often has the support of more senior management.

If you need a decision from this stakeholder, it will be necessary to provide recommendations about the best options. By providing this manager with all the information necessary to make the decision, all that the stakeholder

---

[*] Scott (2006) referred to "bosses"; the analysis here is in the context of senior stakeholder who may be the boss of the project manager or someone with power and influence in the organization whose support is essential for project success.

will have to do is sign the approval sheet. This information is not only data selected according to the decision-making models but also must take into account other factors that affect decision making, including (Frame, 2013):

- Personality of those involved in the decision-making process
- Creative capacity of those involved to develop alternatives that will enhance the quality of the outcomes of the process
- Psychological states of all involved
- Cognitive state: ability to think clearly
- Competence and capability and intelligence

If the outcome of the decision is essential to the continued success of the project, it will be necessary to make an assessment concerning these factors when presenting recommendations to this type of stakeholder. Information such as stakeholder expectations (discussed in Chapter 2), personality, risk profile, or decision-making style* can influence the decision.

Micromanager

The micromanaging stakeholder is generally a detail-oriented person, possibly someone whose career was in the technical domain before a promotion to management. The micromanager is only comfortable with detail and cannot see the strategic "helicopter" view. He or she probably also does not trust the decision making of others and will insist on being given *all* the steps of the decision as part of the briefing. This is annoying and time wasting for most people but is the personality of the stakeholder, so the only option in presenting information is to ensure the complete "story" is presented. If a strong relationship of trust has been developed, it is possible to satisfy the manager with less detail; otherwise, each briefing session will be time consuming and test the project manager's patience: There is no other way.

Gives Unclear Instruction, Is Disorganized

The stakeholder who gives unclear instructions or is disorganized is the opposite of the micromanager. The stakeholder is enthusiastic at the

---

* Williams and Miller (2002) identified five decision-making styles and how to influence them: charismatic, thinkers, skeptics, followers, and controllers. A different but equally useful perspective is offered online (http://toolkit.smallbiz.nsw.gov.au/part/8/42/201).

beginning but soon loses interest or focuses enthusiasm on another project. If this stakeholder is crucial to the success of the project, it will be necessary to continue to provide information, but in a way that is interesting and novel. This stakeholder often feels that by leaving decisions and oversight to the team, he or she is empowering them. If the stakeholder is a roadblock between the project manager and those who actually can provide the information, it may be necessary to work around the stakeholder. It is still essential to brief this stakeholder and possibly even ensure decisions are made or approvals given. In this case, it may be necessary to give information in small chunks; this approach will take more time but may be the only way to ensure that the stakeholder is sufficiently briefed and ensure that the stakeholder cannot later claim to have had no knowledge and did not approve. The team must be involved because the team must help organize the stakeholder to provide the appropriate support or decision for the project.

This type of stakeholder will often make promises to provide the necessary support, or fulfill a task that is necessary for the project, but will not keep that promise. It may be that the boss is just too busy and has not given this project a high priority. If the stakeholder is too busy, the only way to focus his or her attention on the project will be to ensure that the information is presented simply but effectively; keeping the briefings short shows that the stakeholder's time is respected. If this does not work, it may be necessary to use the influence of another, more powerful stakeholder, if this is possible. It is also important to record the promises, follow up with an e-mail summarizing the conversation in which the promise was given, and in further briefings begin the meeting with a reminder of the promise that has been given.

Blames Others or Takes Undue Credit

The stakeholder who blames others or takes undue credit may be a combination of the previous type, claiming he had no knowledge if things go wrong, or may be just becoming one of those who lines up for the "decoration of the nonparticipants" once the work has been successfully completed.* The best way to deal with this stakeholder is to stay calm, whether he or she is claiming credit for others' work or laying blame for a failure—there

---

* The seven steps of project management are wild enthusiasm, disillusionment, confusion, panic, search for the guilty, punishment of the innocent, and decoration of nonparticipants (see http://www.1000advices.com).

is no point in being angry. If all meetings and commitments have been documented and circulated, the options for credit taking or laying blame are limited.

Acts Like a Tyrant or a "Game Player"

The stakeholder who acts like a tyrant or who is a game player may not accept any excuses for failure; the stakeholder will not make allowances for family issues, illness, or even worse, lack of organizational support or involvement. The expectation here is the "whatever it takes" philosophy that has been defined as the way of working of the baby boomer generation.[*] This stakeholder may be of that generation. It may not be possible to change his or her approach, and it will be necessary to ensure good communication with his or her boss. The project manager can still work within these constraints by ensuring that others in the project team are aware of the work and can step in if the project manager cannot.[†]

If the stakeholder is a game player, he or she will take delight in the following games:

- Embarrassing or humiliating the team by reminding them of their failures,
- Drawing attention to personal characteristics, or
- Assigning two people the same task, thinking that the competition will produce better results.

Saying No

Another aspect of the tyrant stakeholder is an inability to take no for an answer. The team member may just want to say yes to avoid confrontation but knows the request is unreasonable and cannot be achieved. If the task cannot be achieved, the individual is perceived as failing, so it is better not to just say yes knowing that the task will fail. This section discusses ways to say no without sounding negative.

We may be unexpectedly asked to do something additional to our regular responsibilities: The only expected answer is yes. If the task is unachievable,

---

[*] This is discussed in more detail in Chapter 7.

[†] This is an important management process. The project manager should not be the "hero"; he or she should ensure that others are briefed on everything that is being done within the project. Not only is it sensible risk management in case illness or other priorities prevent the manager from completing his or her duties, but also it is a useful motivation tool and succession planning approach.

it would be foolish to agree to do it—failure is even more destructive to your reputation. It is important to be able to say no to a senior stakeholder without being perceived as negative for a number of reasons:

- Appearing to be negative gives the wrong signal; it will taint the reputation you are working to develop for credibility, reliability, and trustworthiness.
- Saying no will mean that there is no room to move on the environment or outcomes that you have been asked to work on. The senior stakeholder will feel that he or she has been defied and will not be bothered to have any further discussion. It may be that the stakeholder will "direct" you to do this task anyway.

The most successful project managers will propose or engage in an act of "intelligent disobedience" as a means of actually *establishing* a relationship with a member of the senior management team. Significant relationships are built as a result of the substantial conversations and shared experiences that will result. Discussing a situation of significance with a senior manager and proposing a bold or nontraditional action to solve it forms a basis for extending and expanding the relationship with that senior stakeholder. The leader that does this—after taking the time to "do appropriate homework"—can quickly enrich a relationship. See the sidebar for some suggested dialogue.

The following questions can help clarify the request:

- *About priorities*:
  - How does this fit into the other priorities?
  - What will I need to defer to do this?
- *About process*:
  - How can we set this up to ensure success (people, budget, time)?
- *About people*:
  - Who is this for? (If it is for someone important, ensure that it can succeed.)
  - Who is best to do this?

The idea is also that, in the process of answering the questions (about the business), the senior stakeholder may recognize that the first request was unreasonable and one that can be modified to be achievable should be put in its place.

SAYING NO

When the impossible request comes without warning, further information should be requested to "buy" some time to think. A dialogue such as the one that follows (adapted from Owen, 2012) could be useful[*]:

- *Agree on the goal of the idea*: "I think that this idea will be important for reaching the program's goal; I am not sure, however, how it fits into the overall priorities of the program and, more important, this project. Can you give me more information, please?"
- *Understand the context*: "Can you tell me where this particular task fits into the strategic objectives that this project (or program) must deliver?"
- *Create and evaluate options*: "Now that I understand the context and the objectives, I think that there may be a more cost-effective way to achieve this objective. Can I work with my team and meet with you again later today to discuss the details?"
- *Identify obstacles to success*: "I understand achieving this is important. I need to point out that diverting our energies to this activity will mean that some of the activities of the project may have to be rescheduled. I would like to discuss this with the team and propose a plan for fulfilling this requirement and still delivering the outcomes that the other stakeholders are expecting."

And next steps: Set a meeting to discuss alternative proposals (as soon as possible). You should take this step in any case, working with the project team or other supportive stakeholders to try to build the best argument for the alternative proposal.

---

[*] This approach was originally adapted from a Monty Python sketch, "The Cheese Shop" (http://www.youtube.com/watch?v=vJhq9eq_eJg). In the sketch, the cheese shop has no cheese at all, but the shop owner does not want to admit this, instead offering alternatives or providing reasons why the cheese that was requested is not suitable.

Intelligent Disobedience

The phrase *intelligent disobedience* comes from the world of seeing eye dogs. In the context of training these service pets, intelligent disobedience is

> a concept where any service animal trained to help a disabled person goes directly against their owner's instructions in an effort to make a better decision. (McGannon, 2011:295)

Intelligent disobedience can be adapted for organizations (McGannon, 2011). It is simply having the strength and confidence to ask such questions as have been described and not defaulting to yes. The most successful leaders test situations by asking themselves these questions in specific business and personal circumstances; this is a useful technique for project managers as well. There is some risk involved in asking such questions, as there will be when you suggest that doing this task is not in the best interests of the project. The advice is more likely to be accepted or at least considered when couched in the framework of understanding the business environment and the nature of that specific situation.

The astute leader will strive to understand the workload and capability of his or her management team to contribute to the decision-making process with useful information. In contrast, weaker or less-energetic people in leadership roles do not strive to understand. Taking this course of action will make a *courageous follower,* and your credibility should be enhanced.

If the conversation goes badly, it will probably be necessary to take one of two options:

- Follow the direction of the senior stakeholder: do the task, even if it means sacrificing the project.
- Say yes but follow the alternative course of action that you had proposed* if you are sure that it is the best way to deliver what the senior stakeholder has indicated that he or she really wants. Once you have delivered the desired outcome, even if not by the required means, you will be in a position to either explain what you have done or say nothing.†

---

* Care must be taken with this approach to avoid unethical actions or dishonesty. Often, even ethical project managers are compelled to take this approach anyway, in the best interests of the project and ultimately the organization, despite concluding that the action would not be condoned by the senior leader because they considered such action as "simply the right thing to do."

† Turning the no of senior stakeholders into yes or perhaps is also an important skill for successful project management. It is discussed regarding negotiation techniques in the next chapter.

CONCLUSION

In this chapter, the discussion focused on applying leadership skills to "advising up" while always keeping in mind the importance of project outcomes. Empathy for the stress, uncertainty, and workload of the project's senior stakeholders is an essential starting point when developing strategies and activities to ensure that they are engaged and supportive of the work of the project. Recognizing that often senior stakeholders, even if they are willing to assist, may not know what they should do or how to do it means that sometimes the project manager has to assist with decision making, perhaps even delegating upwards when it comes to dealing with organizational issues that affect the progress of the project. Finally, some guidance was provided on dealing with different types of senior stakeholders, on how to use the team to develop the arguments, and strategies to influence senior stakeholders for the benefit of the project.

The next chapter covers the final two types of stakeholders: sidewards and outwards. The discussions in the next chapter center on ways to influence and engage individuals and groups within these large groups, including networks and the use of social media and negotiation.

6

Focus on Sidewards and Outwards Stakeholders

INTRODUCTION

This chapter analyzes relationships between the project team and the final two groups of stakeholders: *sidewards* and *outwards* stakeholders. *Sidewards* stakeholders are the peers of the project manager within the organization and external to it, but are still stakeholders of the project and have the capability to affect or may be affected by the work of the project. *Outwards* stakeholders are all other stakeholders outside the project—the list is long. There may not be many opportunities to build direct relationships between the project team and each outwards group or individual. Often, the relationships will be indirect, carried out through a third party: the government contact, the account manager, the representative of the project's customer, or the union representative, for example. Without the ability to directly influence this type of stakeholder and build strong relationships when necessary, other options become necessary. These other options are building alliances with these third parties, utilizing networks to influence stakeholders not directly connected with the project manager or team, or negotiating as a final option.

The chapter is organized as follows: First, more detail is provided about sidewards and outwards stakeholders—how they can affect the outcomes of the project or be affected by them and the relationships that need to be built to engage them effectively. The next section focuses on networks: theory and application to the world of projects for the purposes of building alliances, sharing information, and seeking to influence others not directly connected with the project team. This is followed by discussion of the theory and application of negotiation techniques to assist the project manager and team to acquire scarce resources and support for the project in the form of skilled personnel, funding, advocacy, and influence. The final section describes some approaches for coaching to help team members solve problems in a structured way.

SIDEWARDS AND OUTWARDS STAKEHOLDERS

Sidewards Stakeholders

Engaging sidewards stakeholders is about managing the project manager's peers to ensure collaboration rather than competition. The "What's at stake?"* for these stakeholders is usually connected to another project or activity: the project that they manage or the function for which they are responsible. The relationships that need to be developed and maintained are primarily focused on ensuring collaboration between the different projects for the following purposes:

- Management of the interdependencies of outputs from one project that another project needs to meet its own obligations.
- Sharing of scarce resources in the form of personnel with specialist skills. Often, resource management practices in organizations are based on the provision of these skills on an "as-needed" basis. This will occur either because of the scarcity of people with this skill or because it is considered effective financial practice to ensure maximum utilization through the practice of sharing and reduction of "bench time." Not only does this require careful scheduling and cooperation between projects and their managers, but also it may involve some negotiation to take into account schedules that slip or

---

* The "stake" of each stakeholder was described in Chapter 2. It is always a useful question to ask when assessing the importance of a stakeholder and when developing appropriate communication strategies to build and maintain the relationship between each stakeholder and the project. It is important to ask this question when addressing the team as stakeholders and senior stakeholders, but probably it is more important when considering these final two groups of stakeholders because often the relationship, though important, is "arm's length," and communication considerations must also include penetrating the "barrier" of the intermediary.

estimates that were not as accurate as they may have been—resulting in a need to keep the resource within any particular project for a longer period.*

- When there is a need to apply the change management process of an organization to change the time, cost, or scope baselines of one project, part of this process should be developing an impact statement describing how this particular change to one project may have an impact on other projects, programs, or portfolios or operational work. As with management of interdependencies, agreement on changes that have an impact on the outcomes of other projects will often require negotiation with the peers of the project manager.

- Finally, when organizations decide to reduce expenditure, two of the options that apply to the work of projects will involve either discontinuing work on specific projects because their deliverables have lower priority than others or imposing a percentage reduction in the budgets of all the work that is being done at that time. Sometimes, the first option means that some project work is merged with other projects. As with mergers and acquisitions at the organizational level, there are winners and losers in such arrangements. Project managers who have strong collaborative relationships with their peers will be able to ensure that the most important deliverables continue to be worked on and that as many project team members as possible are retained. This is both for the benefit of the individuals and to ensure that the knowledge that they retain is not lost to the organization.

The discussions about the relationships that project managers need to develop with sidewards stakeholders are specifically about how to collaborate with them, ensuring successful outcomes for both people in the relationship. If these collaborative relationships are not developed and maintained, the outcomes of the situations described may not be so beneficial to anyone, particularly if a competitive environment emerges because of the culture of the organization or from poor relationships between project managers and their peers.

---

* This chapter includes a section on negotiation techniques in recognition of the need for project managers to work with their peers and other stakeholders to obtain the best outcomes for the projects, the individuals who are the subject of this overlapping need, and the organization. This should not imply that the project manager does not need to negotiate with team members or their senior stakeholders as well—discussion on both negotiation and networks applies fully to all other types of stakeholders. It is placed in this chapter for convenience as much as any other reason.

Outwards Stakeholders

Any relationship that needs to be developed with outwards stakeholders is usually more complicated, particularly if the project manager or team member has no direct contact with outwards stakeholders.

Managing outwards involves considering the needs and impacts of a large group of stakeholders external to the project and often to the organization. This group will include some (or all) of the following: clients or customers of the organization, users of the solution, their managers and customers, the "public," rate payers, voters, lobby or action groups, government or regulatory bodies, shareholders, suppliers of personnel, material or services, families of these stakeholders, and the media. Each of these outwards stakeholder groups will have different requirements from the project. They are grouped in one "direction of influence,"* but it is important to clarify their requirements of the project and their impacts on the project individually. A further complication is that in many cases there will need to be two layers of relationship: with the stakeholder group or individual and with the individual or group managing that relationship on behalf of the organization. These are usually groups or individuals with titles such as account manager, government relationship manager, regulatory group, media liaison, subject matter expert (SME), and business analyst (BA). In the case of the last two on the list, this "second layer" of relationship occurs when the SME or BA is asked to make decisions about functionality, stakeholders, or process on behalf of the organization they represent. Recognition of the function that alliances and networks play and the consequence of multilayer relationship building are discussed in more detail further in this chapter.† In this next section a discussion of some of the relationships that need to be developed within the outwards stakeholder group is presented. The approach is a general recognition of the expectations of both the liaison group and the stakeholder groups in terms of what is at stake and why they are important to the project's success.

The key feature of outwards stakeholders is that the project manager and team rarely have direct contact with the decision makers in these stakeholder groups. The manager often has to operate through an agent representing the

---

* "Directions of influence" are described in detail in Chapter 2.
† Knowledge of network theory and its application for success of the project are not confined to engaging outwards stakeholders; this chapter is the most logical place for it to be discussed, but the theory can also be usefully applied to downwards and upwards stakeholders.

"real" stakeholder individuals or groups, the regulatory bodies, government departments, investor lobby groups, or even user groups. So, the nature of the relationship is at least once removed. The agent of the outwards stakeholder is also a stakeholder of the project—an important stakeholder who must be engaged and supportive of the work of the project. The agent must be encouraged to promote the benefits of the project with the body represented. The project manager needs to help the agent balance his or her loyalty to the body represented with a commitment to the successful delivery of benefits to that body through successful delivery of project outcomes. The process is helped by involving each agent in the work of the project, almost as part of the project team, with invitations to team meetings and access to information essential for ensuring that the agent can fulfill both roles successfully.

However, it would be too risky to rely only on one communication channel for any important outwards stakeholder groups. To reduce risk, it is essential to establish additional communication channels to other areas within each outwards stakeholder group. Whether it is through peer-to-peer contacts between the project's senior stakeholders and more senior managers within the authority or by establishing other connections into the stakeholder organization it is essential to develop alternative ways to engage outwards stakeholders. Establishing networks that include personnel from the outwards stakeholders will significantly reduce the risk of blocked communication and ensure that the essential connections within the communication ecosystem that sustains the project are robust and enduring.

NETWORKS

Networks help project managers build influence. They bring together people, knowledge, and information that may not otherwise be accessible. Those who use their networks judiciously and work to maintain and grow essential links have broader access to information (and therefore power and influence).

The research of Barabasi (2002) was directed to relationships that each person forms as a result of family, friends, work, and leisure activities. These relationships are not just one to one; through these networks of family, friends, and colleagues, we are connected in ways that allow us to influence and be influenced by people that we do not even know. Networks are present everywhere. Through our own networks, we are linked into the social web within the world beyond the project or the organization. We can know between 200 and 5,000 people by name but are linked to many more through our networks (Barabasi, 2002) and can be influenced by people just because we are connected to the same network.

Definitions

A network is a community defined by structural connections and not necessarily by any particular shared traits. A network defines groups of people and the connections between them (Christakis and Fowler, 2009). There are two main ways to describe social networks: The first is *connection*, who is connected to whom, and the second is *contagion*, what flows across the ties connecting individuals. We tend to associate with people who resemble us, and we seek out people who share our interests, but through the further layers of networks of those we are connected to, we widen our influence and access to information.

Rowley (1997) developed a model of a network that builds on two factors:

- The *density* of the stakeholder network surrounding a project or organization, the number of ties between and among members of the network. *Density* refers to potential communication and influence effectiveness.
- An individual's *centrality* in the network—the position relative to others in the network (Rowley, 1997). Centrality relates to power/influence within the structure of the network and can be different from an individual's personal power. Figure 6.1 illustrates this concept.

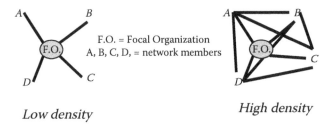

FIGURE 6.1
Density and centrality in networks. (Adapted from Rowley, T. J. *Academy of Management Review*, 22(4), 887–910, 1997.)

We can choose the structure of our network through

- Deciding on how many individuals we want to be connected: We can expand our networks through involvement with different groups of people.
- Influencing how densely we are connected: This influence is on how many of those in our networks we want to communicate with and how often.
- Controlling how central we are to the social network: We may know many by name but are close to only a few if that is what we choose.

By understanding the networks surrounding a project organization, who wields power in networks, and how various coalitions function, project managers can use the networks of the informal organization to solve problems, influence the actions of stakeholders, and improve performance.

> Social networks affect the flow and the quality of information, they are important sources of reward and punishment, and trust, the confidence that others will do the "right" thing despite a clear balance of incentives to the contrary, emerges, in the context of the social network. (Granovetter, 2005:33)

Social networks create agreement through

- "Loyalty systems" within the organization itself or the project organization or even between professionals through a code of ethics[*] (Hersey, Blanchard, and Johnson, 1996).
- The idea of culture—the sharing of ways of thinking and acting without specific coordination or intention.[†]

Different Types of Networks

Christakis and Fowler (2009) identified three types of networks (Figure 6.2) and described them in colloquial terms for easy understanding:

---

[*] The "Code of Ethics and Professional Conduct" developed by the Project Management Institute (http://www.pmi.org/~/media/PDF/Ethics/ap_pmicodeofethics.ashx) is an example.

[†] The "Mexican wave" exhibited by the crowd attending sporting events is an example of the power of networks; it is not usually preplanned and often is a spontaneous activity, frequently within the game itself. The idea of spontaneous networks is further illustrated by the actions of geese flying in formation without central control and shared leadership.

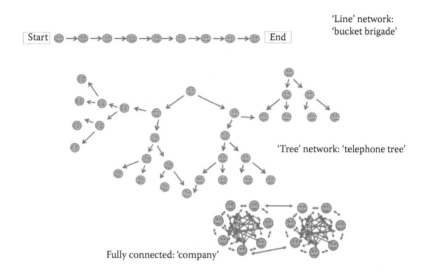

FIGURE 6.2

Common types of networks. (Adapted from Christakis, N. and Fowler, J. *Connected: The Amazing Power of Social Networks and How They Shape Our Lives.* 2009.)

- *Bucket brigade* (line network): Connections are in sequence, such as would form in a group of people attempting to put out a fire that is some distance from the source of water. The lines form to transport full buckets from the water source toward the fire, and another line would form to transport the empty buckets back to collect more water.
  - The feature of networks of this type is that the message (or bucket) only goes in one direction.
  - If someone is missing from the sequence, the message would not go further.
  - Because there is only one source, the content or context of the message may become distorted. This is "Chinese whispers," by which a message is delivered to the person next in the line, who passes it on to the next person, and so on. What generally happens is that the message that reaches the end of the line bears no resemblance to the original message.
- *Telephone tree* (tree network): One person calls two people, who each call two other people to pass on information.
  - The information is transmitted faster and the workload is distributed evenly.
  - If one person cannot be reached the information is not lost completely, only what was originating from that one person. Therefore, the issue arising from a lost connection is limited.

- This reduces the number of steps for information to flow among people in the group.
  - Everyone is connected to three other people, except the first and last persons, with one inbound tie and two outbound. The connection is not mutual but only in one direction.*
- *A company of (100) soldiers* in squads of 10 (fully connected):
  - Each person has nine ties within the group, and therefore everyone in the squad knows everyone else.
  - Each squad is also closely interconnected.
  - There are 450 ties in the company—1 tie for every two people connected.

Within the communication ecosystem of the project, all three types of networks can develop.

- *Bucket brigade*: The line network describes communication to support workflows within a project.
- *Telephone tree*: Generally, this represents normal communication within a project team, where the project manager will instruct and communicate with team leaders, who will instruct and communicate with their teams.
- *Soldier squads*: A fully connected network in a project context can represent an Agile team. With the emphasis on regular and frequent information sharing with all those involved, including senior stakeholders, there will be connections among all team members. If taken to extremes, a network such as this describes a "toxic" team that is totally introspective and does not allow or tolerate any social interactions with anyone outside the group.

Degrees of Separation

Stanley Milgram, a researcher of the 1960s, showed† that any two people are connected by a maximum of six degrees of separation (Christakis and

---

* One example of the telephone tree network is the Ponzi scheme: pyramid selling by which one person can defraud many. A positive example is bushfire trees used by country communities to alert each other in a coordinated manner to fire threat.

† Milgram's experiment consisted of asking 100 people living in Nebraska to send a letter (addressed to someone living in Boston) via their own networks. He asked them to send the letter to someone they knew personally who was more likely to have a personal relationship with the businessman addressee of the letter. On average, it took six readdresses to reach the intended addressee.

Fowler, 2009).[*] The concept has been further tested by other researchers. However, just because a person can link to the US president through six degrees does not mean that she can influence any policy or decisions in that country. It is possible for the person to influence as deep into networks as friends' friends' friends (this is three degrees). Her friends would be one degree, where she would have most influence, and her friends' friends would be at two degrees, where she would have less influence. This influence can apply to their attitudes, behaviors, and feelings; the influence will also flow in the other direction—they can influence the person's attitudes, behaviors, and feelings. Returning to the two characteristics of networks, a person can be connected to anyone else by six degrees (how *connected* we are) but can only influence others up to three degrees away (how *contagious* we are).[†]

Six degrees of separation make our world a "small world" (Barabasi, 2002). But, this does not necessarily mean that things and people are easy to find. Granovetter (1973) first identified the importance of the connections to individuals in the second and third level of the networks. He asked the question: "What connections do people use to get a job?" and found that acquaintances and friends of friends were more useful than people directly connected in the network. The odds were that the individual seeking the job would have many of the same connections of their friends because we often select our networks through shared interests (Christakis and Fowler, 2009). The weak ties are more useful in getting more information or spreading ideas.

The Power of Networks

The connections (ties) are often more important than the individuals themselves to the extent that we care less about our absolute standing in the world than our standing compared to those in our social networks (Christakis and Fowler, 2009). Our networks are *reference groups,* in which we compare ourselves to others in these groups (comparative effects) and in which our behaviors are influenced by people we may not have met (influence effects).

---

[*] The idea was popularized by a play by John Guare in 1990 called *Six Degrees of Separation,* followed by a movie of the same name. This led to a game, Six Degrees of Kevin Bacon, by which it is possible to track the connectedness between Kevin Bacon and any other actor. For example, Elvis Presley has a Bacon number of two even though he never appeared with Bacon. Information is available online (http://oracleofbacon.org/movielinks.php).

[†] There are about 19 degrees of separation in the web (Barabasi, 2002).

Emotions and Networks

We mostly have conscious awareness of our emotions.* Our emotional state may also affect our physical appearance: our faces, voices, or posture. Emotions are also connected to neurophysiological activity: Scary pictures prepare our body for "fight or flight," affecting our physiological state and increasing activity through the neural pathways in the brain. By the same token, we laugh when we see something funny, which often causes others to laugh with us. This "emotional contagion" even takes place among strangers. Emotions spread because this is a key step toward synchronizing feelings and developing emotional empathy that strengthens the connections between others in our networks.

Applying the Theories of Networks to Managing the Expectations of Stakeholders

Social networks assist the project manager by providing the basis for informal (and formal) means to influence activities and people to assist the project. In particular, networks assist the team to communicate with unsupportive stakeholders, whether they are senior stakeholders, team members, or sidewards or outwards stakeholders. By operating through the networks of the project manager and of the targeted stakeholders, it will be possible to send requests for information, approvals, or support through many connections.

Social Media

Social media builds networks with individuals that would not be possible using physical connections. It is now the most widespread technique for connecting with others but probably still not as effective as face-to-face interaction (Kase, Paauwe, and Zupda, 2009). Nevertheless, social media tools such as Facebook, Twitter, and LinkedIn have leapt the intergenerational divide and can be used for making connections and building goodwill and reciprocal relationships and transferring knowledge and information. Time and effort spent in building this "social capital" to achieve personal or project objectives, such as trust or shared knowledge, is a good (time) investment and is essential for delivering successful projects in today's organizations.

---

* The importance of being aware of our own and others' emotional states was discussed in Chapter 4.

Using Social Media Effectively in Projects

Although it is satisfying to have hundreds of "friends" in social media, it is important to remember that the higher the number of friends a person has, the larger the network is. The consequences of larger networks are that there is more access to general (superficial) information but less access to in-depth information. The larger the number of connections funneling the information, the more likely the information will be distorted by the Chinese whispers effect.

LinkedIn and Social Distance

As discussed, weaker network connections can be beneficial for those seeking jobs. When seeking favors, networks such as LinkedIn are useful. People are more likely to do favors for those with whom they have connections: The strongest is first order (direct friend), with friends of friends as second order and friends of a friend of a friend as third order. Power to influence lessens as the connections becomes further from the center (you). However, people will help third-order connections more than strangers (people with whom they have absolutely no connection) (Sacks and Graves, 2012).

Finding Influence Networks around the Project Stakeholder Community

There are many tools available to map influence networks. Social network analysis (SNA) software can build highly complex network diagrams for any organization, project, or social structure. The SNA diagrams are complex; the project team probably needs a simpler technique to understand the networks of a specific stakeholder. The following simple approach requires a limited number of questions to build a customized network for the project stakeholders:

- Who does the stakeholder work with?
- Who does he or she give advice to (or advise)?
- Who does he or she meet with regularly?
- Who does he or she mix with socially?

Having identified connections, the final questions are:

- Which of these connections are the strongest? Last longest?

- Which of these connections is supportive of the project? And is willing to act as the messenger for the project?

With answers to these questions, it is possible to develop a means to reach unsupportive stakeholders.

Traps in Building Networks

There are significant benefits in developing networks within the project's stakeholder community, but it does take time and effort to build and maintain these networks, as it does for any relationship. An inexperienced project manager may encounter obstacles to building effective networks (Cross and Thomas, 2011):

- *Wrong structure*: If the focus is only on the organization's hierarchical structure, valuable people in the informal power structures may be excluded.
- *Targeting busy people*: Reaching out to someone who has many connections and a busy work life may cause a bottleneck.
- *Wrong relationships*: Connecting with an expert with few network connections or someone who relies too much on the opinions of others from similar backgrounds or with similar values could provide wrong relationships.
- *Wrong behavior*: Wrong behavior involves engaging superficially with too many people or with someone who changes personality and attitudes to match the characteristics of whichever group he or she is in at the time.

The sidebar offers some suggestions for an approach to developing a network within and around the project stakeholder community.

Avoiding the Traps

The whole objective of building networks is to enhance the ability and capabilities of the project manager and team. Networking should be considered a means to extend the influence and reach of the project team, beyond the immediate group, using these connections in the ways that we have discussed. Networks can help overcome many of the issues of engaging stakeholders through relationships and information flows that go well beyond the reach of the project manager and team.

HOW TO DEVELOP A USEFUL
NETWORK FOR YOUR PROJECT

First, consider the current stakeholders: Who is important? Who is supportive of the project? The sponsor must be part of the network, and it may be that a sponsor from a previous project could be a useful addition.

- Thinking specifically in terms of the current project and the organization that will benefit, are there individuals in other organizations or countries who have skills and experience in your work areas?
- Remember that one of the key aspects of building a network is about the people you select:
  - Not too many people
  - People who have time or attitude to commit
  - People who are willing to communicate with you
  - People who are connected to other networks
  - People who can fill a gap for you in such areas as information, support, feedback, and challenge

Where will you find these people?

- Finding people for face-to-face connections can start with the five questions described previously for identifying influential supportive stakeholders.
- Membership of user groups, online communities of interest, or other groups of people with similar interests can be a source.
- Social media will connect you with people with the skills and characteristics that you have identified and give you access to wider congregations of potential connections for purposes you have not considered yet.

The networks have to be nourished by continual communication to maintain the necessary relationships. The connections between the project and each person on the network must be used frequently and regularly—intermittent communication may not be effective.

NEGOTIATION

Another important technique is the ability to negotiate. Project managers will benefit from skill in negotiating techniques.

- Negotiating with functional managers and others to acquire scarce resources for the project (generally people with the necessary skills and experience to work within the project team) (see Chapter 4). Often, the negotiations will involve not only making trade-offs to acquire the right person but also ensuring that the individual is willing to work with the project team.
- Requesting additional time or budget will require negotiation: an understanding of the impacts of these changes and ensuring that all affected groups and individuals understand and accept the consequences of that change. If they do not accept and they are important stakeholders, further negotiation may need to occur.
- Turning the no from a senior stakeholder into the yes that will benefit the project.
- Having the senior stakeholder accept your no when the stakeholder expects yes.
- Working with suppliers within the overall contracts developed by the organization to acquire goods, services, or people in a way and a time frame that is best for the project.
- Dealing with conflicts within the team or with stakeholders.
- Agreeing on time frames, deliverables, and standards within the project team.
- Counseling and coaching* team members—implementing any agreements arising from dealing with the negative behaviors of team members.
- Having involvement with corporate negotiations as a technical expert.
- Coordinating with other project managers—on sharing resources or agreeing on time frames for which there are interdependencies between project deliverables.
- Managing project priorities and commitments within the organization.

---

* There is a brief overview of coaching techniques at the end of this chapter.

What Is Negotiation?

Negotiation is defined as a "strategy of conferring with parties of shared or opposed interests with a view towards compromise or reaching an agreement" (PMI, 2012:517). There are two parts to negotiations: reaching an agreement on the problem or issue and implementing the agreement. The primary focus of modern negotiation techniques is on collaboration rather than competition through discussions that focus on "we" and "us" and trying to understand what each side *really* wants. The focus on working together to achieve what each side really wants, or what is of mutual benefit for the organization, means that it should be possible to come to an agreement that promotes an ongoing relationship between both parties. This is obviously essential if the negotiation is between two parties who must continue to work together after the negotiation is complete.

There are two basic types of negotiation:

- *Distributive*: The value available to the parties is essentially fixed, and one party's gain is at the expense of the other. This is the "zero-sum" game or a "win-lose" situation and can only be applied if there is no relationship and no desire for one after the negotiation is complete.
- *Integrative*: The objectives or outcomes are more about relationships and less about the zero-sum approach. Parties will jointly work to create greater value for distribution, through thinking beyond price to other creative trade-offs, such as more time to pay or free consultancy with a software purchase. Trade-offs are really about understanding what each party values most and, from that understanding, recognizing what can be conceded in the interests of the ongoing relationship.

Successful integrative negotiations require trust and shared information to create a "larger pie" so that each party can benefit. It will require both parties to exhibit greater transparency than is the case in distributive negotiations. The more each party can explain the reasons why they want to make this deal and what their real interests and constraints are and are willing to reveal and explain their preferred options, the closer they will actually come to the legendary "win-win" situation. In these circumstances, both parties may actually achieve optimal outcomes.

Four Concepts of Negotiation

The four concepts of successful negotiation (HBR, 2003) that must be an integral part of preparation for a negotiation are deciding your

- BATNA: best alternative to a negotiated agreement
- Reservation price: the point at which you walk away
- ZOPA: zone of possible agreement—the area or range between which an agreement is possible
- Value created through trades.

BATNA: Best Alternative to a Negotiated Agreement

BATNA involves knowing what you will do or what will happen if you fail to reach agreement in the negotiation. It makes no sense to negotiate if you are not clear what your options are if the negotiation fails. If you have no other option but to negotiate around a particular issue, you may be forced to accept an arrangement that is not optimal for the project.[*] If the BATNA has been clearly articulated, the project manager will know when to discontinue the negotiation because there will be other viable options that do not require negotiation.[†]

Reservation Price

The reservation price is derived from the BATNA. It is intended to give the project manager a clear point at which to walk away from the negotiation. It is the least-favorable point at which you should accept the deal and is derived from the discussions and decisions about the BATNA in the negotiation planning phase.

ZOPA: Zone of Possible Agreement

The ZOPA is the area or range in which a deal that satisfies both parties can take place. It is derived from the difference between each party's reservation prices. Figure 6.3 illustrates a ZOPA.

Value Creation through Trade-offs

Negotiating parties can improve their positions through trading off the values at their disposal. Each party is getting something it wants in

---

[*] An example of a BATNA in project environment may be that when you are negotiating with another project for sharing a scarce resource you need to understand how you can complete the specialist work if you do not have access to this one highly skilled person. If options for sharing do not suit the requirements of the project, a BATNA may be to train a team member to do some of this specialized work or to divert some project funds to acquire temporary skills of the same order.

[†] This is good risk management practice.

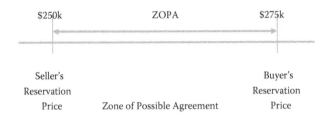

FIGURE 6.3

Zone of possible agreement (ZOPA). (Adapted from HBR. *Negotiation*. Boston: Harvard Business School, 2003.)

return for giving up something it values less.* The focus is not on price but additional services or additional time to pay or more flexible delivery or payment arrangements.

The Negotiation Process

As with any project, planning for a negotiation is the essential step before execution. The sidebar opposite outlines steps recommended in the Harvard negotiation method (Wheeler, 2003). Things to consider apart from the steps in the sidebar are:

- *Roles and responsibilities*: Who will take the lead? If others are involved, what will their roles be? What are the triggers for each role to become "active" in the negotiation?
- *Research about the other party, their project or activity, the people who may be attending*: Is the relationship marked by lack of trust, and is this what the negotiation is about? What could happen if the other party is not willing to reveal any information to assist the negotiation to proceed? What are the contingencies?
- *Risk*: Brainstorm with the project team possible desired outcomes for both parties. Record them and possible trade-offs that the project team is prepared to make to achieve its own desired outcome.
- *Relationship*: What is the current relationship between the other parties? If it is positive and collaborative, what approach will sustain that relationship? If the relationship is troubled, how is it troubled? How did that happen? Do we want an improved relationship as one outcome? What can we do to achieve that?

---

* An example is book collectors (of different collections) who may have a copy of a book that the other desires. Agreement could be reached through trading an unwanted book (perhaps plus an agreed additional sum). Each party can create value for the other rather than claiming it.

PREPARING FOR A NEGOTIATION

The following are the steps recommended by Wheeler (2003):

1. Decide what would be a good outcome for you and the other side. The team may be able to gather information to contribute to this preparation. This is part of the planning that needs to occur before the negotiation begins.
2. Identify potential value creation opportunities: what this project can give up and what is essential for its success. From what you have discovered about the other side, what is essential for their success?
3. Identify the BATNA and reservation price for yourself and the other side.
4. Shore up the BATNA by improving it if possible. This should be an ongoing process; as you learn more about the preferred outcomes of the other side, it is still possible to modify or strengthen your BATNA.
5. Anticipate the authority issue. Be clear about who has authority to approve the negotiated outcome. In negotiations that take place in the environment of the project and its organization, it is likely that both parties will understand who has this authority. But, it is important to be clear on who will make the decision and what the process will be.
6. Learn all you can about the other side's people, culture, goals, and how they have framed the decision. Try to find out beforehand who will attend and research their roles, responsibilities, and personalities to understand potential negotiation style.
7. Prepare for flexibility in the process. As the negotiation progresses, opportunities may emerge that had not been anticipated. If it is a good option, be prepared to work with it.
8. Gather external standards and criteria relevant to fairness.
9. Alter the process in your favor. One of the important first steps of a negotiation is to agree to the terms of reference: What is the subject of the negotiation? What is the agenda?

- *Rehearse*: Develop some scenarios of possible negotiation processes, including scenarios in which the other side has objections to the offers made or makes counteroffers. This helps the team be ready for a range of outcomes.
- *Responses for unreasonable attitudes*: Develop approaches to respond to attitudes such as unwillingness to listen to other points of view, not wanting to "lose," or irrational expectations.

The approach to negotiation outlined in the sidebar may be too formal for many of the negotiation circumstances a project manager encounters in relationships with stakeholders.[*] Owen (2012) suggested a more basic approach that is based on a combination of the Harvard approach and that of Fisher and Ury (1983). The steps are as follows and are further illustrated in the sidebar on turning a no into a yes:

1. *Agree on the problem*: How can we help each other?
2. *Preview the benefits*: Will there be positive outcomes for both?
3. *Suggest the idea*: Provide a range of ideas for discussion.
4. *Explain how it works* so that both sides own the solution.
5. *Preempt objections*: These are potential pitfalls and solutions (together).
6. *Reinforce the benefits*: Benefits are what each side delivers to the other side.
7. Close.
8. Next steps.

TURNING A STAKEHOLDER'S NO INTO YES USING NEGOTIATION TECHNIQUES

Whether the stakeholder is an upwards, sidewards, or outwards stakeholder, there will be occasions when the first response to a request from those in the project will be no. It is possible to use the techniques of negotiation to obtain a more acceptable response, depending on whether there is time to prepare a response and work with the stakeholder to turn no into yes or whether there is no time.

In this case, the request was for funds for an expensive training course for one of the team members. If there is no preparation for the probability that the response would be no, the project manager

---

[*] Typical situations for negotiation for a project were identified previously in this chapter.

has few options: either accept no and leave or try to make an ad hoc case for funds for the training. A far more effective approach would be to recognize that it is most likely that the response will be no and prepare recommendations in business terms ahead of time. Points 1, 2, and 3 form the structure of the recommendation.

1. *Seek agreement for the objective* of the idea or request: "My purpose for making this request for training in the technical specialty is because I know that a number of similar projects have been approved; I can see that these skills will be in high demand and scarce in our organization."

2. *Seek to explain the context* of this request: "In the near future, quite a few projects will have a requirement for similar skills. It is risky to delay in acquiring them; delay may mean that the resources that we acquire hastily may be less experienced and more expensive." *If possible, provide some tangible data to support this assertion.*

3. *Create and evaluate options:*
   a. "It is possible that we can obtain contributions to the cost of the training from other projects and possibly from the customer as well. If that is the case, would you reconsider?"
   b. "If we could identify a number of candidates for this training, say four, would you consider arranging in-house training? This will reduce the unit costs and mean that there is no cost for travel and accommodation."

If there has been no preparation for the negative response, a second meeting may prove useful if the sponsor can be persuaded. In this case, options 1–5 will need to be presented.

4. *Identify obstacles:* "Just so I can understand the reasons for this response, would you please explain them to me?"

5. *AND next steps:* "Would you like me to investigate further these options and some others and produce a business case for the issue? Are there some options that you think may be acceptable?" With this question, there is an assumption that

the stakeholder is now prepared to consider agreeing to the request in a modified form: This is the first step to changing the no into a yes.

If you have prepared, the case for funding is stronger because the request is supported by tangible data that show you understand the issues that the sponsor faces. Even turning no into maybe is a step toward success.

CONCLUSION

The focus of this chapter was on the final two groups of stakeholders: sidewards and outwards. Each stakeholder group brings unique challenges and opportunities. Sidewards stakeholders are in either a collaborative relationship or a competitive one—it is rarely neutral. Collaboration brings the benefits of sharing information or resources for mutual advantage. Along with the respect and support such a collaborative relationship brings, there is the added benefit of knowing that reciprocal agreements or arrangements are relatively simple. When the relationship is competitive, there will often be a need to negotiate either formally or informally to share resources or agree on finding arrangements.

Outwards relationships, on the other hand, are complicated by the need for communication through an intermediary, who may not necessarily have the interests of any one project at heart. Here, the relationships will need the knowledge of networks connecting the project and its stakeholders and the ability to exploit the connections for the benefit of the project and its stakeholders.

As always, all actions to build and maintain relationships with stakeholders, for the benefit of the project, need to be made in the environment of sustaining those relationships. "Winning" in a negotiation may be a personal victory but not necessarily in the best interests of the project or its stakeholders. The only tool for building and maintaining relationships is communication: the exchange of appropriate information. It is important to remember that networks are the connections for communication within the ecosystem, as is negotiation. The next chapters focus on effective communication and the information that is necessary to achieve effective communication.

7

Culture and Other Factors that Influence Communication

INTRODUCTION

Previous chapters focused on understanding relationships between the project, the project manager and the team, and their stakeholders. These relationships are as unique as the individuals themselves and have different applications depending on the type of stakeholder. The different types of stakeholders, whether they are categorized by "directions of influence" (upwards, downwards, sidewards, and outwards) (Bourne, 2012) or by typology (stake owner, stake watcher, stake keeper, or stake seeker)* (Fassin, 2012) or any other typology, will have different relationships and by extension will require different communication strategies.

Communication is all there is to build and sustain these important relationships, but the process of communication is complicated by the uniqueness of the project's stakeholders. Communication requires more than a standard process and a standard set of reports to build the relationships that really matter to the project and its success. Processes for effective communication are described in the next chapter; this chapter analyzes the factors that make the individuals and social groups within the project's stakeholder community unique. The answer to the question, What makes us who we are and how we operate in our social world? lies in the complex web of our own "reality" formed by our life experiences (and how our brain makes sense of those experiences), our culture, and

---

* Chapter 2 describes stakeholder theories and typologies.

our gender. This web influences how we live, work, and relate to others. In addition to these personal factors, within the work environment, the culture of the organization also affects the project and its stakeholders.

This chapter is organized as follows: First, how each of us perceives the world and how that perception filters what each person "sees" and thinks are discussed. The second section focuses on personality and preferences of the individual and how those may affect sending and receiving information to maintain the relationship. The next section analyzes culture in its various forms. Finally, there is a brief section on organizational culture as an influence on the structures, ecosystems, outcomes, and success of projects and those who work within them.

PERCEPTION AND "REALITY"

Researchers have long taken an interest in the different ways that individuals make sense of their surroundings—"their world." Weick (1995) developed the concept of "sensemaking" to describe how we make sense of the environment. Sensemaking is the starting point for learning new things, resolving current issues, or adapting to a new environment. To illustrate this concept, Weick (1995:55) related the story of a small military unit that was sent on a training mission into the Swiss Alps and which became lost in a snowstorm. There was a map, and they used this map to plan their journey back to their base. When the storm subsided, they began their journey, but noticed that they did not always find the landmarks on the map. With the help of residents of the villages they passed through, they found their way back to base, tired, hungry, and cold. That was when they discovered that the map was a map of the Pyrenees and not the Alps. This example of sensemaking shows that even with a bad map the soldiers survived because they had a sense of purpose (survival) and had an image of where they were and where they were going even though they were in many ways mistaken. The map was not accurate, and it only helped them get started; the rest of the journey was facilitated by cues from the environment, incorporating new information and acting with purpose. What was important were the stories and maps (their frameworks) and encouragement for those involved as they discussed and contributed ideas and then acted. Weick (1995:15) summarized:

To talk about sensemaking is to talk about reality as an ongoing accomplishment that takes form when people make retrospective sense of the situations in which they find themselves and their creations. ... People make sense of things by seeing a world on which they already imposed what they believe.

The starting point for sensemaking, then, is a "reality" that is unique to the individual. It is the filter through which everything they experience, either consciously or unconsciously, is passed. Weick (1995) has interpreted this process in one way; neuroscientists have taken a completely different approach for how we construct our reality and how we learn and make sense of new situations.[*]

The Role of the Brain

The primary function of the brain is one of finding associations, connections, and links between bits of information (Rock, 2006). Our thoughts, memories, skills, and attributes are vast sets of connections or "maps" joined together via complex chemical and physical pathways.[†] Every thought, skill, and attribute is stored in the brain, but not necessarily in the same part of the brain. New ideas are processed by comparing them to existing maps and creating a new map that becomes a part of the layout of the brain. Brains work to create order out of the chaos of data they receive, making links between information so that our lives make more sense. The more frequently we repeat an action or a thought or receive information, the stronger the connection within the brain. This is hardwiring: freeing up working memory for higher-level tasks that require conscious thought.

The Brain Hardwires Everything It Can

The brain is constantly trying to automate processes so that the unconscious part of the brain can manage them. If you observe a young baby learning to walk, the baby struggles to stay upright, perhaps holding on to furniture, walls, or people in early attempts. As the baby's muscles become stronger, balance improves and the baby becomes more confident and

---

[*] There are obviously many other theories contributing to an understanding of how we construct reality. It has long been a question that philosophers have grappled with: reality and the relationships between the mind and reality through the means of language and culture.

[†] These can also be referred to as circuits, wiring, or neural pathways (Rock, 2006).

requires less thinking about the process of putting one step after another. Before long, walking is automatic—this function has been transferred to an instinctive process. Normally, we will never have to think about walking again unless a misfortune affects us (e.g., such as a stroke) and we have to learn to walk all over again. Our habits are equally unconscious: A person sitting near you with an annoying whistle or pencil tapping may not even be conscious that he or she is doing it and even less conscious that it is annoying you.

"You Create Your Own Reality"

When new information is presented to us, these new data are compared to our existing mental maps to find connections between new data and existing frameworks. If there are no connections, the brain will try to make the connections fit into the existing framework. The brain is continually bombarded with new information and stimulation, so it will take shortcuts. For example, when we read something we glance at the first part and guess the rest in the context of all the words in the sentence. We have expectations about what we are going to read; therefore, we "see" the sentence in that frame—not necessarily what is actually written. Such approximation means that often we misunderstand or misinterpret what we read.

There is no reality "out there," only the reality we decide to see through the filters of our experiences, our knowledge, and interests. Each person has constructed a different reality, so that each may describe the same scene in totally different ways.* Each brain truly sees the world according to its own wiring, selecting and ignoring information depending on its filters.

Up to the end of the twentieth century, scientists thought that the brain was "fixed" by early childhood and then over time slowly declined as the neurons deteriorated and the connections became weaker with age. Within this paradigm, the theory was that the brain could not regenerate new connections; this seemed to be supported by observations about how as people aged they became more forgetful. With the advent of functional magnetic resonance imaging (fMRI) in the 1990s, a noninvasive way to see how the brain works enabled scientists and other researchers to

---

* Horowitz (2013) described what happens when she turns a daily "walking around the block" with her dog into an exercise of perception by inviting people from different professions to walk with her and describe what they "saw." Each one of them drew her attention to different aspects of the same pathways she had walked on many times before: psychiatrist, economist, her 19-month-old son, an architect, and eight others. They all saw aspects of that block that she could never have imagined.

observe activity in the brain. Scientists now believe the brain is "plastic" and adaptive. This means that a person's current reality can be adapted with sufficient stimulation and hard work.

How Do We Know These Things?

The fMRI measures and records *changes* in blood flow that occur in response to neural activity. When the brain is active, it consumes more oxygen, which causes more blood to flow to this area. What is shown in the fMRI picture is a map of the areas of the brain involved in any particular mental process. It is important to note that the fMRI does not measure neuronal activity directly; it measures *change* in the blood flows and oxygen levels. Using fMRI to understand the brain and how it works is a new science, with many claims that may or may not be substantiated through research and the passage of time.[*]

PERSONALITY

Each person's brain has been developed by experiences and the knowledge acquired. Personality is a second factor to consider. The term *personality* is derived from *persona* meaning "mask" and refers to an individual's distinct pattern of thoughts, motives, values, attitudes, and behaviors. There are many typologies for categorizing personality. In this section, the focus is on the Myers–Briggs Type Indicator® (MBTI®), the most well known of the personality tests that categorize personality.[†] It measures psychological preferences in how people perceive the world and make decisions (Kroeger and Thuesen, 1988).

The MBTI uses four pairs of alternative preferences:

- Introversion (I) or Extraversion (E): *attitudes*
- Sensing (S) and Intuition (N): *functions*

---

[*] Its meteoric rise as the new science has been compared with phrenology in the nineteenth century. Phrenology is a process that involved observing or feeling the skull to determine an individual's psychological attributes (Fine, 2010). This measurement of the skull and consequent categorization of individuals accordingly led to assumptions about individuals now considered misleading.

[†] A quick assessment to obtain a feel for the MBTI process is available online (http://www.personality pathways.com/type_inventory.html).

- Thinking (T) and Feeling (F): *functions*
- Judging (J) and Perception (P): *lifestyle*

The combination of these 4 alternatives results in 16 possible preferences. Table 7.1 provides a summary of each of these preferences and an example of how they would probably talk about salary.

Understanding a stakeholder's personality can provide useful clues about the type of communication to use to engage the stakeholder effectively.

CULTURE

Schein (1985) defines *culture* in terms of systems of symbols, ideas, beliefs, and values and of distinctive forms of behavior. Culture can be defined as "how we do things around here"; cultural norms are the "unwritten rules of behaviour." A person's culture (national, generational, or professional) influences how messages will be sent and received (their communication style); this in turn influences how people from different backgrounds can work together harmoniously. Understanding the communication styles used by different cultures prevents misunderstandings and helps build empathy.

Culture manifests itself through patterns of thinking, feeling, and acting that have been learned throughout the person's lifetime. Culture is learned from parents, teachers, peers, and "heroes" throughout childhood and well into adult life through

- Language and other symbols,
- Role models and heroes, such as parents, friends, celebrities,
- Rituals, such as recognizing "coming of age," courtship, marriage, and
- Basic values.

Hofstede, Hofstede, and Minkov (2010) have defined four ways to describe how culture manifests itself: symbols, heroes, rituals, and values. Analyzing them helps develop an understanding of culture and provides a means to compare cultures. First, it is important to define the four typologies; the first three are visible to individuals and groups outside the cultural group, but their meaning is not necessarily accessible to outsiders.*

---

* Even within a culture, meaning may not be obvious.

TABLE 7.1

Summarizing the MBTI Types

MBTI Types	Summary	Typical Approach to Talking about Salary
ISTJ	Doing what should be done	"I'm not concerned with what the other person will think of me. I'm more concerned with what they'll think of the data."
ISFJ	A high sense of duty	"I'm always surprised when someone looks you right in the eye and tells you how much they charge."
INFJ	An inspiration to others	"I know I could make more money as a consultant, but I'm still in government because I can't be bothered with selling myself. I need a structure to support me."
INTJ	Everything has room for improvement	"I have a high sense of ethics, but I'm not going to be taken advantage of."
ISTP	Ready to try anything once	"I wouldn't leave a salary figure up to them. I'd figure out first what I wanted and be prepared to be totally in command of the direction of the discussion."
ISFP	Sees much but shares little	"If I see the other person wince at what I ask for in negotiating, I try to take care of the person."
INFP	Performing noble service to aid society	"I keep asking myself, 'Can they afford it?' I have to remind myself that the work is valuable, and I am just the vessel the work flows through."
INTP	A love of problem solving	"I don't consider negotiating a game, but a point of clarification. You work together to define the conditions and the logical consequences of taking a job."
ESTP	The ultimate realist	"I just make up a number. Depending on how they react, we usually settle on one between my number and their number."
ESFP	You only go around once in life	"Two things in my favor when negotiating salary: focus on details for breakdown of my costs and chance to negotiate."
ENFP	Giving life an extra squeeze	"I hate money, and I hate talking about it. I'd rather change jobs than ask for more."
ENTP	One exciting challenge after another	"I constantly go around putting a value on my time."
ESTJ	Life's administrators	"It's fun to ask for a raise. I love going in and telling the boss why I deserve more."
ESFJ	Hosts and hostesses of the world	"Accomplishments should be acknowledged and rewarded without my having to ask."
ENFJ	The great communicators	"I always cringe when people ask me what my daily rate is. Every doubt of my self-worth flashes before my eyes."
ENTJ	Life's natural leaders	"I don't expect supervisors to know how good I am, so I send them periodic updates."

Source: Adapted from Kroeger, O. and Thuesen, J. *Type Talk: The 16 Personality Types that Determine How We Live, Love, and Work.* New York: Dell, 1988:66–71.

- Symbols are words, gestures, pictures, or objects that carry a particular meaning that is recognized as such only by those who share the culture. This can be in the form of dress, language, flags, and status symbols. Symbols from one group are often copied by others.*
- Heroes are persons, alive or dead, real or imaginary, who possess characteristics that are highly prized in a culture and thus serve as models for behavior. Heroes such as Gandhi, Nelson Mandela, or Mother Teresa may be supplanted in the younger generations by sporting heroes or celebrities such as Lady Gaga or Justin Bieber.†
- Rituals are collective activities that are technically superfluous but are considered socially essential within a culture. They are carried out for their own sake. Rituals can range from how and who we pay respect to, religious ceremonies, or business conferences (a way of reinforcing group identity). Rituals include the way that language is used in text and talk, in food preparation and eating rituals, in daily interaction, and in communicating beliefs.
- Values are broad tendencies to prefer certain states of affairs over others. Because they are acquired early, many values remain unconscious to those who hold them. However, a value system is central to culture. The value system is best understood through understanding pairings such as
  - Good/evil, dirty/clean, dangerous/safe,
  - Forbidden/permitted, decent/indecent, moral/immoral, ugly/beautiful, unnatural/natural, or
  - Abnormal/normal, paradoxical/logical, irrational/rational (Hofstede, Hofstede, and Minkov, 2010).

In-Group/Out-Group

Within any culture there is clear understanding of who is part of the group (the in-group) and who is not (the out-group). People in the in-group will develop a feeling of relatedness through sharing symbolic group membership, whether it is shared admiration for a celebrity or a sports team.

---

* A good example of this is the way the current (social media) generation has adopted tools such as Twitter or Facebook only to move on to a newer social media tool as the established tools become used by the older generations. Similarly, as the middle classes have been able to acquire more expensive cars or fashion accessories, the rich have attempted to acquire even more expensive or rare items. This is not just the behavior of the Anglo-American cultures; it now occurs in other developing countries where there is a wealthy class.

† Celebrities have also led the trend to a focus on outward appearance.

The relatedness often extends to willingness to fight and die for the country or group (culture). Moral rights and duties such as this are built into the cultural development of everyone within that culture.

Cultural diversity may take the following forms:

- *Generational and gender*: A project team or civilization may contain representatives from as many as four different generational groups: baby boomers and Generations (Gen) X, Y, and Z. Differences in rituals, values, heroes, and symbols between these groups may cause misunderstandings based on communication preferences, attitudes to work, and even language.
- *Industrial or professional*: This includes managers; professionals (engineers, accountants, teachers); blue-collar workers. Once again, they will have different communication styles, language, and approaches to work.
- *National*: Consider a mix of Asian, Anglo-American, and Latino cultures: Here also, there will be different communication styles, language, and approaches to work.
- *Organizational*: Corporations, government departments, and universities will all have different structures, language, values, and focus.

Much of the literature on leadership, teams, management, and organizations has been developed in the Anglo-American countries—primarily the United States, but also Canada and the United Kingdom. Therefore, it is culturally specific. When operating in a culturally diverse environment, a theory or approach that was developed within the Anglo-American context may not translate well into the various cultures represented in the team.

DIMENSIONS OF CULTURE

Hofstede, Hofstede, and Minkov (2010) developed typologies of culture from research carried out for IBM in the 1980s and updated in 2010. They defined five dimensions, and with recent collaborations with other researchers, added a sixth:

- Power distance index (weak/strong) (PDI),
- Collectivism/individualism (IDV),

- Femininity/masculinity (MAS),
- Uncertainty avoidance index (weak/strong) (UAI),
- Long-term/short-term orientation (LTO and STO, respectively), and
- Indulgence/restraint (IVR).

The dimensions should be considered as points along a continuum; there are no absolutes. They were developed in the context of countries and define as much as possible national culture. Not included are different groupings that may have been absorbed into a national entity, such as the Karen in Burma and Western Thailand or the various tribes within African nations.

Power Distance

Power distance is an indicator of dependence relationships in a country. It is defined as the extent to which the less-powerful members of institutions and organizations within a country expect and accept that power is distributed unequally. Institutions are the basic elements of society: home, school, community.

Where PDI is small, there is

- Limited dependence of subordinates on bosses,
- Preference for consultation (interdependence between bosses and subordinates), and
- Emotional distance is small. Subordinates will be more likely to approach and contradict their bosses.

Table 7.2 shows a selection of differences* within the power distance typology from the extensive examples provided by (Hofstede, Hofstede, and Minkov, 2010).

Individualism/Collectivism

Individualism defines societies in which the ties between individuals are loose: Everyone is expected to look after him- or herself and his or her immediate family. Collectivism defines societies in which people from birth onward are integrated into strong, cohesive in-groups that continue to protect people throughout their lifetime in exchange for unquestioning

---

* These tables only show a small selection of differences.

TABLE 7.2

Some Differences between Small Power Distance and Large Power Distance

Small Power Distance	Large Power Distance
Inequalities among people should be minimized.	Inequalities among people are expected and desired.
Parents treat children as equals.	Parents teach children obedience.
Students treat teachers as equals.	Students give teachers respect, even outside class.
Teachers expect initiatives from students in class.	Teachers should take all initiatives in class.
Hierarchy in organizations means an inequality of roles, established for convenience.	Hierarchy in organizations reflects existential inequality between higher and lower levels.
There is a narrow salary range between the top and the bottom of the organization.	There is a wide salary range between the top and the bottom of the organization.
Subordinates expect to be consulted.	Subordinates expect to be told what to do.
This occurs mostly in wealthier countries with a large middle class.	Mostly poorer countries with a small middle class are involved.
All should have equal rights.	The powerful should have privileges.

Source: Adapted from Hofstede, G., Hofstede, G. J., and Minkov, M. *Cultures and Organizations: Software of the Mind. Intercultural Cooperation and Its Importance for Survival.* New York: McGraw-Hill, 2010:72.

loyalty. Table 7.3 shows some differences between collectivism and individualism. Individualist societies value, and people within them expect, the following:

- *Personal time*: The job will allow time for personal and family life.
- There is *freedom* to adopt one's own approach to the job.
- *Challenge*: Work gives a sense of accomplishment.
- *Training*: This is available to improve or acquire skills.
- *Physical conditions*: Good working conditions are expected.
- *Use of skills*: Skills are used fully on the job.

Figure 7.1 shows comparisons between IDV and PDI for selected countries.

Masculinity/Femininity

Masculine societies have the following characteristics:

- *Earnings*: opportunity for high earnings,
- *Recognition*: receive the recognition deserved for doing a good job,
- *Advancement*: opportunity for advancement to higher-level jobs, and

TABLE 7.3

Some Differences between Collectivist and Individualist

Collectivist	Individualist
People are born into extended families or other groups that continue protecting them in exchange for loyalty.	Everyone grows up to look after him- or herself and his or her immediate (nuclear) family only.
Children learn to think in terms of "we."	Children learn to think in terms of "I."
Harmony should always be maintained and direct confrontations avoided.	Speaking one's mind is a characteristic of an honest person.
Resources should be shared with relatives.	Individual ownership of resources exists even for children.
Adult children live with parents.	Adult children leave the parental home.
Trespasses lead to shame and loss of face for self and group.	Trespasses lead to guilt and loss of self-respect.
Brides should be young, industrious, and chaste; bridegrooms should be older.	Criteria for marriage partners are not predetermined.
Use of "I" is avoided.	Use of "I" is encouraged.
Showing sadness is encouraged and happiness discouraged.	Showing sadness is discouraged and happiness encouraged.
A social network is a primary source of information.	Media are the primary source of information.
Laws and rights differ by group.	Laws and rights are supposed to be the same for all.
Lower human rights rating exist.	Higher human rights rating exist.
Ideologies of equality prevail over ideologies of freedom.	Ideologies of freedom prevail over ideologies of equality.
Imported economic theories are unable to deal with collective and particularistic interests.	Native economic theories are based on pursuit on individual self-interests.
Harmony and consensus in society are ultimate goals.	Self-actualization by every individual is an ultimate goal.
Diplomas provide entry into higher-status groups.	Diplomas increase economic worth or self-respect.

Source: Adapted from Hofstede, G., Hofstede, G. J., and Minkov, M. *Cultures and Organizations: Software of the Mind. Intercultural Cooperation and Its Importance for Survival.* New York: McGraw-Hill, 2010.

- *Challenge*: have challenging work to do that gives a personal sense of accomplishment.

A society is called masculine when emotional gender roles are clearly distinct: men are supposed to be assertive, tough, and focused on material success, whereas women are supposed to be more modest, tender, and concerned with quality of life. A society is called feminine when emotional gender roles overlap. In feminine societies both men and women

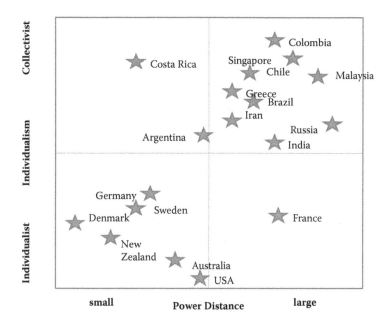

FIGURE 7.1

Comparison between IDV and PDI. (Adapted from Hofstede, G., Hofstede, G. J., and Minkov, M. *Cultures and Organizations: Software of the Mind. Intercultural Cooperation and Its Importance for Survival.* New York: McGraw-Hill, 2010.)

are supposed to be modest, tender, and concerned with the quality of life. (Hofstede, Hofstede, and Minkov, 2010:140)

Table 7.4 illustrates some of the differences between feminine and masculine societies.

Uncertainty Avoidance

Uncertainty avoidance is defined by the extent to which the members of a culture feel threatened by ambiguities in unknown situations. It is compared to MAS in Figure 7.2. There is a need for predictability in the form of written and unwritten rules. Table 7.5 illustrates some of the differences between weak and strong uncertainty avoidance cultures.

Long-term/Short-term Orientation

This fifth dimension of culture—LTO and STO—was not part of Hofstede's earlier research. When he became aware of the work of other researchers that included this dimension, he was interested in including it in his

TABLE 7.4

Some Differences between Feminine and Masculine Dimensions

Feminine	Masculine
Relationships and quality of life are important.	Challenge, earnings, recognition, and advancement are important.
Both men and women should be modest.	Men should be assertive, ambitious, and tough.
Both men and women can be tender and focus on relationships.	Women are supposed to be tender and focus on relationships.
In families, both mothers and fathers deal with facts and feelings.	In families, mothers deal with feelings, and fathers deal with facts.
Girls' beauty ideals are influenced by the father and mother.	Girls' beauty ideals are mostly influenced by the media and celebrities.
Parents share earning and caring roles.	The standard pattern is that the father earns and the mother cares.
Both boys and girls are allowed to cry, but neither should fight.	Girls cry but boys do not; boys should fight back, and girls should not fight at all.
Boys and girls play for the same reasons.	Boys play to compete; girls play to be together.
Husbands should be like boyfriends.	Husbands should be healthy, wealthy, and understanding; boyfriends should be fun.
Women's liberation means that men and women take equal shares both at home and at work.	Women's liberation means that women are admitted to positions so far occupied by men.
There is a single standard: Both sexes are subjects.	There is a double standard: Men are subjects, women objects.
Jealousy exists regarding those who try to excel.	Jealousy exists regarding those who try to excel.
Failing in school is a minor incident.	Failing in school is a minor incident.
Competitive sports are extracurricular.	Competitive sports are part of the curriculum.
Children are socialized to be nonaggressive.	Aggression by children is accepted.
Management is regarded as *ménage:* intuition and consensus.	Management treated as *manège:* decisive and aggressive.
Resolution of conflicts is by compromise and negotiation.	Resolution of conflicts is by letting the strongest win.

Source: Adapted from Hofstede, G., Hofstede, G. J., and Minkov, M. *Cultures and Organizations: Software of the Mind. Intercultural Cooperation and Its Importance for Survival.* New York: McGraw-Hill, 2010.

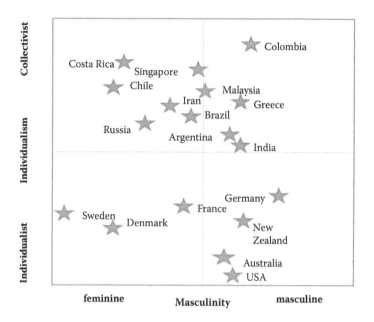

FIGURE 7.2

Comparison between MAS and UAI. (Adapted from Hofstede, G., Hofstede, G. J., and Minkov, M. *Cultures and Organizations: Software of the Mind. Intercultural Cooperation and Its Importance for Survival.* New York: McGraw-Hill, 2010.)

own research because of its correlation with economic growth. Table 7.6 illustrates some of the differences between STO and LTO.

LTO and STO are defined as follows:

> Long-term orientation stands for the fostering of virtues oriented towards future rewards—in particular perseverance and thrift. Short-term orientation stands for the fostering of virtues related to the past and present—in particular, respect for tradition, preservation of "face" and fulfilling social obligations. (Hofstede, Hofstede, and Minkov, 2010:239)

Indulgent/Restrained

The indulgent/restrained dimension has as its focus "happiness"—a universally cherished goal. It is compared to LTO in Figure 7.3. There are two main aspects:

- Evaluation of one's life, and
- Description of one's feelings.

TABLE 7.5

Some Differences between Weak and Strong Uncertainty Avoidance Index (UAI)

Weak UAI	Strong UAI
Uncertainty is a normal feature of life, and each day is accepted as it comes.	The uncertainty inherent in life is a continuous threat that must be fought.
Low stress and low anxiety exist.	High stress and high anxiety exist.
Aggression and emotions should not be shown.	Aggression and emotions may at proper times and places be vented.
In personality tests, higher scores on agreeableness occur.	In personality tests, higher scores occur on neuroticism.
Individuals are comfortable in ambiguous situations and with unfamiliar risks.	There is acceptance of familiar risks and fear of ambiguous situations and of unfamiliar risks.
Lenient rules exist for children on what is dirty and taboo.	Tight rules exist for children on what is dirty and taboo.
There are many nurses but few doctors.	There are many doctors but few nurses.
Work hard only when needed.	There is an emotional need to be busy and an inner urge to work hard.
Time is a framework for orientation.	Time is money.
There is tolerance of ambiguity and chaos.	There is a need for precision and formalization.
What is different is curious.	What is different is dangerous.
If a country is affluent: There is satisfaction with family life.	If a country is affluent: Individuals are worried about the cost of raising children.
Individuals are positive or neutral toward foreigners.	Xenophobia is prevalent.
Refugees should be admitted.	Immigrants should be sent back to their countries.

Source: Adapted from Hofstede, G., Hofstede, G. J., and Minkov, M. *Cultures and Organizations: Software of the Mind. Intercultural Cooperation and Its Importance for Survival.* New York: McGraw-Hill, 2010.

There appears to be a correlation between nations with a higher percentage of people who state that they are very happy and lower incidence of deaths from cardiovascular diseases (Hofstede, Hofstede, and Minkov, 2010). This still holds true even if national differences in wealth and quality of health care have been taken into account. The dimension indulgence/restraint (Table 7.7) has the following as central components:

- Happiness
- Life control
- Importance of leisure
- Having friends

TABLE 7.6

Some Differences between STO and LTO

Short-Term Orientation (STO)	Long-Term Orientation (LTO)
Social pressure toward spending	Thrifty: being sparing of resources
Efforts should produce quick results	Perseverance: sustained efforts toward slow results
Concern with social and status obligations	Willingness to subordinate oneself for a purpose
Concern with "face"	Having a sense of shame
Respect for traditions	Respect for circumstances
Concern with personal stability	Concern with personal addictiveness
Marriage is a moral arrangement	Marriage is a pragmatic arrangement
Living with in-laws is a source of trouble	Living with in-laws is normal
Young women associate affection with a boyfriend	Young women associate affection with a husband
Humility is for women only	Humility is for both men and women
Old age is an unhappy period but it starts late	Old age is a happy period but it starts early
Preschool children can be cared for by others	Mothers should have time for their preschool children
Children receive gifts for fun and love	Children receive gifts for education and development
Focus is on the "bottom line"	Focus is on market position
Importance of this year's profits	Importance of profits 10 years from now
Managers and workers are psychologically in two camps	Owner-managers and workers share the same aspiration
Service to others is an important goal	Children should learn to save money and things
Proud of my country	Learn from other countries
Tradition is important	Children should learn to persevere
Family pride	Family pragmatism

Source: Adapted from Hofstede, G., Hofstede, G. J., and Minkov, M. *Cultures and Organizations: Software of the Mind. Intercultural Cooperation and Its Importance for Survival.* New York: McGraw-Hill, 2010:

Then the two poles of this dimension are:

For indulgence:
- Perception that one can act as one pleases
- Freedom to spend money
- A capacity to indulge in leisurely and fun-related activities with friends or alone

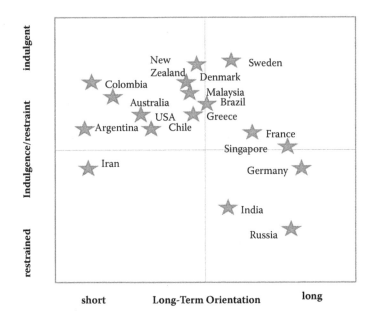

FIGURE 7.3

Comparison between IVR and LTO. (Adapted from Hofstede, G., Hofstede, G. J., and Minkov, M. *Cultures and Organizations: Software of the Mind. Intercultural Cooperation and Its Importance for Survival.* New York: McGraw-Hill, 2010.)

For restraint:

- Perception that one's actions are restrained by various social norms and prohibitions
- Feeling that enjoyment of leisurely activities is somewhat wrong

GENERATIONAL CULTURE

From time immemorial, the older generations have complained about the transgressions and lack of respect of the younger generations; complaints about the loss of respect of the "younger generation" were found in Egyptian scrolls 2000 BC (Hofstede, Hofstede, and Minkov, 2010).

Zemke, Raines, and Filipczak (2013) categorized the four potential generations that operate in the workplace today as

- *Traditionalists:* born before 1943,
- *Baby boomers:* born 1943 to 1960,

TABLE 7.7

Some Differences between Indulgent and Restrained Cultures

Indulgent	Restrained
Higher percentage of very happy people	Lower percentages of very happy people
A perception of personal life control	A perception of helplessness; "what happens to me is not my own doing"
Higher importance of leisure	Lower importance of leisure
Higher importance of having friends	Lower importance of having friends
Thrift is not very important	Thrift is important
Less moral discipline	Moral discipline
Positive attitude	Cynicism
More extroverted personalities	More neurotic personalities
Higher percentages of people who feel healthy	Lower percentages of people who feel healthy
Higher optimism	More pessimism
In countries with well-educated populations, higher birth rates	In countries with well-educated populations, lower birth rates
Lower death rates from cardiovascular diseases	Higher death rates from cardiovascular diseases
More satisfying family life	Less satisfied with family life
Household tasks should be shared between partners	Unequal sharing of household tasks is no problem
Freedom of speech is viewed as relatively important	Freedom of speech is not a primary concern

Source: Adapted from Hofstede, G., Hofstede, G. J., and Minkov, M. *Cultures and Organizations: Software of the Mind. Intercultural Cooperation and Its Importance for Survival.* New York: McGraw-Hill, 2010.

- *Gen Xers:* born 1960 to 1980, and
- *Gen Yers:* born 1980 to 2000.

Table 7.8 highlights only some of the differences in the generations. But, even from the brief information in the table, it is clear that there can be many areas of potential conflict and misunderstanding in the form of

- Values and points of view,
- Ways of working and thinking, and
- Talking and communicating.

From the perspective of effective stakeholder engagement and effective communication to build strong relationships and bridge the inevitable gaps between the project and its stakeholders, it is important to understand these differences.

TABLE 7.8

Some Comparisons between Generations

	Traditionalists: Born before 1943	Baby Boomers: Born 1943 to 1960	Gen Xers: Born 1960 to 1980	Gen Yers (Millennials): Born 1980 to 2000
Defining events	Great Depression WWII	Television Vietnam Birth control	Watergate AIDS Internet	Facebook Climate change 9/11
Symbols	Swing, big band Jukeboxes Radio	Rock and roll Fallout shelters Peace sign	Personal computers John Lennon assassination	Spice Girls Coldplay Digital media
Heroes	Jack Welch Warren Buffet General MacArthur	Gandhi Martin Luther King, Jr.	None	Their parents Firefighters (9/11)
Values	Sacrifice Hard work Conformity Law and order Respect for authority	Growth/expansion Optimism Team orientation Personal gratification Health/wellness	Survivor mentality Self-reliance Diversity Fun Pragmatism Balance (work/life)	Optimism Civic duty Confidence Achievement Sociability
Other defining characteristics	"Big is beautiful" Logic/not magic Law and order	Civil rights Workaholics	Technology Project management knowledge	Overprotective parents Involved parents

Consumer style	Thrifty and "make do" Before credit cards	Designer brands Buy now, pay later	Cautious Conservative	New emphasis on saving and getting out of debt—college loans
Work ethic	Stable Detail oriented Loyal Uncomfortable with ambiguity Uncomfortable with conflict	"Go the extra mile" Good team players Uncomfortable with conflict Judgmental to those who believe differently	Casual approach to authority Cynical Distrustful of authority Inept at office politics	Tenacity Adept at change Need supervision and structure Family events are more important than work
Leadership style	Directive Hierarchical Command and control Theory X and Y	Consensus "Stewardship" "Managing with heart" Participative management	Less attracted to leadership Egalitarian Flexibility Altruistic	Collaborative
Team structure	Large (Army) "One right answer"	Community size "It takes a village"	Virtual: sometimes no more than three people	Large civic-minded teams Volunteers
Communication	Formal, written chain of command	One-on-one in person	Direct, as needed	E-mail, with many courtesy copies, instant messaging

Source: Crumpacker, M. and Crumpacker, J. *Public Personnel Management*, 36(4), 349–369, 2007; and Zemke, R., Raines, C., and Filipczak. *Generations at Work: Managing the Clash of Boomers, Gen Xers, and Gen Yers in the Workplace.* New York: Amacom—American Management Association, 2013.

Generational studies only seem to be focused on the differences between and influences of the cohorts that have been identified in studies of the cohorts now. It is also important to recognize that each age group will have distinguishing characteristics that may also have an influence on how the different generational groups operate and how the other generational groups view them.*

Generational differences, such as the following, can affect project teams (Crumpacker and Crumpacker, 2007):

- Communication preferences and styles,
- Work ethic and values,
- Leadership styles,
- Attitudes to and knowledge of technology, and
- Motivation strategies.

Because of these differences, conflict and misunderstanding may occur and undermine the efforts of the leader.

Professional Culture

Even teams from the same generations and national groupings may be made up of different communities; these are professional cultures that exist within any project or organization today. Schein (1996) identified three distinct cultures in manufacturing organizations:

- *Operators*: Exist within the part of the organization that builds the product or delivers the service. Their structure and values are unique to the organization or at least to the industry where they operate. Their culture and norms are built on trust and teamwork.
- *Technical specialists*: Designers and implementers of technology. These categories include project managers, engineers, and hardware specialists.
- *Executives*: Fiscal responsibility. They favor command-and-control systems and management techniques based on command and control.

---

* For example, 20-*somethings* are ideological and believe that the older generations are cynical and complacent; at 30, most individuals will have met a life partner and may even have begun to raise a family—this will change their worldview. At 40, individuals will begin to recognize that many of their dreams may now never be fulfilled; this can lead to the phenomenon of changing jobs or making lifestyle changes. At 50, people have more money and fewer expenses and can indulge in things that they could not afford in their youth, such as fast cars or motor bikes. These opinions are based on my own observations of Western individuals and groups and some conversations with people in these age groups.

There are now far more occupations that will contribute to success of the project or the organization, but these three categories still serve the purpose of understanding the different types of professional cultures in a project. This understanding will assist communication by reducing the possibility of misunderstanding. Communication between these different groups can be improved through the effort of each group understanding the values, symbols, and rituals of the other groups* (Schein, 1996).

GENDER

The previous sections on perception, personality, and culture have focused on factors that cause individuals to think and act in the way that they do; this also illustrated how each individual is unique. Individuals are not all the same; they cannot be treated all the same. There remains one more point of difference that needs to be considered in this chapter: gender.

The Social Context of Gender

> The more I was treated as a woman the more woman I became. I adapted willy-nilly. If it was assumed to be incompetent at reversing cars or opening bottles I found myself becoming. If a case was thought too heavy for me inexplicably I found it so myself. (Morris, 2002, quoted in Fine, 2010)

We think of ourselves in terms of gender—even if we do not realize it (Fine, 2010). The social context we grow up in influences who we are, how we think, and what we do. All our social expectations and stereotypes are formed at an early age.

Gender Stereotypes

In the Western world the gender stereotypes fit within the framework of the following (to a greater or lesser extent):

---

* This will require the involvement of the groups that will be the recipients of the information to ensure that the message, format, and content are appropriate. This is discussed in more detail in the next chapter.

Female traits:
- Communal personality characteristics
- Compassionate, loves children, dependent, interpersonally sensitive, nurturing
- Serves the needs of others

Male traits:
- Agentic personality tendencies[*]
- Aggressive, leader, ambitious, analytical, competitive, dominant, independent, and individualistic
- Bend the world to your command and earn a wage for it[†]

Gender Priming

A person grows and changes in response to social environment. Each person develops a "wardrobe of self" (Fine, 2010) to match the many social identities one person can adopt.[‡] "Priming gender" can influence a person's ideas about gender and the appropriate wardrobe. Research that sought to understand the effect of gender priming included a math test with both male and female participants. Some of the participants were told that previously both women and men did well, others were told nothing. With this gender priming, the group that was told that both men and women did well, did do well. But, the group that did not have this information matched the stereotype of women not being good at math. A further test reinforced gender identity by starting with a request to state sex (male/female) by ticking a box. This seemingly innocuous request has been shown to prime (reinforce) the gender stereotype:

- Women are more confident with verbal skills and less confident with math skills (this is the stereotype).
- Men succeed at math and sciences and are not so good at verbal skills.

One that asks for ethnicity would have a different effect depending on the social stereotypes for the ethnic factor (Fine, 2010).

---

[*] This is the capacity to exercise control over the nature and quality of one's life: the capacity to act in the world (National Center for Biotechnology Information: http://www.ncbi.nlm.nih.gov/).

[†] This is the case for white middle-class heterosexual men (Fine, 2010).

[‡] My wardrobe is as follows: Melbourne resident, teacher, grandmother, woman, university professor, writer, baby boomer. Depending on which identity I need to "wear," I will have different approaches, perhaps use different language and tone; I will socialize in different ways. Who I am is sensitive to the social context at that moment.

Workplace Discrimination

Perception, and self-perception, of gender roles spills over into the workplace through the lingering stereotypes of women as caregivers and men as breadwinners. Even now that "equal pay" legislation has been enacted in many countries, particularly the Anglo-American countries, men still occupy the higher-paying jobs, and women in those roles often face covert (and sometimes overt) hostility.*

One of the issues that women in executive roles face is the lack of role models and the minority position in which they find themselves. According to Fine (2010), this situation is partly caused by homophily, the tendency for people, in this case males in executive positions, to select and mix with people "just like them." Homophily creates barriers to all minority workers, not just women, to the extent that clients who are white males will prefer to work with white males and exhibit resistance to working with people who are not white males. The resulting hostility and isolation can cause women to be unsure about their approach and to have doubts about their own ability. And, without other female executives as role models, they have to battle in isolation.

Gender Differences

What is clear is that there exists in every society a men's culture and a women's culture.

In masculine countries, men are supposed to deal with facts, women with feelings (Hofstede, Hofstede, and Minkov, 2010). In the United States, boys choose games that allow them to compete and excel; girls chose games for the fun of being together and for not being left out (Tannen, 2013). Boys play very differently from girls: They focus on status dimension. They usually play in larger groups in which more boys can be included and emphasize rather than downplay their status. They maintain status by displaying their abilities and knowledge, challenging others and resisting challenge. In these games, one or several boys will be seen as leader or leaders.

Women focus on rapport building and speak in ways that save face for others, using "we"; this is often interpreted as lack of confidence or lack

---

* This hostility can be in the form of needing to walk the razor edge between being "nice" and ineffective and being effective but "too aggressive." It is often seen in the names that powerful women are given by their staff: "the queen," "she who must be obeyed," or "the bitch." I have encountered all of this treatment in my own experiences in executive roles, but the most demeaning of all was to be called "love."

of knowledge. According to Tannen (2013), this is the result of socialization. Girls play in games that support the relationships in much smaller groups than those of boys and seek to downplay disagreement. In the same way, women downplay their certainties, and men downplay their doubt. Women take failure personally and men much less so: sometimes even blaming others.

In feminine countries, men and women are allowed to deal with the facts and with the soft things in life. In the Netherlands, for example, the research of Hofstede, Hofstede, and Minkov (2010) found no significant differences in goals that children seek in playing games.

Discourse: The Sharing of Information

In dealing with communication to stakeholders, whatever category they fall into, it is essential to consider all the differences in culture that we have discussed so far. The reason that it is important to understand gender differences is the way the men and women transmit and choose to interpret information. Tannen (2013) described these differences as follows:

- *Report talk*: the way that men communicate both formally and informally, transferring information to establish and maintain status that displays their abilities and knowledge.
- *Rapport talk*: the way that women communicate both formally and informally to build and maintain connections, first validating the relationship to build rapport and then dealing with any business.

Neither of these ways of communicating is necessarily superior to the other—this is just how men and women have been socialized. It also explains why there can be misunderstandings in both formal and informal conversations in which men try to "fix" the problem by giving advice and women want to talk about the problem without necessarily needing the advice the men are seeking to provide. This will also explain the impression that many male managers have of the linguistic styles of their female colleagues. For example, women ask more questions, usually for clarification or deeper understanding; this has been interpreted by male managers as not knowing enough and therefore not being good candidates for executive roles (Tannen, 1995).[*]

---

[*] And of course, there is the story of how women are willing to ask for directions and men are reluctant to do so.

A person's approach to the world can depend on social expectations. Gender stereotypes are perpetuated through cultural expectations, from parents, teachers, peers, and their environment, where gender is labeled by clothes, hairstyles, and accessories. Even when parents try to avoid gender stereotyping in the home, as soon as the child goes to school or other places outside the home, the socialization starts. Other children have clear views of what girls do and what boys do; teachers classify the children, often organizing activities for "the boys" and "the girls"; media and other advertising support gender stereotyping; even most children's books support the idea of boys being active and curious and of girls being passive and needing to please.

Organizational Culture

The final aspect of culture is the specific culture of an organization. When companies are part of international corporations, their planning and control systems will be influenced by the national culture specific to the country in which this branch of the company practices, even though headquarters will attempt to influence decision making, processes, and controls.

Different types of organizations will display different characteristics, depending on their structure and mission:

- Corporation (for profit)
- Not for profit, such as charities
- Government departments or agencies

Within these higher-level characteristics will be other distinguishing features based on the following:

- *Risk tolerance*: Are they risk avoiding or risk seeking?
- *Charter*: Are they entrepreneurial or public service?
- *Who benefits*: Shareholders? Selected groups of society? The public at large?
- *Product orientation*: Is manufacturing, product sales, service providers, or a mixture involved?
- Is there a national, regional, or multinational focus?

The culture of the organization will be formed from the mix of features; in turn, the culture of the organization will influence how management is "done" within the organization. Part of people's mental software consists of their ideas about what an organization should be like, with power distance and uncertainty avoidance affecting our thinking about organizations (Hofstede, Hofstede, and Minkov, 2010). Understanding these dimensions requires answering two questions:

- Who has the power to decide what (power distance)?
- What rules or procedures will be followed to attain the desired ends (uncertainty avoidance)?

Individualism and masculinity affect our thinking about people in organizations and not the processes, practices, and symbols of the organizations themselves. Some specific features of organizations are manifested in practices such as meetings, concepts of planning and control, and motivation theories.

Meetings

Meetings in organizations with feminine characteristics are primarily for discussion of problems and seeking of solutions through consensus. In masculine cultures, meetings provide opportunities for the participants to assert themselves to show how good they are. Decisions are generally made by others in other situations (not meetings). In masculine cultures, the stress is on results (not the process of achieving them) and people are rewarded for performance.

Planning and Control

Planning is important in an organization or a project to reduce uncertainty; control can be considered a form of power. The mix of the application of planning and control will vary according to the level of uncertainty avoidance and power distance for any country or organization. Planning and control systems are usually considered to be rational tools but are really partly ritual, for which there will be believers and nonbelievers in the effectiveness of these practices (Hofstede, Hofstede, and Minkov, 2010).

Where power distance is high, the underlying drivers will be political rather than strategic thinking. Where it is lower, control systems that place more trust in the subordinates will be the norm. Higher uncertainty avoidance usually has the following features:

- It is less likely that strategic planning activities are practiced.
- Planning that is more detailed and more short-term feedback will be the norm.
- Planning is usually the domain of specialists.
- There is a more limited view of what information is relevant (Hofstede, Hofstede, and Minkov, 2010).

Theories of Motivation

In a previous chapter, the theories of management of Herzberg, Maslow, and McGregor were discussed in terms of managing project teams. This section does not aim to repeat what has already been covered but instead seeks to understand these theories in terms of the cultural dimensions of Hofstede, Hofstede, and Minkov (2010) and the assumptions that may have led to the development of these theories. One assumption was that values, symbols, and rituals observed in the Western cultures were universal—an assumption that has been built into most of the leadership, management, and organizational development texts available today.

Herzberg (2003) assumed that his theories of extrinsic (hygiene) factors and intrinsic (motivator) factors were universal and that the *job content* not the *job context* is what makes people act. This theory fits the environment in which power distance is small and uncertainty avoidance is weak, and employees do not depend on more powerful superiors to make decisions for them on a day-to-day basis.

McGregor, in developing his theory X and Y, assumed the following (Crainer, 2003):

- Work is good for people. It is God's will that people should work.
- People's capacities should be maximally utilized. God's will is that people should use their capacities to the fullest extent.
- There are "organizational objectives" that exist apart from people.
- People in organizations behave as unattached individuals.

These assumptions could only have been developed in an individualist, masculine society such as in the United States; they have no application in Southeast Asia, where cultural assumptions about work are the following:

- Work is a necessity but not a goal in itself.
- People should find their rightful place in peace and harmony with their environment.

- Absolute objectives exist only with God. In the world, persons in authority positions represent God, so their objectives should be followed.
- People behave as members of a family or group. Those who do not are rejected by society.

CONCLUSION

This chapter looked at factors that must be considered when planning and implementing communication strategies to engage and influence stakeholders. The chapter described three major influences on an individual's perceptions: previous experiences, knowledge, and an individual's personality. The actions, reactions, and ways of thinking of both individuals and groups will be influenced by their national culture, the culture of the profession to which they belong, and of course their gender. Organizations influence individuals and groups to the extent that the processes, practices, and hierarchies affect how the work is done and how decisions are made. All of these influence the way people communicate; therefore, it is the best way to structure a communication with them.

The next chapter discusses elements of communication, considerations for developing strategies for general and specific information sharing (communication), and factors to ensure that the time and resources spent on this complex, time-consuming but crucial activity are beneficial to the project, its stakeholders, and the organizations to which they belong.

8

Communication

INTRODUCTION

We all communicate, consciously or unconsciously, through words, facial expressions, gestures, and other actions; this is part of being human. Communication is the only tool for developing the relationships necessary for successful outcomes of projects and programs.

To improve the chance of project success, communication must be planned and implemented, taking into account the uniqueness of every stakeholder or stakeholder group. Effective communication is more than putting data into templates and reports. The key to effective communication is understanding the complexity created by different cultural backgrounds and different "realities" of each stakeholder. Each stakeholder's culture and reality must be factored into the development of the communication plan. Additional focused communication and information sharing is necessary to build relationships with important stakeholders. The threads of leadership, culture, personality, and communication techniques such as negotiation or networking developed in previous chapters are brought together in this chapter to show how to communicate effectively in the complex environment of organizations, projects, programs, and people.

This chapter is organized as follows: First, a description of the three types of stakeholder communication—reporting, project relations (PR), and directed communication—is provided. This is followed by a definition of communication and descriptions of the mechanisms necessary to perform the act of communication. The next section contains a discussion of the Aristotelian view of communication that translates into three essential components of successful project communication: defining the purpose of the communication, organizing appropriate format and content, and targeting the needs of the project and its stakeholders. Next is a description of how to prepare the communication strategy and implementation plan, taking into account the type of stakeholder and the characteristics that make each stakeholder unique. Finally, ways of measuring successful (and effective) communication are described.

TYPES OF STAKEHOLDER COMMUNICATION

There are three general classes of stakeholder communication that must be considered: reporting, PR (marketing), and directed communication.

Reporting fulfills at least two useful purposes:

- It demonstrates effective and efficient management of the project and its outcomes to project stakeholders. Project managers are expected to provide regular reports, maintaining a steady stream of information about project progress to project governance bodies, such as steering committees. These reports will usually be in the form of updates or progress reports or may just be in the form of the artifacts of the project: schedules and plans, risk documentation, and budgets.
- It maintains a line of communication with essential stakeholders and builds credibility and "brand recognition" as insurance against the time when their support or urgent response is essential to deal with a project issue or meet a project need.

Reporting is basic communication in that it provides information about the project and gives a perception that the project manager is in control through ordered, regular updates on progress and issues. Even if the reports are never read, their very existence provides the recipients of these reports with a feeling of "comfort" that predefined processes of information production and distribution are occurring. It is reassurance that the project manager possesses the attributes of being well organized, is able to plan and implement the necessary project processes and practices, and is equipped to deal with the unexpected. The circulation of reports also serves to acknowledge the position of the senior stakeholders and their right to receive this consideration. Whitty (2011) described reports and bar charts as essential "clothing" for a project manager (and as Mark Twain *did not say*, "Clothes make the man. Naked people have little or no influence in society.").

Reports are required by the organization and often by law. Generally, project software will generate the format and content that are required. Some examples include the following:

- Project status reports
- Meetings with the sponsor or project steering committee and the minutes from these meetings
- Required reports to shareholders or the board of directors
- Government-mandated reports, such as safety reports and regulatory compliance reports

The information contained in reports is typically "pushed" (that is, sent directly to) recipients. This creates a consistent set of data in a time series. However, reports have limited potential as communication, primarily because they are rarely read, even though they serve the purpose of supporting the status quo. This is not to say that the production and distribution of reports is a waste of time or effort. Information provided through reports can be used as part of directed communication (discussed further in this section) for specific project needs, such as alerts of potential risk events or warning that the budget or schedule may need attention.

Project relations† or project marketing is probably the most underrated and underused communication process. PR includes all of the broadcast communications needed to provide information about the project to the wider stakeholder community. The purpose of this type of communication is to market the value of the project and to prevent information "black holes" developing that breed misinformation and rumor. The power of social media to feed on rumors and amplify bad news is massive: It is almost impossible to kill the rumors once they have started even if the information circulated is completely false. Once a perception of a disaster is created in a person's mind, the tendency to reject any other information is innate.

---

* Mark Twain (and Albert Einstein) has been credited with many wise sayings. This is not one of them.
† This is similar to the idea of public relations except for the purpose of marketing the work of the project.

Effective PR uses a range of media, including web portals and social media, to mitigate the insidious effect of rumors and half-truths. The challenge is to be first, to be understood, and to be credible to build a recognizable brand for your project that symbolizes "successful" and "effective." Some of the options include:

- Project blogs focused on positive information and accomplishments.
- Travelling road shows and awareness-building sessions that people can attend at various locations to explain the project and benefits.
- Presentations about the project at other meetings within the organization or at stakeholder organizations.
- Testimonials from senior stakeholders describing how the project deliverables provided value to them.
- Being open to "pull" communication by placing useful information such as frequently asked questions (FAQs) and project documentation in a common repository, directory, or website that people can access subject to appropriate security processes.
- Investing in project memorabilia with project name or image portrayed, such as pins, pencils, cups, T-shirts. The project team members and their personal networks are part of the project's greatest assets; anything that builds the identity of the team internally and externally strengthens the team culture and enhances the effectiveness of the team.

Developing an effective PR campaign is a skilled communications process designed to build buy-in and enthusiasm for the project and its deliverables. It requires knowledge and understanding of the power relationships within the organization and the stakeholder community and is the domain of the experienced project leader.

PR is well worth the effort on almost every project. It is far easier to create a good first impression than to try to change a negative impression among stakeholders; this is particularly important if the project is going to cause disruptive change within the organization. The project will experience far lower levels of opposition and, even more important, is likely to receive higher levels of support if only through the recognition factor that the branding exercise has provided.

Directed communication is focused on the important stakeholders (both positive and negative) identified through the *five-step* process of the **Stakeholder** *Circle.* It includes providing direction to team members and suppliers and influencing the attitude or expectations of other key stakeholders.[*]

Directed communication needs to be planned, starting with a clear view of the intended effect (such as reducing resistance to change or seeking enhanced levels of support from key stakeholders). Planning is essential for any directed communication; part of the planning should include the purpose of the communication, understanding of characteristics of the receiver, receiver's expectations of the project outcomes, and anything else that may be relevant to achieving the best outcomes for the project. Some of the tactics that can be used to make communication effective include the following:

- WIIFM ("What's in it for me?"): Try to align the needs of the project with the expectations of the stakeholder (or group) (mutuality).
- WIFMF ("What is in it for my friend?"): If there is no practical WIIFM, is there something that may benefit the stakeholders' friends or colleagues or the overall organization?
- Using networks to build peer pressure through the stakeholder's network of contacts: It is hard to hold out against a group.
- Delivering information incrementally in a carefully planned way with different people playing different roles in the communication plan.[†]
- Making as much information as possible easily accessible, "pull" communications on a project "web portal," and then directing the specific stakeholder to the information you want them to respond to (this works for reports as well).

Directed communication is hard work and needs to be carefully focused on the stakeholders that matter at any point in time.[‡] As with risk management, a regular review of the stakeholder community is essential to reassess the relative priorities of all new and existing stakeholders, to understand if the communication efforts of the team are being successful, and to ensure the most effective focus of any additional, or future, communication efforts.

---

[*] The process of understanding these aspects of important stakeholders has been described in previous chapters.

[†] Anecdotally, any message must be repeated at least three times for it to achieve its intended outcome.

[‡] Additional discussion about defining the purpose of the communication appears in the next section.

Communication Competence

Research has found that it is the "communication competence" that determines success of a project or organizational activity (Clutterbuck, 2001). Communication competence is defined as the combination of appropriate and effective communication skills (tailored to meet the needs of the organization and the stakeholder community) (Bourne, 2012; Payne, 2005) accompanied by the willingness of the individual to operate within the organization's political environment (Bourne and Walker, 2003).

Communication competence is developed through the following factors:

- *Clarity of purpose*: Focus on a few key messages and constantly reinforce them.
- *Effective interfaces*: Trust and openness in key relationships exist: between leaders and employees, managers and direct reports, business and customers, and within the team.
- *Effective information sharing*: Provide the right information at the right time for people to do their jobs, share opinions, discuss ideas, and learn from each other.
- *Consistent leadership behaviors*: What leaders say and do, both formally and informally, should be consistent.

WHAT IS COMMUNICATION?

Communication is the exchange of information, whether ideas, demands, or knowledge. Shannon and Weaver (1949) developed the "exchange model" of communication, designed to mirror the technologies of the time and considering three types of problems that might be encountered:

- How accurate is the transmission of the message?
- How well is the meaning transferred from sender to receiver?
- How well does the meaning of the message affect behavior? How effective is it?

This model has been adopted today as the basic process of communication (Project Management Institute [PMI], 2012).

The exchange of information based on this model but adapted to incorporate the complexity of human beings as sender or receiver has some basic steps:

- *Formation*: The idea is formed in the brain and is translated into symbols—usually language in the form of speech, writing, or graphical images. These symbols are then transmitted through physiological processes to the muscles that drive speech, writing, or development of graphical images.
- *Transmission*: The symbols are coded in a form that can be sent through the appropriate medium: air, electronic means, or perhaps the post.* The signals make their way to the receiver, perhaps encountering noise on the way. Noise can be in the form of an actual noisy environment, lack of interest or attention of the person who is receiving the message, or inability to understand the message through lack of clarity or misunderstandings due to cultural differences. At the receiving end, the message is decoded to enable the recipient to hear or see it. This involves further use of physiological processes and then the processes of the brain to edit and interpret the information received.
- *Feedback*: The symbols must be recoded and returned to the originator. If the message that reaches the originator matches the message first sent, the sender has some assurance that it was received without distortion. The feedback mechanism is straightforward in a data communications context but more complicated in organizational communication. Feedback in the human context seeks to confirm if the intent of the message was understood. One mechanism that can be used in a feedback process in the human dimension is active listening.

ASPECTS OF SUCCESSFUL COMMUNICATION: THE POWER OF WORDS

The main source of communication is through words—spoken or written. In most of the communication we do, particularly the informal communication, we tend to assume that we will be understood by the receiver,

---

* The description of the transmission of communication messages that is described here is derived from the procedures for understanding the transmission of electronic messages and data developed in the early days of computing. Its primary purpose was to ensure that the data had been transmitted accurately. Distortion and corruption of data could be so severe that information was lost. In digital communication, the information is represented by individual bits (0s and 1s); the message is broken into these smaller parts, transmitted sequentially, and reassembled at the receiver. To ensure that the message has been received in its entirety, it is sent back to the source as a series of bits. If the *checksum* (the sum of bits transmitted and bits re-sent to the source) results in 0, there is assurance that the data have been transmitted without distortion or corruption.

particularly if we are using the same language. However, misunderstandings in communication often come from the poor choice of words. The main reasons for misunderstandings come from the following:

- *The assumption that within a language, words and phrases have the same meaning*: We assume that if both sender and receiver speak the same language (e.g., English) there is common understanding. There are many differences between the English spoken in the United Kingdom and Australia and the English spoken in the United States and even more differences in the English spoken by native English speakers and those who speak English as a second language even when they are fluent. Research indicates that the way we learn to use our first language (mother tongue) affects how our brain processes information and even how we construct sentences (Boroditsky, 2011).
- *The use of the words and phrases that sit comfortably with our own peer group*: Matching the vocabulary of communication to the audience reduces misunderstandings and makes the sender appear more accessible and credible to the audience.* Beware of using words that are innocent in one language but have different, darker meanings in others.
- *The use of jargon*: Every profession and many organizations have developed internal sublanguages: jargon. This is often in the form of acronyms that simplify communication within that particular subgroup but have other meanings, or no meaning at all, to outsiders.
- *Words should adapt to the purpose of the communication*: Language will be different for persuasion or explanation, for example. See the sidebar for elements of effective explanation.
- *Use of negative language*: Even giving bad news or negative feedback to team members can be couched in a positive way. The use of negative language reduces the options for understanding by minimizing opportunities to explore or understand the information you are trying to convey. The first response to negative language is usually emotional; this reaction reduces the options to move beyond recriminations to developing constructive outcomes or solutions (Rock, 2006).

---

* Even simple words such as *plan* can have very different meanings, depending on the "group." Architects will immediately think of large drawings, such as "the plans of a house"; project managers think of schedules and other documents that make up the "project plan."

KEY ELEMENTS OF A GOOD EXPLANATION

- *Make your audience feel smart*: It is not about how smart you will appear. Fancy vocabulary and extensive background information are more likely to confuse listeners. Make the audience feel smart by building their knowledge and confidence. Dazzle them with clarity.
- *Not too much detail*: Too much information will not help someone who is already confused. Start with the big idea and "why" it might be important to them and add a layer of detail.
- *Remember the audience is only human*: Simple stories offer a way for the audience to empathize and imagine themselves solving similar problems.
- *Focus on why*: The best explanations answer one question: Why? Why does this idea or service make sense? Why should I care about it? Why does this matter to me? By answering the why question early in an explanation, you create a foundation for understanding on which to build more complex ideas.
- *Your job is to engage people through words, ideas, and solutions*: Often, the audience will have more power and authority and less available time than you and your team. Use this important point to set the tone of your explanation. Your job is to inform busy people, so do not waste their time; focus on what they need to hear and what the project needs from the result of this explanation.

The use of appropriate words and phrases can reduce misunderstandings and increase the chances that the intent of the message is understood and received. There are two other important uses of words: building credibility through storytelling and supporting sensemaking with the use of metaphors. Connected to the use of metaphors is persuasion.

Metaphors

In the Aristotelian view of communication, *pathos* is best conveyed through stories and personal experiences, often through the use of metaphors. Metaphors are defined as the understanding of one thing in terms of something else (Lakoff and Johnson, 1981). What we perceive and how we interact with people within our social systems depend on how we make sense of that environment, how we describe it conceptually, and how we share information; mostly, this is automatic.* Our mother tongue—the language of our everyday life—is a good indicator of this. Lakoff and Johnson (1981) used the example of the conceptual metaphor: Time is money. This metaphor is expressed by phrases such as:

- You are *wasting* my time.
- This gadget will save you *hours.*
- How do you *spend* your time these days?
- I have *invested* a lot of time in her.
- You need to *budget* your time.
- He is living on *borrowed* time,
- *Thank you* for your time.

Time does not really equate to money, but in the Western world, time has great value. The work of Taylor (see Chapter 2) was focused on reducing the time spent on tasks; a key determinant of project success is "on-time delivery," punctuality is important in the English-speaking culture, and we have all become so busy at work that leisure time is scarce and extremely valuable. Many other cultures do not assign the same value to time.

Metaphors are useful for communication even in the world of organizations and projects because many concepts in organizational communication are either abstract or not clearly delineated in our experience, such as emotions, ideas, or time. Metaphors can assist in building a clear picture, but only if everyone in the communication relationship sufficiently agrees on the basis of the metaphors; this will require similar backgrounds or experience and is only achievable once the team has developed its own culture, including shared vision, shared experiences, and shared language.

Persuasion

Using words or phrases that match the personality of the decision maker can be effective for persuading senior stakeholders (Williams and Miller,

---

* Use of our mother tongue occurs automatically. In general conversation, much of communication transactions occur without too much analysis, driven by our cultural framework and our habitual processes of using language in social situations. I had to learn Spanish for my visits to South America for business and my teaching roles—the process of communication in a language that I am not entirely comfortable with and within a culture very different to my own means that communication is not a habitual process; every word requires conscious thought.

2002). Using words that match the language preferences that the stake-holder would use can help build rapport and increased levels of support of the stakeholders. For example, one type of stakeholder, the *charismatic*, is naturally enthusiastic but recognizes that this enthusiasm must be modified by balanced information not just emotions. This stakeholder responds best to words such as *proven, results,* or *focus.* A second type of stakeholder, the *controller*, is comfortable with uncertainty and a focus on facts and analysis. The words that provide the most response are *details, facts, logic,* or *reason.* Matching these "buzzwords" to the personality of the executive or other stakeholder was shown in the research of Williams and Miller (2002) to be most effective for persuasion.

ACTIVE LISTENING

No matter how well the message is crafted and transmitted, it may not be properly understood by the receiver; its content or intent may have been distorted by "noise," cultural misunderstandings, or other "barriers," such as

- *Personal reality*: conscious and unconscious thought.
- *Cultural differences*: but beware of stereotypes.
- *Personal preferences*: personality and communication style of sender and receiver.
- *Environmental and personal distractions*: noise, lack of interest, fatigue.

Active listening is a process to confirm accurate receipt of content or intent; it is recommended for use in point-to-point communication. Active listening is the process in which the receiver summarizes or repeats the message and the meaning that he or she understood so that the sender is assured that it was received correctly. Alternatively, the sender can ask the receiver to summarize the context of the message.[*]

Active listening requires concentration, focus, and attention to

- Listening rather than talking.
- Listening for information.

---

[*] To begin the active listening process, the question, "Can you summarize the message so that I can be certain that I have sent it successfully?" or "Let me just summarize so that we can be certain that I have received the message that you intended."

- Avoid listening for opportunities to sound intelligent, important, or funny.
- Avoid listening for opportunities for personal benefit.
- Avoid internal distractions such as focusing on your own thoughts.

Active listening is supported by actions that accompany the words or symbols:

- *Eye contact*: This gives the perception of openness and trustworthiness in many cultures, but there are cultures for which eye contact has different meanings, so make sure that eye contact is a positive action during the planning of the communication.
- *Facial expressions*: In every culture, smiling transmits friendliness. Smiling can be contagious, helping those you want to share information with feel more at ease and more prepared to receive your information.
- *Gestures*: Some animation in face-to-face communication adds to the appeal of your information. Too much animation can be distracting.
- *Posture and body orientation*: These augment the words and contribute to, or counteract, successful communication.
- *Proximity*: Different cultures have different rules about comfortable distances between people in conversation. "Personal space" is extremely important in some cultures, but not at all important in others.

These guidelines for understanding and accepting the content and intent of the message apply well to face-to-face communication. Face-to-face communication is easier because the sender can modify the message in response to the reactions of the audience. Point-to-point communication such as e-mail or word-based information exchange, compared with face-to-face communication, is more complicated. Misunderstandings can be reduced but not eliminated through using the five Cs of written communication in composing a traditional (nonsocial media) written or spoken message:

- *Correctness* of grammar and spelling: Poor use of grammar or inaccurate spelling can be distracting. It can also introduce distortions of meaning of the message.
- *Conciseness* of expression through elimination of excess words or redundancy: A concise, well-crafted message eliminates prospects for misunderstanding the intent of the message.

- *Clarity* of purpose and expression with direction to the needs of the readers: This ensures that the needs and interests of the audience are factored into the message.
- *Coherence* through a logical flow of ideas and use of "markers" such as introduction and summaries of the ideas throughout the writing.
- *Control* of flow of words and ideas: This may involve graphics or just summaries throughout the message.

Much modern communication is broadcast, through either e-mails to multiple addresses, through the use of social media such as Twitter or Facebook, or through an organization's internal channels (e.g., intranet or shared drives). The evolving language of social media does not support use of the 5Cs.

COMMUNICATION ESSENTIALS

The essential aspects of effective communication are:

- Defining the purpose—clarity on the purpose of the communication;
- Understanding as much as possible about the receiver of the communication; and
- Monitoring implementation and measuring the effectiveness of the communication.

Defining the Purpose

The first consideration in developing effective communication is defining the purpose of the communication. It can be for

- *Distributing information*: Sometimes support can be improved by providing more information about what is happening in the project, typically either as reports or PR. It can be progress reporting, comparing the estimates of time or cost to what is actually happening—the comparison of planned and actual. It might be in the form of a newsletter in addition to the regular structured reports; the newsletter could address the more informal aspects of the work, such as when people leave or join the team, issues that have been addressed, or updates on what has been delivered and how it is benefiting the organization or individual stakeholders. It may be in the form of ad hoc reports requested by important stakeholders.

- *Reducing anxiety or resistance*: If the project is delivering change, there will be various degrees of resistance from the stakeholder groups affected by the implementation of the project's outcomes, such as employees, suppliers, or even those within the team. Directed communication is best in this situation. The information that they need most will be about how the change will affect them personally. The first responses will be: "How will this change affect me and my family?" "Will I still have a job?" Information about the strategic or business reasons for the change may be useful later; however, the immediate need for information will be at the personal level and should be delivered by the immediate supervisor of the individual or groups most affected (Hiatt, 2006).

- *Problem/issue solving*: There is specialized information exchange for the purpose of resolving conflicts to avoid damaging relationships between the project and important stakeholder groups or within the project team itself. This was described in detail in a previous chapter.

- *Giving bad news*: It is important to share bad news with senior stakeholders as early as possible to enable early resolution or minimization of the consequences.

- *Motivation*: Motivation also involves specialized communication, discussed in detail previously. Motivation in the form of additional challenging activities or responsibilities within the project team are recognized as strong motivators. Any allocation of additional motivators must be accompanied by information about details of the task, boundaries, and standards, as well as ensuring that the rest of the team and any other stakeholders who may need to know have been informed. This will ensure a smooth transition and operating within the framework of the new role.

- *Negotiation*: Another specialized communication technique described in detail previously is negotiation. This is essential for project managers and team members who do not necessarily have the power necessary to fulfill all the requirements of their respective roles. Influence, acquisition of resources, and cooperation must often be negotiated to ensure successful outcomes for the project.

Understanding the Recipient of the Communication

The recipient of the communication may be an individual who is recognized as important, groups with special information needs, or stakeholders who require information to maintain or improve their levels of support for the work or outcomes of the project. These are all stakeholders but with different expectations for information about the project and with different backgrounds—culture, gender, or personality. The challenge is to ensure that the messages sent from the project will be received by the intended recipient, or recipients, without too much distortion. This means that the following factors must be considered when developing the message:

- *Who*: Individual or group?
- *Needs*: What are their expectations?
- *Influences*: What cultural, gender, or personality characteristics must be considered?
- *Preferred means of communication*: Face to face, reports only, special meetings?
- *Messenger*: Is it necessary to match the personality, style, or hierarchical position?
- *Attitude*: Supportive or antagonistic? (See discussion that follows.)

In most cases, the regular reporting regime of an organization will be enough to provide information to stakeholder groups or individuals. However, if a stakeholder is important and is not supportive of the project's outcomes, additional directed communication activity is necessary. Each of the following aspects of a project's stakeholders may need to be considered once directed communication activity has become necessary[*]:

- *Hierarchy*: Where is the person in the organization's structure compared to the project manager: higher/lower, internal/external, colleague or competitor?
- *Influence*: How well connected is the person (step 1, identify)?
- *Interest*: Does the person have an active interest, passive interest, or no interest (step 1, identify)?
- *Legitimacy*: Does the person have some level of "right" to be consulted (step 1, identify)?
- *Power*: What is the person's ability to instruct or cause change (step 2, prioritize)?
- *Proximity*: How involved is the person in the work (step 2, prioritize)?

---

[*] Most of this information can be gathered during the data collection activities included in *Stakeholder Circle* methodology steps.

- *Urgency*: Does the person perceive the work as important (step 2, prioritize)?
- *Attitude*: Will the person help or hinder the work (step 4, engage)?
- *Receptiveness*: How easy is it to communicate with this person (step 4, engage)?
- *Support*: Does the person support or oppose the work (step 4, engage)?

Monitoring Implementation and Measuring Effectiveness

The third of the three essentials of effective communication is ensuring that the planned communication is implemented and measuring the effectiveness of that communication. Much of this book has been about planning for communication, whether describing the characteristics of different groups of stakeholders or the unique aspects of individual stakeholders. Planning is important, but it is a wasted effort if the plans are not implemented efficiently and monitored to gauge their effectiveness. The actual communication activities to implement the plan should be shared among the project team members and supportive senior stakeholders. By sharing the communication load, the project manager can free time for other tasks. There is the added benefit that team members will be given opportunities for working with the project's stakeholders that they may not otherwise have. All communication activities must be reported at team meetings. This provides incentive for the team members given the task of communication activities to share their communication successes and challenges with their colleagues.

Chapter 2 provided details of step 5 of the **Stakeholder** *Circle* methodology. Compare data collected about the support and receptiveness of the stakeholders who were to receive more directed communication. This information is the key to managing the project's communication activities in support of project success (see Figure 2.6).

ARISTOTELIAN COMMUNICATION

In the Aristotelian view (see the sidebar opposite), there are three parts to effective communication:

- *Logos*: a logical focus on the questions:
  - o Why should the listener hear what you have to say?

o What is the problem, opportunity, or perspective that you need to share with the listener?

o What are you going to say? How will you say it? (Remember to summarize the main points.)

- *Ethos*: To build credibility, provide evidence to support what you are saying.
- *Pathos*: Use pathos to make the emotional connection by relating your message to the experiences and needs of the audience. The application of pathos often involves use of metaphor.

APPLICATION OF ARISTOTELIAN COMMUNICATION TECHNIQUES

An example of using the Aristotelian approach to giving negative feedback can take the following path:

1. Thorough preparation consisting of recognition of the experience, culture, gender, and personality of the individual who is to be given the negative feedback will help to reduce misunderstandings and upset during the feedback process.
2. Prepare for any defensive responses, such as "This was what I was told to do." "The other team members let me down." This type of preparation enables the conversation to proceed more smoothly with fewer emotional moments.
3. Begin the interview by stating why you are both meeting, in simple terms, providing some details about the issue, what happened, and how often. This is logos: The 5Cs (discussed previously this chapter) will prove useful in ensuring the ideas are expressed clearly.
4. The description of the issue should be supported by evidence—what you observed and what was reported to you. This is *ethos*.
5. The next part of the process will be to talk about how the issue has affected the rest of the team or other stakeholders, perhaps even describing how it may have affected you. This is *pathos*.

Use of this structure should lead easily on to next steps: What must occur to resolve or remediate the issue?

PREPARING FOR EFFECTIVE COMMUNICATION

One of the most common mistakes in communication is filling out a template for a report or developing a message without considering the purpose, format, content, or audience for the communication activity. The Aristotelian concept of successful communication provides a useful approach for preparing and delivering effective communication. Customizing the format and content of the message is essential for ensuring the intent of the message is understood by important stakeholders and that the information is readily accessible to them.

The Message: Format and Content

Effective understanding and appropriate responses to messages can be enhanced by matching the format and content of the message to the communication preferences of the stakeholder or stakeholder group. The next section analyzes some of the most effective ways to create and deliver messages that meet the information access needs of stakeholders: upwards, downwards, sidewards, and outwards (see Table 8.1).

The guidelines for developing communication strategies for upwards, downwards, and sidewards stakeholders are relatively straightforward. However, developing an understanding of the expectations of each individual, each group, or each individual in the outwards group is more complicated if there is a need to work through a third party. The third party—the connection between the organization and the decision makers in the stakeholder institution—is also a stakeholder whose expectations must be understood and whose support for the outcomes of the project must be encouraged. This third-party support is necessary to engage any of the groups of outwards stakeholders when there are "relationship managers" or "gatekeepers." In other organizations when direct communication is possible with outwards stakeholders, the guidelines from Table 8.1 apply.

IN CONCLUSION: PUTTING IT ALL TOGETHER

Chapters 2–7 contain analyses of stakeholders, how to identify and prioritize strategies, and then how to recognize where to focus the attention of

TABLE 8.1

Effective Ways to Communicate

Types of Stakeholders	Expectations and Focus of Message	Format and Content
Upwards: Sponsor, steering committee, and other senior managers responsible for keeping commitments of the organization	Usually exception reports: to provide early advice about potential risk events or assurance that whatever is important to this upwards stakeholder is on track or at least being monitored	Presentation in formats that enable swift access to the information: Summaries in the form of graphs, spreadsheets, high-level data
Downwards: Staff, contractors, specialists Anyone who applies knowledge and experience to work with the project manager (PM) to achieve the project goals	Acknowledgment, overview of progress, and issues or requirements that affect the team as well as the individual	Details on what is required of the individual or team; the more focused information that is included in the communication, the more useful it will be for understanding standards and expectations Detail of work, reporting and presentation requirements, roles and responsibilities, work teams
Sidewards: Other PMs and individuals at your level in the organization	To share all news and encouragement or have the opportunity to negotiate with peers who are in competition for scarce resources	Informal discussions or e-mails Gossip, coaching, and sharing of experiences
Outwards: Included in this category are the typologies of Fassin (2012). Government, public, users, suppliers, lobby groups Stake watchers, stake keepers, stake seekers	Because there are usually no direct communication opportunities with this type of stakeholder, working with or through the person responsible for managing relationships between this stakeholder group and the organization or project	Often no direct access to individuals working within the institutions; any access is through allocated contact persons responsible for all relationships between the stakeholder group and the organization Briefing notes, regular meetings for both giving information and receiving feedback

the team for the benefit of the project. The guidelines include how to apply different techniques and approaches depending on each stakeholder's culture, gender, personality, and importance to the project. The sidebar on page 214 summarizes some of the questions and data that need to be collected to ensure that when it counts the most, communication strategies

GATHERING INFORMATION TO DEVELOP CUSTOMIZED COMMUNICATION

Gathering information to develop customized communication will require some planning:

- What does the team know about the stakeholder? There should be sufficient information collected in the process of analyzing the stakeholder and his or her place in the project's stakeholder community. What is the role in the organization? What information has been gathered about the stakeholder's power, proximity, and urgency? What are the stakeholder's expectations of the project?
- What does the team know about the individual's connections with other stakeholders in the project's stakeholder community? Are there supportive stakeholders in the stakeholder community who are willing to act as ambassadors for the project?
- What does the team know about the reasons that the stakeholder has been assessed as unsupportive? Are there competing projects? Is the stakeholder too preoccupied with his or her own role? Is the stakeholder new in the job and struggling to master that role? Is there a personal reason? This information can possibly be sourced from other supportive stakeholders—the stakeholder's colleagues.
- Is the stakeholder interested in meeting with the project manager or other members of the team? Perhaps the stakeholder would like to meet one of the project's ambassadors who is also a colleague?
- What other options does the project manager have to make contact with the stakeholder or to find out the reason for lack of support from the stakeholder?
- Does the stakeholder have preferences for the type of communication he or she might welcome? Does the stakeholder prefer graphics, words, face-to-face meetings, or numbers?

Based on information about the unsupportive stakeholder collected through questions such as these, the additional communication effort will be as focused on his or her information needs and preferences as possible. Developing a clear plan and efficient delivery of the information is the next step.

- Who should be the messenger? The project manager may not be the best person to deliver the message. Perhaps a supportive stakeholder from the project's stakeholder community is a better option.
- Is the message in line with what the team understands to be the stakeholder's expectations of the project? For example, if the stakeholder expects benefits for the group he or she leads, this is what the content of the message should focus on: how the outcomes of the project will provide value to the stakeholder's part of the organization.

If there is no useful information available about the stakeholder, perhaps a meeting can be organized to try to identify expectations and, even more important, to try to identify the reason for his or her lack of support. Often, this can be approached as follows: "In the project team we have identified you and your group as important stakeholders. But, we also recognize that we are unclear about how the project outcomes can improve the workload or product delivery capability of your team. Your support is important to us: Can you give us some information that will assist us in providing better information to ensure that we can deliver benefits to your team?"

The unsupportive stakeholder may not want to spend the time providing the project with that information. It may be necessary to set up another meeting or invite one of the stakeholder's team members to attend project meetings or brief the team. The important thing is making the connection with the stakeholder and the stakeholder's group and establishing a stronger relationship through this process.

Additional consideration may need to be factored into the communication for any differences in background, such as culture or gender.

and implementations will work to ensure the project delivers its outcomes to meet the needs of its stakeholders.

Communication is not just a process of developing lists, gathering information, and sending the message. It is not a mechanical process. The lists in this chapter are intended to act as guidance to assist project teams to build robust and sustainable relationships with their stakeholders. Effective communication does require planning, but at a fundamental level, successful communication and stakeholder engagement still require recognition that the subject of all the processes and lists are people—they cannot be categorized in the same way inanimate objects can be, but on the other hand, communication will always be more successful with preparation, provided each interaction is managed sensitively.

The most important messages of this book are:

- People make projects possible. Projects are done by people for the benefit of other people.
- Robust effective relationships with stakeholders are essential for project success.
- Communication is not just monthly reports and progress meetings.
- The most effective communication is achieved by applying the appropriate techniques for building relationships.
- Communication uses project artifacts, such as the schedule or the risk register.
- Communication includes negotiation, coaching, problem solving, and decision making.
- The project manager does not have to "do it alone."
- By working with senior stakeholders, particularly the sponsor, and obtaining their involvement, the organization moves toward the perfect communication ecosystem in which everyone recognizes that *project success is everybody's business.*

SUMMARY OF COMMUNICATION STRATEGIES

Communication type:

- **Reporting:** usually preset format and content and at regular intervals.
- **Project relations:** to maintain awareness of the project and to build credibility.
- **Directed:** for changing attitudes, enhancing support, dealing with issues or conflict.

Questions to ask to plan for directed communication:

- **Importance:** How important is this stakeholder to the success of the project?

- **Hierarchy**: Where is the person in the organization's structure?
- **Influence**: How well connected is the person?
- **Interest**: Does the person have an active interest, passive interest, or no interest?
- **Power**: What is the person's ability to instruct or cause change?
- **Proximity**: How involved is the person in the work?
- **Urgency**: How important is the work to the stakeholder?
- **Attitude**: Will the person help or hinder the work?
- **Receptiveness**: How easy is it to communicate with this person?
- **Support**: Does the person support or oppose the work?

Developing the message:

- **Expectations:** What does this stakeholder expect to gain or lose from supporting this project?
- **Who will be the messenger?** The message should be delivered by someone who can influence the outcomes of the communication or has credibility or empathy with the message's recipient.
- **Cultural, gender, or personality characteristics that can assist or hinder effective transmission of the message:** Focus on the characteristics of the stakeholders that are clearly different from the culture of the team and individual team members. Information about the differences, whether different cultural backgrounds, age, or gender, can be gathered through research, advice from others from similar backgrounds, or the stakeholders themselves. More credibility is gained from seeking information than from assuming that you know.

These data must be considered for each directed message intended to change minds or attitudes or to increase credibility of the team or project manager. It is worth any additional effort involved—communication is the key to success of the project.

References

AccountAbility. (2006). *Stakeholder Engagement Standard (AA1000SES)*. London: Institute of Social and Ethical Accountability.

AccountAbility. (2011) *AA1000 Stakeholder Engagement Standard (AA1000SES)*. London: Institute of Social and Ethical Accountability.

Adkins, L. (2010). *Coaching Agile Teams: A Companion for ScrumMasters, Agile Coaches, and Project Managers in Transition*. Boston: Pearson Education.

Association of Project Management (APM). (n.d.). *Directing Change: A Guide to Governance of Project Management*: Association of Project Management.

Baldoni, J. (2010). *Lead Your Boss: The Subtle Art of Managing Up*. New York: Amacom.

Barabasi, A. (2002). *Linked: The New Science of Networks*. Cambridge, MA: Perseus.

Bass, B. M. (1985). *Leadership and Performance Beyond Expectation*. New York: Macmillan.

Bergstrand, J. (2009). *Reinvent Your Enterprise through Better Knowledge Work*. Earning Organization Series. Charleston, SC: BookSurge.

Blake, R. R. and Mouton, J. S. (1964). *The Managerial Grid: The Key to Leadership Excellence*. Houston, TX: Gulf.

Boehm, B. and Turner, R. (2004). *Balancing Agility and Disipline*. Boston: Addison-Wesley.

Boroditsky, L. (2011). How language shapes thought: the languages we speak affect our perceptions of the world. *Scientific American*, February 2011. http://www.scientificamerican.com/article/how-language-shapes-thought/.

Bourne, L. (2012). *Stakeholder Relationship Management: A Maturity Model for Organisational Implementation*. Rev. ed. Farnham, UK: Gower.

Bourne, L. and Walker, D. H. T. (2003). Tapping into the Power Lines—A Third Dimension of Project Management Beyond Leading and Managing. Paper presented at the 17th World Congress on Project Management, June 2003, Moscow, Russia.

Chabris, C. and Simons, D. (2009). *The Invisible Gorilla: How Our Intuitions Deceive Us*. New York: Broadway Paperbacks.

Chartered Institute of Internal Auditors. (2004). Corporate Governance: https://www.iia.org.uk/; Accessed January 4, 2013.

Christakis, N. and Fowler, J. (2009). *Connected: The Amazing Power of Social Networks and How They Shape Our Lives*. Harper-Collins ebooks.

Clutterbuck, D. (2001). *Communication Competence and Business Success*. San Francisco: International Association of Business Communicators.

Collins, J. (2001). Level 5 leadership: The triumph of humility and fierce resolve. *Harvard Business Review, 79*(1), 66–77.

Conway, M. E. (1968). How Do Committees Invent? http://www.melconway.com/research/committees.html; accessed June 2014.

Crainer, S. (2003). One hundred years of management. *Business Strategy Review, 14*(2), 41–49.

Crawford, L. and Brent, C. (2008). Exploring the Role of the Project Sponsor. http://www.projects.uts.edu.au.

Crosby, P. B. (1979). *Quality is Free: The Art of Making Quality Certain*. NY: McGraw-Hill.

Cross, R. and Thomas, R. (2011). A smarter way to network. *Harvard Business Review*, July–August, 142–153.

Crumpacker, M. and Crumpacker, J. (2007). Succession planning and generational stereotypes: Should HR consider age-based values and attitudes a relevant factor or a passing fad? *Public Personnel Management, 36*(4), 349–369.

Csikszentmihalyi, M. (1997). *Creativity: Flow and the Psychology of Discovery and Invention.* New York: HarperCollins.

DeFeo, J. (2001). The tip of the iceberg, *Quality Progress. 24*(5), 29–37.

Dinsmore, P. C. (1999). *Winning in Business with Enterprise Project Management.* New York: AMA Publication.

Donovan, S. (2006). *Using Cost of Quality to Improve Business Results.* Milwaukee, WI: American Society for Quality Press.

Fassin, Y. (2012). Stakeholder management, reciprocity, and stakeholder responsibility. *Journal of Business Ethics, 109,* 83–96.

Fine, C. (2010). *Delusions of Gender: The Real Science Behind Sex Differences.* London: Icon Books.

Fisher, R. and Ury, W. (1983). *Getting to Yes: Negotiating an Agreement without Giving In.* London: Penguin Books.

Frame, J. D. (2013). *Framing Decisions: Decision Making that Accounts for Irrationality, People, and Constraints.* San Francisco: Jossey-Bass.

Freeman, R. (1984). *Strategic Management: A Stakeholder Approach.* Boston: Pitman.

Freeman, R. Harrison, J., Wicks, A., Parmar, B., and deColle, S. (2010). *Stakeholder Theory: The State of the Art.* Cambridge, UK: Cambridge University Press.

Friedman, M. (1970). The social responsibility of business is to increase its profits, *New York Times,* September 13, p. 33.

George, B. (2003). *Authentic Leadership: Rediscovering the Secrets to Lasting Value.* San Francisco: Jossey-Bass.

Gladwell, M. (2000). *The Tipping Point.* London: Abacus.

Goldman, L. R. (1990). An alternative "description of personality": The big-five factor structure. *Journal of Personality and Social Psychology, 59,* 1216–1229.

Goleman, D. (2000). Leadership that gets results, *Harvard Business Review, 78*(2), 78–90.

Goleman, D. (2006). *Social Intelligence: The New Science of Human Relationships.* London: Hutchinson.

Goleman, D. (2011). *The Brain and Emotional Intelligence: New Insights.* Northampton, MA: More than Sound.

Granovetter, M. (1973). The strength of weak ties. *American Journal of Sociology, 78*(6), 1360–1380.

Granovetter, M. (2005). The impact of social structure on economic outcomes. *Journal of Economic Perspectives, 19*(1), 33–50.

Gray, C. E. and Larson, E. W. (2008). *Project Management: The Managerial Process.* 4th ed. New York: McGraw-Hill Irwin.

Green, C. H. and Howe, A. P. (2012). *The Trusted Advisor Fieldbook: A Comprehensive Toolkit for Leading with Trust.* Hoboken, NJ: Wiley.

Hatfield, E., Cacioppo, J. T., and Rapson, R. L. (1993). Emotional contagion: current directions. *Psychological Science, 2,* 96–99.

HBR. (2003). *Negotiation.* Boston: Harvard Business School.

Hersey, P., Blanchard, K., and Johnson, D. E. (1996). *Management of Organizational Behaviour.* 7th ed. London: Prentice Hall International.

Herzberg, F. (1987 and 2003). One more time: How do you motivate employees (reissue of 1968 paper)? *Harvard Business Review,* January, 87–96.

Hiatt, J. M. (2006). *ADKAR: A Model for Change in Business, Government and Our Community*. Loveland, CO: Prosci Research.

Hofstede, G., Hofstede, G. J., and Minkov, M. (2010). *Cultures and Organizations: Software of the Mind. Intercultural Cooperation and Its Importance for Survival*. New York: McGraw-Hill.

Horowitz, A. (2013). *On Looking: About Everything There Is to See*. London: Simon and Schuster.

Jenner, S. (2012). *Managing Benefits: Optimizing the Return from Investments*. London: APMG-International.

Kahneman, D. (2011). *Thinking, Fast and Slow*. London: Penguin Books.

Kase, R., Paauwe, J., and Zupda, N. (2009). HR practices, interpersonal relations, and intrafirm knowledge transfer in knowledge-intensive firms: A social network perspective. *Human Resources Management, 48*(4), 615–639.

Katzenbach, J. R. and Smith, D. K. (1993). *The Wisdom of Teams: Creating the High-Performance Organization*. Boston: Harvard Business School Press.

Kroeger, O. and Thuesen, J. (1988). *Type Talk: The 16 Personality Types that Determine How We Live, Love, and Work*. New York: Dell.

Lakoff, G. and Johnson, M. (1981). *Metaphors We Live By*. Chicago: University of Chicago Press.

Lencioni, P. (2002). *The Five Dysfunctions of a Team*. San Francisco: Jossey-Bass.

Loosemore, M. (2011). Managing stakeholder perceptions of risk and opportunity in social infrastructure projects using a multimedia approach. *International Journal of Project Organisation and Management, 3*(3/4), 307–315.

Maslow, A. H. (1943). A theory of human motivation. *Psychological Review, 50(4), 370–396.*

McClelland, D. and Burnham, D. (2003). Power is the great motivator (reprint from 1976). *Harvard Business Review*, January, 117–125.

McCrae, R. R. and Costa, P. T. (1997). Personality trait structure as a human universal. *American Psychologist, 52*, 509–516.

McGannon, B. (2011). Intelligent disobedience: The art of saying "no" to senior managers. In L. Bourne (Ed.), *Advising Upwards: A Framework for Understanding and Engaging Senior Management Stakeholders* (pp. 297–316). Farnham, UK: Gower.

McGrath, J. E. (1984). *Groups: Interaction and Performance*. Englewood Cliffs, NJ: Prentice Hall.

Mersino, A. (2007). *Emotional Intelligence for Project Managers: The People Skills You Need to Achieve Outstanding Results*. New York: Amacom.

Meyerson, D., Weick, K., and Kramer, R. M. (1996). Swift trust and temporary groups. In R. M. Kramer and T. R. Tyler (Eds.), *Trust in Organizations: Frontiers of Theory and Research* (pp. 166–195). Thousand Oaks, CA: Sage.

Mintzberg, H. (2005). *Managers Not MBAs: A Hard Look at the Soft Practice of Managing and Management Development*. San Francisco: Berrett-Koehler.

Mitchell, R., Agle, B., and Wood, D. (1997). Towards a theory of stakeholder identification and salience: Defining the principle of who and what really counts. *Academy of Management Review, 22*(4), 853–886.

Morrell, M. and Capparell, S. (2001). *Shackleton's Way: Leadership Lessons from the Great Antarctic Explorer*. London: Brearly.

Morris, P. (2013). *Reconstructing Project Management*. Oxford, UK: Wiley-Blackwell.

Northouse, P. G. (2013). *Leadership: Theory and Practice*. Thousand Oaks, CA: Sage. E-book downloaded October 2013.

Office of Government Commerce UK. (2008). Project sponsor. https://www.gov.uk/government/publications/best-management-practice-portfolio; accessed June 13, 2008.

Organization for Economic Cooperation and Development (OECD). (2004). Revised principles of corporate governance and their relevance to non-OECD countries. In D. f. F. a. E. Affairs (Ed.), *Report on the Observance of Standards and Codes of the World Bank Group.* Paris: OECD.

Owen, J. (2012). *The Leadership Skills Handbook.* 2nd ed. London: Kogan Page.

Paloma Vadillo, M. (2012). *Liderazgo y Motivacion de Equipos de Trabajo.* 7th ed. Madrid: ESIC Editorial.

Payne, H. J. (2005). Reconceptualizing social skills in organizations: Exploring the relationship between communication competence, job performance *Journal of Leadership and Organizational Studies,* Winter. http://jlo.sagepub.com/content/11/2/63.abstract. 63–77.

Phillips, M. (2014). *Reinventing Communication: How to Design, Lead and Manage High Performing Projects.* Farnham, UK: Gower.

Pinto, J. (2014). Project management, governance, and the normalization of deviance. *International Journal of Project Management, 32*(3), 376–387.

Pinto, J. K. (2000). Understanding the role of politics in successful project management. *International Journal of Project Management, 18,* 85–91.

Project Management Institute (PMI). (2012). *A Guide to the Project Management Body of Knowledge (PMBOK®).* 5th ed. Newtown Square, PA: PMI.

Porath, C. and Pearson, C. (2013). The price of incivility: Lack of respect hurts morale and the bottom line. *Harvard Business Review,* January–February, 116–121.

Reeson, A., and Dunstall, S. (2009). *Behavioral Economics and Complex Decision-Making.* South Clayton, Australia: CSIRO.

Robbins, H. and Finlay, M. (2000). *Why Teams Don't Work—What Went Wrong and How to Make It Right.* London: TEXERE.

Rock, D. (2006). *Quiet Leadership: Six Steps to Transforming Performance at Work.* New York: HarperCollins.

Rowley, T. J. (1997). Moving beyond dyadic ties: A network theory of stakeholder influences. *Academy of Management Review, 22*(4), 887–910.

Sacks, M. A. and Graves, N. (2012). How many "friends" do you need? Teaching students how to network using social media. *Business Communication Quarterly, 75*(1), 80–88.

Salas, E., Cooke, N., and Rosen, M. (2008). On teams, teamwork and team performance: Discoveries and developments. *Human Factors, 50*(3), 540–547.

Salovey, P. and Mayer, J. D. (1990). *Emotional Intelligence, Imagination Cognition and Personality* (Vol. 9). Amityville, NY: Baywood.

Samphire, M. (2014). Dream or reality? *Project,* May, 28–31.

Schein, E. H. (1985). *Organizational Culture and Leadership.* San Francisco: Jossey Bass.

Schein, E. H. (1996). Three cultures of management: The key to organizational learning. *Sloan Management Review,* Fall, 9–20.

Scott, G. G. (2006). *A Survival Guide for Working with Bad Bosses: Dealing with Bullies, Idiots, Back-Stabbers, and Other Managers from Hell.* New York: AMACOM.

Shannon, C. and Weaver, W. (1949). *The Mathematical Theory of Communication.* Urbana: University of Illinois Press.

Snowden, D. and Boone, M. (2007). A leader's framework for decision making. *Harvard Business Review,* November, 69–76.

Stacey, R. D. (2001). *Complex Responsive Processes in Organizations; Learning and Knowledge Creation.* London: Routledge.

Stoney, C. and Winstanley, F. (2001). Stakeholding: confusion or utopia? Mapping the conceptual terrain. *Journal of Management Studies, 38*(5), 603–626.

Sveiby, K. E. (1997). *The New Organizational Wealth: Managing and Measuring Knowledge-based Assets*. San Francisco: Berrett-Koehler Publishers, Inc.

Tague, N. R. (2004). *The Quality Toolbox*. 2nd ed. Milwaukee, WI: ASQ Quality Press.

Talbot, P. A. (2003). Management organisational history—a military lesson? *Journal of European Industrial Training, 27*(7), 330–340.

Tannen, D. (1995). The power of talk: who gets heard and why. *Harvard Business Review, 73*(5), 139–148.

Tannen, D. (2013). *You Just Don't Understand: Women and Men in Conversation*. E-book; accessed February 2014. http://www.harpercollins.com/9780062210098/you-just-dont-understand.

Terry, R. W. (1993). *Authentic Leadership: Courage in Action*. San Francisco: Jossey-Bass.

Thompson, L. (2011). *Making the Team: A Guide for Managers*. Englewood Cliffs, NJ: Prentice Hall.

Tuckman, B. W. (1965). Developmental sequence in small groups. *Psychological Bulletin, 63*(6), 384–399.

Tuckman, B. W. and Jensen, M. A. (1977). Stages in small group development revisited. *Group and Organisation Studies, 2*, 419–427.

Vroom, V. and Jago, A. (1988). *The New Leadership: Managing Participants in Organizations*. Englewood Cliffs, NJ: Prentice Hall.

Walker, D. H. T., Bourne, L., and Shelley, A. (2008). Influence, stakeholder mapping and visualization. *Construction, Management and Economics, (26)*, 645–658.

Watkins, M. (2003). *The First 90 Days*. Boston: Harvard Business School Press.

Weaver, P. (2013). Where did the misuse of the names Gantt and PERT originate? *PM World Journal, 11*(4). Retrieved from http://www.pmworldjournal.net; accessed June 2014.

Weick, K. E. (1995). *Sensemaking in Organizations*. Thousand Oaks, CA: Sage.

Wheeler, M. (2003). *Harvard Business Essentials: Guide to Negotiation*. Boston: Harvard Business School Press.

Whitty, J. (2005). A memetic paradigm of project management. *International Journal of Project Management, 23*, 575–583.

Whitty, J. (2011). How to train your manager: A Darwinian perspective. In L. Bourne (Ed.), *Advising Upwards: A Framework for Understanding and Engaging Senior Management Stakeholders*. Farnham, UK: Gower.

Whitty, J. and Schulz, M. (2007). The impact of Puritan ideology on aspects of project management. *International Journal of Project Management, 25*, 10–20.

Williams, G. A. and Miller, R. B. (2002). Change the way you persuade. *Harvard Business Review, 80*(5), 65–73.

Yukl, G. (2002). *Leadership in Organisations*. 5th ed. Englewood Cliffs, NJ: Prentice Hall.

Zeithaml, V., Parasuraman, A., and Berry, L. (1990). *Delivering Quality Service: Balancing Customer Perceptions and Expectations*. New York: Free Press.

Zemke, R., Raines, C., and Filipczak, D. (2013). *Generations at Work: Managing the Clash of Boomers, Gen Xers, and Gen Yers in the Workplace*. New York: Amacom—American Management Association.

Index